Secretarial Procedures

By the same author

Telephone and Reception Skills
Typing Skills — Book 1
Typing Skills — Book 2
Advanced Typing Skills
Office Skills Exercises and Assignments
Office Skills Documents
Office Skills (and Office Skills Answer Book)

Secretarial Procedures

Thelma J Foster

Fellow of the Royal Society of Arts, Dip RSA

Lecturer Member Institute of Qualified Private
Secretaries (LIQPS)

Formerly Chief Examiner to the Royal Society of
Arts for General Reception

Formerly Senior Lecturer, Business Studies Department,
Worcester Technical College

Stanley Thornes (Publishers) Ltd

First published in 1990 by:
Stanley Thornes (Publishers) Ltd
Old Station Drive
Leckhampton
Cheltenham GL53 0DN
England

British Library Cataloguing in Publication Data

Foster, Thelma J
    Secretarial procedures.
    1. Secretaries. Duties
    I Title
    651.3741

    ISBN 0-7487-0172-9

Typeset by Tech-Set, Gateshead, Tyne & Wear.
Printed and bound in Great Britain at The Bath Press, Avon.

Acknowledgements

I am grateful to the following members of my family for their never-failing help and advice: Mr R A D Foster (my husband) who contributed Chapter 7 on visual aids; Mr R W Foster (my elder son) for the section on VDU health and safety; Mr T J Foster MA Oxon (my younger son) for the section on computers.

Other people who have contributed their time, patience and expertise of which I am very appreciative are: staff of Stanley Thornes (Publishers); Maureen Cummins, freelance editor.

The author and publishers are grateful to the following for permission to reproduce copyright material:

ABC Travel Guides (pp. 318–25)

W & R Chambers Ltd (World Time Zones Chart, p. 307)

Formecon Services Ltd (p. 280)

Girobank PLC (p. 211)

The Controller of Her Majesty's Stationery Office for the Crown copyright forms (pp. 271, 274–7)

Midland Bank PLC (p. 205)

The Post Office (Chapter 8)

To

Carrie, Becky and Katy; three very special people

Contents

SECTION 1

Acknowledgements   **v**

Preface   **xi**

CHAPTER 1   **Business Organisation**   **3**
The people and departments in a large firm   5
Office services   12
The secretary's role   16
Office automation and information technology   18
Location and planning of offices   20

CHAPTER 2   **Telecommunications**   **37**
Answering the telephone   37
Making telephone calls   40
Sources of reference for telephoning   42
Telephone services   43
International telephone services   46
Telephone equipment   48
How a switchboard operator should deal with calls   52
Today's switchboards   52
Other forms of telecommunication   53
Teleprinters and telex   56
Telemessages   58

CHAPTER 3   **Reception**   **63**
Dealing with callers   63
The reception area   65
The receptionist's desk   66
Security and reception   68
The secretary and reception   68
Reception reference books   70

CHAPTER 4   **Office machinery**   **73**
Typewriters   73
Audio-typing equipment   77
Word processing   79

		VDU health and safety	81
		Computers and printers	83
		Calculators	87
		The Data Protection Act	88
		Copying and duplicating	89
CHAPTER 5	**Retrieval and storage of information**		**97**
		Reasons and general rules for filing	97
		Folders and filing cabinets	103
		Safety	108
		Classifying filing	110
		Indexing	114
		Microfilming	117
		The filing clerk and supervisor	121
CHAPTER 6	**Sources of information**		**124**
		General reference books	124
		Reference books about people	125
		Reference books about firms and organisations	126
		Other useful reference books	126
		Other sources of information	126
CHAPTER 7	**Visual Aids**		**129**
		Charts and graphs	129
		Wall planners	137
CHAPTER 8	**Mail Handling**		**140**
		Incoming and outgoing mail	140
		Mail room equipment	150
		Mail room sundries	156
		Mail room reference books	157
		Parcels	157
		Mail handling by the secretary	160
		Inland and overseas mail and Post Office services	161
		Electronic mail	174
CHAPTER 9	**Stationery supplies**		**179**
		Paper sizes	180
		Envelope sizes	181
		Stock control of stationery	181
		Reordering stationery	182
CHAPTER 10	**Money at banks and post offices**		**186**
		Bank accounts	186
		Other bank services	204
		Postal orders	210
		Girobank	210

CHAPTER 11 **Petty Cash and VAT** **214**
What is petty cash? 214
Value Added Tax (VAT) 218

CHAPTER 12 **Business Documents** **222**
Buying 222
Selling 225

SECTION 2

CHAPTER 13 **Written communications** **233**
Addressing envelopes 233
Forms of address 238
Form letters, compliment slips and memoranda 241
Business letters 247
Dictation 249
Typing speeches and drafts 251

CHAPTER 14 **Safety and security in the office** **256**
The secretary's responsibilities 256
Safety legislation 258
Reporting accidents 259

CHAPTER 15 **Staff Recruitment** **262**
Advertising 262
Interviewing 263
Job description and specification 267
Induction courses 268
Deductions from salaries 270
Fringe benefits 278
Sickness benefit 279
Employment legislation 279
Contract of employment 281

CHAPTER 16 **Meetings** **285**
Types of meetings 285
The secretary's responsibilities 286
The chairman's role 287
Agenda and notice of meeting 288
Minutes 290
Terms used in connection with meetings 291

CHAPTER 17 **Planning ahead** **296**
Diaries 296
Other reminder systems 300

CHAPTER 18	**Travel**	**304**
	Itineraries	304
	Documents	308
	Health	308
	Currency and tickets	309
	Hotel bookings	310
	Rail and road travel	311
	Travelling with your executive	312
	Travel reference books	313
CHAPTER 19	**Business entertaining**	**326**
	Formal and informal	326
	General arrangements	327
	Invitations	328
	Seating plans	331
	The secretary's role	331
CHAPTER 20	**Conferences**	**334**
	Arrangements	334
	Venues	334
	Safety and security	337
	After the conference	337
CHAPTER 21	**Public relations**	**340**
	Public relations officer	340
	Press release	340
	Press conference	343
CHAPTER 22	**Designing forms**	**346**
CHAPTER 23	**General assignments**	**349**
CHAPTER 24	**Information for lecturers**	**351**
INDEX		**353**

Preface

A survey into how secretaries spend their working day (carried out by the Personnel Research Unit at City University Business School in London) showed that almost a quarter of their time was spent on duties such as filing, photocopying, switchboard, reception, and mail handling. On areas usually considered to be 'secretarial' (e.g. arranging travel, taking minutes, organising conferences and business entertaining, making appointments) secretaries spent a tenth of their time. Producing letters absorbed just over a quarter of the working day, with the remainder allocated to other tasks, such as wages, petty cash, supervising staff, interviewing applicants, preparing precis or drafting reports. It is therefore obvious that any textbook which aims to provide guidelines for trainee secretaries has to include at least 25 per cent office practice. Students who have used my book *Office Skills* will have a head start, finding familiar material in a condensed form, with new exercises and assignments providing useful revision.

It is heartening that at last secretarial training is to be realistically assignment-based throughout most secretarial courses, with continuous assessment eliminating the dreaded three-hour examination on which depended the success or failure of the previous year's work on secretarial duties. This seems to me to make it even more important for students (and hard-pressed lecturers) to have information at hand in the form of a textbook such as *Secretarial Procedures*, the aim of which is to provide all the necessary facts concisely and clearly, while giving adequate scope to students for further research on their own initiative.

Since I produced *Office Skills* in 1981, my subsequent books – *Typing Skills I, Typing Skills II, Advanced Typing Skills* and *Office Skills Documents* – have been linked by the use of the same firms' names, executives' names and business documents, addresses, telephone, telex and fax numbers, making them ideal for assignment work. *Secretarial Procedures* follows the same pattern thus helping lecturers to organise realistic continuity in assignments.

Because of the wide range of subjects to be covered, I have included quick revision sections at the end of each chapter, together with brief practical secretarial tips where appropriate – the latter in the hope that they will prove useful in job situations long after training is finished. Each chapter is followed by its own relevant assignments. Chapter 23 contains several general assignments.

A handbook is to be published to accompany *Secretarial Procedures*, giving answers to revision questions, and guidelines on the form assignments could take.

Secretarial Procedures covers the syllabuses of the Royal Society of Arts and London Chamber of Commerce and Industry examinations, together with BTEC National, and NVQ.

THELMA J. FOSTER

SECTION 1

CHAPTER 1

Business Organisation

There are three main groups of business organisations:

- Those providing a service, but which do not have to make a profit because they are financed by public funds — hospitals, educational establishments such as universities, charities, and local government.
- Those making goods for sale or dealing in the re-selling of goods (wholesaling).
- Those providing a service (e.g. legal, banking, advertising, accounting).

Many businesses are run and owned by one person, who takes the profits and also runs the risks of any losses – a 'sole trader'.

Anyone can set up in business, providing they operate within the law. Under the Business Names Act, 1985, if the owner of a business trades under a name which is not his own, then he must:

- display the name, type of business and the real name of the owner conspicuously where he trades from,
- print both names on all business stationery,
- ensure that the name of the business will not bring it into conflict with another business of the same or a similar name,
- notify the Inspector of Taxes and the DSS (for VAT, see pp. 218–19).

When a sole trader needs more capital, or help in the business, he often takes a partner or partners. Each partner is entitled to a share of the profits according to the amount of capital invested. He is also liable for any losses, to the frightening extent of having to sell his own possessions. To avoid the possibility of this, a limited partnership relates the amount of liability for loss to the amount of capital invested, but there must still be at least one partner in a limited partnership whose liability for loss is not limited. Partnerships are regulated by the Partnership Act, 1890.

As the firm prospers and enlarges, more capital may be needed. This can be provided by shareholders. The company registers under the Companies Act and the word 'Limited' appears at the end of its name, e.g. A.L. Carter & Co. Ltd. It then becomes a private limited company. There is no limit to the number of shareholders, except that the general public are unable to buy shares in a private limited company.

A public limited company's shares are offered to the public and the letters PLC or plc (public limited company) appear after its name.

Every large business organisation has a structure of management which is responsible for its control. The members of the management 'team' are the executives or managers, headed by a managing director, under a board of directors (or committee, depending upon the type of organisation) and a chairman. These executives are known as 'top management'.

In a large firm, the senior managers or executives have assistants or deputies with their own areas of responsibility. These deputies are known as 'middle management'.

An organisation chart shows departments within an organisation. In a large firm, there may be organisation charts of each department.

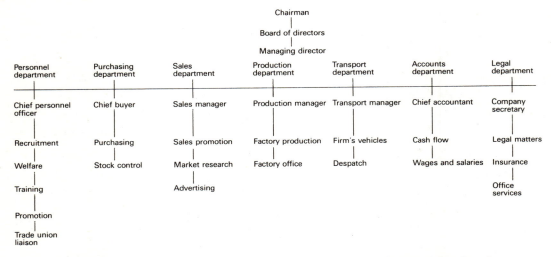

A typical organisation chart. The exact structure of any firm will of course depend on the particular type of business being conducted

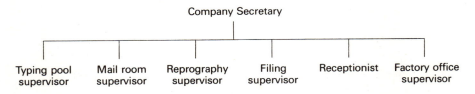

The organisation of office services in a typical large firm may look like this

The Purpose of the Office

An 'office' is a place where any clerical work is done, and the word 'clerk' means any office worker – typist, book-keeper, receptionist, for example. Offices exist in firms mainly to receive, record and find information. In a small

A modern office

business, separate office services will not be necessary. The manager can receive and give information him or herself. In large businesses the managing director cannot deal personally with all inward and outward communications; nor can he or she supervise everything that takes place. The office services are there to carry out these functions.

THE PEOPLE AND DEPARTMENTS IN A LARGE FIRM

The Chairman of a Company

The chairman is the most important member of the board of directors (and is usually elected by them). He or she represents the company both outside the firm to the public (shareholders, for example) and inside the firm. The chairman takes the 'chair' (i.e. presides) at board meetings and presents the annual report on the company's progress to shareholders. He or she depends upon fellow directors for information and advice.

Board of Directors

Each director may be responsible for a particular section of the business – production, sales or buying, for example – but they are also responsible to the managing director and have to accept the board of directors' decisions.

Managing Director

The managing director's chief responsibility is to see that the decisions made by the board of directors are carried out. Close cooperation with the chairman and the managers (known as 'executives') of the various departments is essential. It is through the managing director that important matters are passed to the board of directors for discussion and decision.

The Company Secretary

The company secretary is mainly responsible for making sure that the company does not break the law. He or she also acts as a link between the company and the shareholders and sends them information about their shares, and the company's financial position, i.e. how much profit or loss it has made in the previous 12 months. The company secretary is responsible for keeping an account of proceedings at all meetings (minutes: see pp. 290–1) and that the company keeps proper records of its financial transactions (buying, selling, borrowing, paying wages). The company secretary works closely with the chief accountant and deals with insurance and, in many firms, with office services. In all firms it is the company secretary who is the link between the board of directors and the office staff.

The Personnel Department

The word 'personnel' means 'the persons employed in any service', and the main duties of the staff working in a personnel department are connected with people. Such duties may include:

- Advertising vacancies for jobs.
- Training employees; promoting them.
- Transferring employees from department to department.
- Keeping staff records.
- Looking after the welfare of staff.
- Organising negotiations with trade unions.
- Dealing with resignations and dismissals.
- Helping to run social events and 'public relations' exercises such as open days for visitors.

The first step towards obtaining a job in a large firm is usually taken by completing an application form for the personnel department. This may be a general form, suitable for any vacancy in the firm, or a specialised one, suitable for office staff only, for instance. A completed application form will tell the firm whether an applicant is suitable enough to be interviewed. If so, he or she is put on a 'short list' containing the names of the best applicants.

EMPLOYMENT APPLICATION FORM (Office Staff)

Surname (in CAPITAL letters, please) . . . .

Forename(s) . . . . Mr/Mrs/Miss

Address . . . .

. . . .

Date of birth . . . .   Nationality . . . .

Education

	Name	From	To
Last school attended	. . . .	. . . .	. . . .
Further education	. . . .	. . . .	. . . .

Examinations passed

Subject	Board	Grade
. . . .	. . . .	. . . .
. . . .	. . . .	. . . .
. . . .	. . . .	. . . .
. . . .	. . . .	. . . .
. . . .	. . . .	. . . .
. . . .	. . . .	. . . .

Previous office experience

Name of firm	Position held	From	To
. . . .	. . . .	. . . .	. . . .
. . . .	. . . .	. . . .	. . . .
. . . .	. . . .	. . . .	. . . .

Any other work experience

. . . .	. . . .	. . . .	. . . .
. . . .	. . . .	. . . .	. . . .

Hobbies and other interests

. . . .

. . . .

Please tick any of the positions below in which you are interested and for which you consider you would be suitable. Number them in order of interest and suitability.

☐ Audio-typist	☐ Filing clerk	☐ Secretary
☐ Book-keeper	☐ Word processor operator	☐ Shorthand-typist
☐ Copy-typist	☐ Receptionist	☐ Switchboard operator

Signed . . . .   Date . . . .

An application form for employment

After interview, and appointment, details on an application form are transferred to a staff record sheet. In the one shown this will go on the left-hand side; the right-hand side is for information relating to the employee's career with the firm and this will be kept up-to-date continuously.

Personnel records contain a great deal of information which is confidential and must be filed in lockable cabinets, which should never be left open when the office is unattended. Staff working in a personnel department have to be trustworthy and discreet – never passing on information about staff to anyone outside or inside the firm.

It is of importance to employees working in the Personnel Department to be aware of legislation which affects the rights of all members of staff.

STAFF RECORD SHEET

Name .... First name(s) ....   Department ....

Position ....

Address ....   Salary (starting) .... Date ....

....   Salary increases .... Date ....

Date ....

Tel No .... Nationality ....   Date ....

Next of kin .... Address ....   Date of appointment .... Age on appointment ....

Tel No ....

Date of birth .... M/F Married/single   Transfers or promotions: .... Date ....

Children ....   Date ....

....   Date ....

Education: To/From   To/From   Date ....

Secondary .... Further ....   Training record:

In the firm: To: From ....

Qualifications   Day release   To: From ....

Subjects	Examining boards	Dates
....	....	....
....	....	....
....	....	....
....	....	....
....	....	....
....	....	....

Block release   To: From ....

Additional qualifications gained: Date

....

....

Periods of illness

From: To: Nos of days absent ...... Reason ....

From: To: Nos of days absent ...... Reason ....

Absences for reasons other than illness:

Date   Cause

....

....

Previous employment

Firms	Positions held	Dates
....	....	....
....	....	....

....

Pension scheme   Joined .... Due to retire ....

National Insurance No ....

Retired ....

Referees given ....   Date of leaving ....

....   Reason (other than retirement) ....

A staff record sheet

Discretion is vital in the personnel department

Purchasing Department

The purchasing department is the responsibility of the purchasing officer or 'chief buyer'. The chief buyer carries out three important duties:

- He or she must make sure that value for money has been received.
- He or she must make sure that accurate records of money spent are kept by his or her department.
- He or she must authorise all payments made on behalf of his or her department.

The purchasing department arranges for the buying of raw materials to be used by the production department, as well as office equipment, stationery and possibly the food and other requirements of the canteen. Frequent visitors to the purchasing department are sales people from other firms, hoping to be given orders for the goods they are trying to sell. Invoices from suppliers are sent to the purchasing department for checking, after which they are sent to the accounts department for payment. Other forms used are orders and enquiries. Another important responsibility of the purchasing department is stock control.

The 'stock' in a firm consists of supplies of everything likely to be needed. Because it costs money, it is very important to make sure that too much stock

Stocktaking

is not piling up on the shelves. Money can earn interest – idle stock on shelves which is not likely to be required for months earns nothing. The supervisor in charge of stock control has to arrange security for the goods in store so that they cannot easily be stolen, and he also has to prevent stock being wasted. Stock record cards (see p. 182) enable him to see at a glance how much of any article is in stock, and who is 'requisitioning' it from him. Stock requisitions are forms completed by employees requiring goods from the stores.

Trade Directories available for reference:

Directory	Contains information about:
Guide to Key British Enterprises	major British firms
British Middle Market Directory	important British private companies
Who Owns Whom	British companies owned by American firms
Kelly's Manufacturers and Merchants	Great Britain and Ireland
Kompass	manufacturers and suppliers
Machinery Buyers' Guide	manufacturing industries

Sales Department

The organisation of the all-important sales department is carried out by the sales manager who may attend directors' meetings at which sales policy is decided. The sales manager also supervises his or her assistant managers and sales representatives. A large sales department may be divided into two sections – one for supervising sales overseas (export market) and one for supervising sales in this country (home market). An advertising section often forms part of the sales department, and its main job is to arrange sales 'promotion' – to bring the products of the firm to the attention of the public by free offers, advertising in magazines, newspapers, on television and arranging exhibitions and special campaigns. Other ways of advertising are by 'direct mail' – sending circulars through the post to people living in a selected area or having a particular interest. Market research (interviewing passers-by in the street or calling at their homes in certain neighbourhoods and asking them to fill in questionnaires) enables the advertising section to find out what the public wants to buy.

Clerical workers in the sales department spend part of their time sending out catalogues and price-lists to customers, and typing invoices.

Customers' complaints may also be dealt with by the sales department and, in some firms, this department provides a repair service to customers for goods they have purchased from the firm.

Production Department

The production manager is responsible for the factory which manufactures the goods sold by the firm. A works manager is usually in direct control of the factory, and the factory office is the link between the factory and all the other departments in the firm. When an order is received by the sales department, it is sent to the factory office, and the factory office must ensure that the goods are manufactured and delivered correctly without delay. The production manager may also be responsible for maintenance, which is carried out by supervisors with technicians and workers under their control.

Transport Department

The manager in charge of transport has the responsibility of arranging for the goods manufactured by the firm to be delivered to the customers. This may be done by the firm's own vehicles or by British Rail or transport firms. The transport manager has to decide upon the safest, quickest and cheapest methods. If the firm's own vehicles are used, he also has to make sure that they are always in a good state of repair and available when required.

The transport manager and the works manager have to work closely together.

Accounts Department

The chief accountant is the head of the accounts department, which is one of the most important in the firm. It is the job of the accounts department to see that all the bills sent to the firm by its suppliers are paid promptly and, similarly, that all bills are sent out punctually to the customers of the firm, and that they are also paid promptly.

At the end of the 'financial year' (this is often the income tax year (see p. 273) the records kept by the accounts department are checked by an independent outside accountant (this is known as an 'audit').

A copy of the audited accounts is sent to the shareholders. These audited accounts enable the accounts department to produce details which show how much profit or loss the firm has made during the preceding financial year.

Payment of wages and salaries is often a part of the accounts department's responsibilities, although it may be dealt with by a separate section. The wages section calculates weekly or monthly deductions, such as income tax and national insurance, and will almost certainly use calculating machines and computers to do this.

OFFICE SERVICES

Typing Pool

Word processor operators have taken the place of copy-typists to a large extent and typing pools contain fewer copy-typists than formerly, but audio-typists and shorthand-typists with good speeds are still in great demand. The typing pool provides an excellent training for the school or college leaver, as they work directly under experienced supervision. The work in a typing pool may include circular letters, form letters, schedules, reports, envelopes or letters.

Mail Room

Many school-leavers are first appointed to work in a mail room, which gives them an opportunity to get to know the employees in a large firm, and where the various departments are situated.

Reprography Department

The reprography department is where all the duplicating and photocopying needed in the firm is done. In conjunction with typists the workers in a reprography department may produce a wide variety of jobs – staff handbooks, price-lists, instruction sheets, office stationery, internal telephone directories, copies of minutes and agenda.

Filing Department

In many firms, one department is responsible for the sorting and filing of all papers which are required to be stored for future reference. Centralised filing saves space and ensures the use of a uniform method.

The disadvantage is that files may be out when required, and the filing department may be some distance from many of the offices, thereby causing a waste of time when clerical workers go to borrow files.

Don't let this happen!

Factory Office

Clerical workers in the factory office have to work closely with the factory workers who are the people actually engaged in making the firm's products. The factory office keeps records of all manufacturing and production operations and is the link between the factory and all the other departments in a firm.

Office Juniors

It is possible to start work as an office junior without being able to type. Some firms have their own training departments where office staff learn typing, shorthand, audio-typing, and how to use a computer. Other organisations release their office staff for one day a week to attend the local technical college for training. An office junior would learn to help with filing, photo-copying, answering the telephone, handling the mail, and reception.

Copy-typists

Copy-typists type from handwritten material or corrected manuscript. Their typing speeds range from 35 words a minute (a junior copy-typist) to about 60 words a minute (an experienced copy-typist). Because of the increasing use of word processing, fewer copy-typists are employed in today's offices.

Shorthand-typists

A shorthand-typist has to have a good typing speed (50 words a minute) and a shorthand speed of about 80–100 words a minute. Her standard of English must also be very high.

Audio-typists

An audio-typist listens to a cassette through headphones and types what she hears. Her standard of English must be high.

An audio-typist

VDU Operators

A visual display unit (VDU) is a screen resembling a television screen, on which the 'input' (see p. 84) from a computer or teleprinter is displayed.

Keyboard operators should be accurate typists. Speed is less important than accuracy when operating a computer keyboard as mistakes are not so easy to correct. Keyboard operators may be computer programmers or computer terminal operators.

A VDU operator

Receptionist

The receptionist is almost the first person callers see when they come to a firm and therefore this role is most important. The receptionist must be pleasant, polite, tactful and well groomed, and should be well informed about the firm and what it does in order to answer callers' questions. To learn about reception work, a school- or college-leaver should look for a job as an assistant receptionist (see Chapter 3).

A receptionist

A switchboard operator

Telephonists

Another important key post in a firm is that of the telephonist or switchboard operator. They must be efficient, polite, tactful, calm and helpful (see Chapter 2).

In some firms the jobs of receptionist and switchboard operator are combined.

A secretary dealing with callers

THE SECRETARY'S ROLE

Both top and middle management employ secretaries. Top management secretaries may have their own assistants. The duties of today's secretaries are no different from those of their predecessors – what has changed in most firms is the way in which repetitive work is now carried out by office technology. This frees the secretary to take more responsibility for administration and supervision. It may enable her also to work for more than one person as a 'team' secretary, which can make for a more interesting and involved role. A great deal depends on the personality of the secretary, her interest in and knowledge of the organisation she works for, and the attitude of the firm towards promotion for secretarial staff.

The other factors affecting secretarial responsibilities are the size of the firm (the smaller it is, usually the more varied the work) and the extent to which an employer is prepared to delegate.

Qualifications

Intermediate standards of typing, word processing, shorthand and/or audio-typing, with speeds of 80–100 words a minute shorthand and 50 words a minute typing, are the minimum requirements for a secretary. Equally important is a high standard of English – a good GCSE grade or equivalent.

Allied to the 'secretarial skills', which most employers take for granted, is the essential training in all other aspects of secretarial responsibilities, any of which *may* be part of a secretary's job and she must be aware of them when she finishes her course. Training in the basic clerical functions is essential also, as supervision of junior colleagues may be an important part of a secretary's responsibilities.

The top secretarial qualifications are the Royal Society of Arts Diploma in Secretarial Procedures and the London Chamber of Commerce Private Executive Secretary's Diploma.

Even armed with one of the above, an applicant for a secretarial post still lacks one vital factor – experience. No one who has not worked in an office under pressure has any idea of the difference between the calm of a college classroom and the busy atmosphere of an office, with its constant interruptions. Any sort of job in an office, however low down the scale, will quickly give valuable insight into this, and enable a trainee secretary to apply for a more responsible job (perhaps in the same firm) with greater confidence, in a matter of only a few months.

Personal Qualities

Above everything else, an efficient secretary has to be a good organiser. She needs to be able to get her own priorities right, and to plan her employer's day so that he or she puts his or her own time to the best use. In addition to this, the ability to get on with people is a great asset, especially when supervision of other staff is part of the job – it 'oils the wheels' of everyday life. Other valuable personal qualities are diplomacy ('screening' telephone callers and visitors is a vital part of a secretary's job), loyalty and discretion, common sense and initiative. Added to these, it is important for a secretary to regard all the information which passes through her hands as completely confidential and to be able to resist all temptations to pass on anything.

It is a formidable list, and these qualities cannot be taught or learnt in any training course – they are acquired the hard way, by experience.

The Future for Secretaries

There will be a great impact on jobs in 1992, when the 'single market' brings down trade barriers in Europe. Training will continue to be of critical importance with especial emphasis on European languages.

English will remain the most common language of business, but knowledge of European languages will be essential if advantage is to be taken of the free flow of labour between European countries. Many more jobs will be available but only to people willing to face the twin challenges of different environments and cultures.

OFFICE AUTOMATION AND INFORMATION TECHNOLOGY

The office scene has changed very little for generations but suddenly, everyone is expected to be familiar with new technology, and equipment is often installed in the expectation that it will solve every problem.

Automation in the office began with the calculator, followed by the computer terminal linked to the mainframe. Ten years ago, most companies used their computers solely for accounts. The cost of computers falling dramatically and swiftly during the past few years has meant that personal computers (PCs) have become a part of the desk-top equipment of over 90 per cent of the large firms in the United Kingdom. Word processing has widened the scope of computers.

Office automation means the complete integration of word processing, electronic filing, diary management and communications, including electronic mail and telex. Every department of every organisation is likely to need these functions at some time and one terminal on the desk of a manager, secretary or typist can perform all the required tasks.

The other effect of office automation has been to reduce dramatically the number of clerical workers carrying out routine tasks such as processing forms and keeping records – these are ideal for transferring to computer databases and spreadsheets. The number of typists employed by large firms will continue to drop, probably more slowly, for the simple reason that many firms are still equipped with conventional typewriters and will only replace them gradually over the next few years. There is also resistance by some typists to learning how to operate word processing programs and this does not help small offices to change over to new technology. On the other hand, typists who remain and learn word processing skills will find that they are then in a position to cope with the other electronic equipment in offices and in so doing will not only enlarge the scope and interest of their jobs, but ensure that they become more useful employees.

The latest development is electronic mail (see p. 174), also known as electronic data interchange (EDI). Messages are sent to an electronic mail-box or any number of different mail-boxes, and stored in an electronic memory until the mail-box is opened. This has considerably reduced the amount of paper used in large firms, especially in sending memos. Electronic mail is making the 'paperless' office, which has been widely forecast during the last few years, more of a possibility, although computers are able to produce so much information so quickly in the form of 'hard copy' that the amount of paper consumed by them probably offsets the savings effected by electronic mail. However, in addition is the undoubted saving in paper made by word processing, where text can be completely accurate before it is printed. There must be a considerable reduction here in the quantity of letterheading and bond paper used.

What is becoming a possibility is that commuting to an office to work will not be necessary in the twenty-first century for many office workers using electronic information systems. They will be able to work at home, with a much smaller central office for occasional important consultations with executives, and for meetings with other employees. This will eventually have the effect of changing the appearance of the centres of large cities, at present dominated by huge office blocks – they will no longer be necessary.

Voice recognition by computers, cutting out the need for keyboarding, will have a dramatic effect on the number of junior typists and clerks in offices. It will enable a manager to dictate straight into a machine, thus eliminating the shorthand- or audio-typist, as his words will appear on a screen. So far, voice recognition is far from perfect and is unlikely to become widely used for some years, but it is a real development for the future, and prospective office workers should be aware of it. This office of the future is not so far away.

LOCATION AND PLANNING OF OFFICES

Siting of Firms

The following are important considerations to all employees (not just office workers) when decisions have to be made about the situation of a firm:

- nearness to public transport,
- nearness to shops, banks, building societies, post office, cafes, restaurants and hairdressers,
- nearness to a source of labour with the appropriate skills.

Also, increasing in importance is the provision of adequate parking space. A site outside a city in pleasant peaceful surroundings may be miles from most of the above and make recruiting employees difficult.

The Location of Offices Inside a Building

Near the main entrance must be the reception area, so that visitors can easily find it (see p. 63). The personnel department should not be too far away from the main entrance, as there will be many callers here from outside – people coming for interviews, for instance. The other department that will receive outside visitors is the buying department, so this should not be too far from the main entrance.

It makes good sense to site on the ground floor any department using heavy machinery – the reprographic department, for example.

Services which are centralised in many firms – mail room, filing, typing pool, messenger, reprography, wages and accounts – should be sited centrally, convenient to other departments, *not* on the top floor which causes waste of time and energy to all staff (and lifts are often on the wrong floor, or out of order).

There must be cloakroom facilities and toilets on every floor, with fresh drinking water available, as well as hot water for washing.

The canteen and surgery should be close to offices to avoid employees walking long distances in cold or wet weather.

Office Conditions

Conditions under which office staff work are important to their standard of efficiency:

- Their work may require peace and quiet – under the Health and Safety at Work Act (see p. 258) it is illegal for noise to rise above a certain level).
- They may need to be accessible to frequent outside callers or to staff from other departments.

- Privacy may be necessary – some interviews with other members of staff should not be overheard.
- Good lighting is essential for all office workers. Special lighting is necessary where VDUs are used (see p. 82).
- Ventilation (or air-conditioning) is vital – in summer and winter.

Modern offices have work stations which contain computers, printers, typewriters, dictating machines, telephones and clear working surfaces on which to write. It is possible to link work stations so that the 'work flow' may be organised more efficiently.

Planning Offices

Before choosing furniture and equipment, it is important to decide on the layout of an office.

Cellular Offices

These are the traditional type of offices, similar to a medium-sized room, with doors and windows. Their advantages are:
- lockable, providing security,
- private,
- there is peace and quiet for work which needs concentration,
- special conditions can be provided for equipment which needs controlled temperature and humidity (mainframe computers),
- they can be used as status symbols for senior employees.

The disadvantages of cellular offices are:
- partitioning, doors and windows take up extra space in a building,
- one employee may not need all the space in his/her office,
- maintenance (redecoration, heating and lighting) is more expensive,
- more supervision is required, as staff work behind closed doors.

Open-plan Offices

These consist of one large space furnished as an integrated whole, with or without the use of screens (sometimes provided by plants in pots or plant stands). An open-plan office generally accommodates several grades of staff from typists and clerical workers to managers and directors.

Advantages of Open-plan Offices
- Easier supervision, as all staff are on view.
- Communications between staff easier, for the same reason.

Cellular office for an executive

Plants and screens in an open-plan office

- Flow of work is from desk to desk instead of from office to office, and is therefore quicker.
- Centralisation of office services organised easily.
- Senior staff are in constant contact with the work of all staff.
- Maintenance is cheaper – lighting, heating and cleaning.
- More efficient use of space.
- Layout can be changed quickly if necessary.

Disadvantages of Open-Plan Offices

- Noisier, because of lack of partitions.
- Distraction for workers of people passing by.
- Security is reduced, without lockable doors.
- Little privacy.
- Colds, coughs and influenza spread more easily.
- Noisy equipment (typewriters, computer printers) are unsuitable for open-plan areas.
- Senior staff prefer their own offices (regarded as status symbols).

23

An open-plan office combined with cellular offices for managers

- Difficult to suit all tastes with regard to lighting, heating and ventilation.
- Impersonal atmosphere – many people like office walls on which to hang pictures, calendars, postcards, etc.

Many firms adopt a compromise between open-plan and cellular offices. Services which can be centralised in open-plan areas and give a more efficient service by this means are: filing, mail room, typing pool, reprography, wages and accounts.

Centralisation

This is an arrangement in firms where services used by all departments are under the control of one or two supervisors – e.g. the typing pool, the mail room, the filing and reprography departments and the wages and accounts departments.

The Advantages of Centralisation

- The work load can be spread more evenly among specially trained staff.
- All noisy machinery can be contained in one area and away from other staff.
- Expensive equipment can be installed in one area, rather than in several offices or departments.
- A more efficient service can be provided by the specialist staff.

The Disadvantages of Centralisation

- Centralised services may be a long way from some offices and time is wasted while staff walk to and fro.
- The staff engaged on work in a centralised office may find it monotonous.
- Contact may be lost with staff in other departments.
- Staff do not have direct access to records but have to follow a procedure to obtain them which may result in an inconvenient delay.

Planning the Layout of an Office

Under present legislation covering office workers, the minimum space to be allocated to each one is 13 square metres (or 40 square feet) and when planning the layout of a new office it is essential to make a scale plan on graph paper with cardboard templates also cut to scale representing all the desks, chairs, tables, storage cabinets and equipment to be placed in the office. Test the layout by stretching string across to demonstrate the flow of work and movement of people. Gangways, power and telephone points must be taken into consideration, as well as doors and windows, and heating (radiators or warm air grilles). It is possible to obtain models of furniture and equipment to help with planning an office. These can be attached to a base so that it is possible to see clearly how the office will look when it has been fully furnished and equipped.

Making a Plan

- use scale 1 cm to 30 cm,
- mark doorways, windows, power points, telephone points,
- make templates from thin cardboard of furniture and equipment to scale,
- arrange templates on plan,
- check with senior member of staff space required for each worker,
- mark in names of workers.

When new offices are being planned, provision should be made for wheelchairs – doorways should be wide enough to admit them, ramps instead of stairs, and suitable lifts, toilets and cloakrooms.

Office Furniture

Well-designed office furniture, suitable for the work of the user, helps health and efficiency. Desks and chairs should be the right height for the user as poor posture causes aches and pains.

Steel furniture is less of a fire risk than plastic, which causes suffocating smoke within seconds after the outbreak of fire. Flame-retardant fabric must be used for upholstery.

For typists and computer operators, shaped modules provide a working and typing area. A swivel chair enables both areas to be used easily. The height of seat and back should be adjustable. Footrests should be available for all

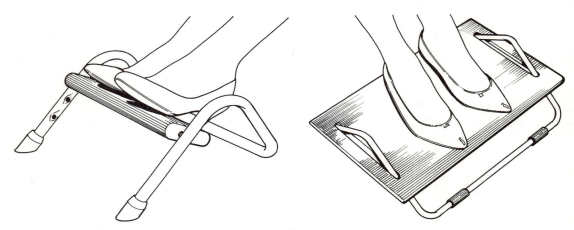

Footrests for typists

typists and clerical workers. An Anglepoise desk lamp gives adjustable lighting and may be necessary in addition to overhead lighting. Carpets must be antistatic.

A secretary in today's office will have at hand not only a typewriter and a telephone, but a computer, a printer, and possibly audio-typing equipment.

A single desk will not comfortably accommodate all of these and an efficient way to make use of space is by means of 'work stations' (see illustration p. 28) where desks are linked together with wedge-shaped extensions or connectors into 'modules', which enable the office workers to share equipment such as printers and computers when necessary. When planning work stations, areas should be left to provide surfaces on which to do written work, open the post, sort filing, etc. Lockable deep drawers under the work surfaces can be used for filing confidential papers, or petty cash (see p. 214), and storage for stationery.

Specialised furniture is required for drawing office workers and artists in the advertising department, and also for visitors in the reception area, where people need to be able to relax while they wait.

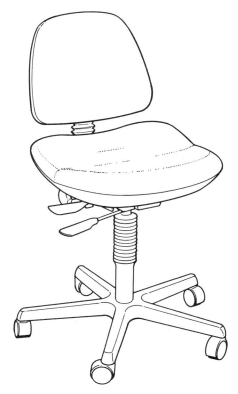

Typist's swivel chair with adjustable seat and back

A work station in an office

QUICK REVISION

1 The three main types of business organisation are those providing a non-profit making service, those manufacturing goods for sale and ....

2 Anyone can set up in business, providing they operate within the law. If they trade under a name other than their own, there are regulations under the ....

3 Partnerships are regulated under the Partnership Act, 1890. To share liability in the event of loss, the safest form of partnership is ....

4 A company becomes a private limited company when ....

5 When a private limited company's shares are offered to the public, it then becomes ....

6 The management team in a large firm consists of the chairman, board of directors, managing director and ....

7 'Middle management' consists of ....

8 In many firms, the responsibility for office services is under the ....

9 The main duties of the personnel department are connected with people – filling job vacancies, training, welfare of staff, staff records, ...
....

10 The Employment Protection (Consolidation) Act, 1978, which is an important piece of legislation for the personnel department, covers ....
....

11 The Act which eliminates discrimination with regard to pay and conditions of employment between men and women is ....

12 The purchasing department is responsible for the buying of raw materials to be used by the production department as well as ....

13 Work in the sales department may include market research, advertising, dealing with complaints and repairs, as well as ....

14 The production department is where the goods sold by the firm are made. The production manager may also be responsible for ....

15 The accounts department has to ensure that all money due to the firm is paid in and is often also responsible for sending audited accounts to the shareholders. An 'audit' is ....

16 Wages and salaries may be dealt with by a separate department or is often a part of ....

17 The typing pool is where typists, shorthand-typists and audio-typists provide a centralised service for executives. The number of copy-typists has dropped because ....

18 The department working closely with the typing pool where all the photocopying and duplicating is carried out is the ....

19 In some firms, filing is centralised because it saves space, but there are disadvantages, such as ....

20 The receptionist is a key person in a firm because she is the first person visitors see. In addition to courtesy, tact and good grooming, she must ....

21 The factory office keeps records of all manufacturing and production operations. It is ....

22 An opening for a school-leaver, with no knowledge of typing, would be possible in a firm as an office junior. Her duties could include ....
....

23 A copy-typist, if experienced, should have a speed of about ....

24 A shorthand-typist has to have a typing speed of 50 words a minute and a shorthand speed of ....

25 An audio-typist needs a high standard of English. She listens to a cassette through head-phones and ....

26 Telephonists often act as receptionists too, and hold a key position in a firm. Many tele-phonists are trained by ....

27 Today's secretary is often freed from much repetitive work by modern technology and this enables her to ....

28 Factors affecting secretarial responsibilities are the size of the firm ....

....

29 An efficient secretary needs to be, above all, a ....

30 Other valuable personal qualities are ....

....

31 The year 1992 is important because ....

32 Offices which should (ideally) be situated near to the main entrance of a firm are

....

33 Departments on the ground floor should be ....

34 Three of the services which may be centralised in some large firms are: ....

....

35 The traditional type of office, similar to a medium-sized room is a ....

36 The main advantage is ....

37 The main disadvantage is ....

38 Open-plan offices consist of ....

39 One of the main advantages of open-plan offices is ....

40 One of the main disadvantages of open-plan offices is ....

41 Centralisation is an arrangement in firms where ....

42 One of the advantages of centralisation is ....

43 One of the disadvantages of centralisation is ....

44 The minimum space allocated to each office worker (under present legislation) is

....

45 Equipment on a secretary's work station might consist of a typewriter, computer, telephone, printer and ....

ASSIGNMENTS

1 You work as a secretary to the owner of a small firm. She has taken on a partner, in consequence of which your workload has increased. You have been authorised to advertise for a junior, at bottom salary level. Which of the advertisements on p. 32 would you consider to be a suitable guide for drafting yours? Using one of them as a guide, draft your own advertisement.

2 As a college leaver with RSA Diploma in Secretarial Procedures or the London Chamber of Commerce Private Executive Secretary's Diploma, which vacancies on pp. 32–6 would you apply for?

3 Write (or type) a covering letter and enclose your CV for the above, using the form below as a guide for layout.

4 Since leaving college two years ago, you have worked for a firm as secretary to the Export Manager, and now feel that to obtain promotion you will have to move to another firm.

You have 100 words a minute shorthand, and 60 words a minute typing, together with experience of audio-typing and word processing, also good English and maths qualifications. Which of the vacancies advertised on pp. 33–6 appeal to you, and you feel you have the necessary abilities for?

5 Measure up a classroom and make a plan to scale on graph paper for the following:
(a) typist's desk and chair
(b) two filing cabinets
(c) work station for computer and printer with chair.

Decide whether your classroom would have room for a bookcase(s) and if so, what sizes.

Measurements for these (in varying sizes) can be obtained from catalogues which most printing retailers will be pleased to supply.

CURRICULUM VITAE

Name   Nationality

Address   Marital Status

Telephone

Education

Qualifications

Experience

Other Interests

Hobbies

Referees

Bright, capable and keen to develop?

JUNIOR SECRETARY

*c.£7,500 p.a. +
finance sector benefits*

If you have around 6-12 months' sound experience, good all-round office skills and are keen to develop further, we can offer you an excellent opportunity. We are looking for a very capable and enthusiastic young person to join our lively Personnel and Finance teams within the Estate Division of Reliant Portfolio Managers.

It's a busy environment, where you'll need good accurate typing, lots of initiative and a well-organised approach to your work. W.P. experience would be an advantage, but training will be given to someone who is quick to learn and eager to develop their skills.

(a)

OFFICE JUNIOR

To learn reception, accounts, word processing, switchboard and general office duties.

Full training to the right person.

(b)

ADVERTISING AGENCY
W2 AREA
require bright well presented

SECRETARY/TYPIST
MUST HAVE GOOD SKILLS (80 SH/TYPING 50 WPM). SUIT COLLEGE LEAVER 18+

(c)

JUNIOR SECRETARY

Required to assist Director's Secretary

Aged 18. Duties audio/copy typing, telex, filing, general office duties.
Must be non smoker
Apply for application form to

(d)

JUNIOR SECRETARY

Required to assist Directors Secretary. Age 18-20
Duties: Audio/copy typing, telex, filing, general office duties. Experience on Wordstar Professional an advantage but not essential.

Must be non smoker

(e)

★JUNIOR SECRETARY★
★FASHION★
★£7,000 - £7,500★
A willing and helpful secretary with some Sh. to work in showroom. Lots of varied duties.
Age 17-20.

(f)

TYPIST/CLERK
(Shorthand not essential)

Flexible hours, 5 day week. Successful applicant joining this expanding company would be working mainly unsupervised on various clerical duties. Must be nimble, diligent, tidy-minded and with a resourceful patient personality to fit in with the semi-organised chaos that emanates from fashion buyers of National Department Stores, Mail Order Companies, etc.... and the Directors ... coffee and aspirins ad lib.
Ring for interview.

(g)

JUNIOR
REQUIRED FOR SMALL OFFICE
Duties to include switchboard, reception, filing, post and must be able to type.

Apply in writing

(h)

OFFICE ASSISTANT
Bright numerate person required, 19+ for small friendly Head Office. Must be willing to tackle any duties required.

SALARY CIRCA £7,000
PLEASE CONTACT:.

(i)

PRIVATE SECRETARY

An experienced confidential secretary is required to work for the Business Manager. As well as the normal secretarial skills, this position requires good organisation, and audio experience. The ability to work on own initiative is essential as well as providing a full secretarial service to other sales and marketing personnel. This position offers a salary depending on age and experience.

(j)

SECRETARY TO MANAGING DIRECTOR

We are looking for someone experienced in secretarial work who is reliable, capable of working on their own initiative, good at figures, able to deal with customers on the phone as well as sales invoicing. Some word processor experience would be a help as we are about to be computerised. A generous hourly rate is available, hours 9.00am to 5.30pm, Monday to Friday. Four weeks paid holiday per annum. Own transport essential.

(m)

TEAM SECRETARY
ENGINEERING DEPT.

Mature, self-motivated person needed to look after and co-ordinate this small, friendly team and work for 4 managers. As well as using your secretarial skills (audio, WP, Sh. useful but not essential), you will have a wide variety of clerical and administration responsibilities + making travel arrangements for overseas visits. However, you will not be able to escape the filing and other normal but repetitive duties! Co. benefits include: Hrs. 9.30–5.30, £420 LV's pa. Discount on holidays, nr. Waterloo/Blackfriars tube, luxury surroundings. £9,000–£9,500 pa.

(k)

SUPERB AUDIO SEC
£12,000 W1

A fast and very accurate Audio Sec who has WP experience and excellent written and spoken ENGLISH to deal with highly confidential work close to Bond St. Appetite for hard work will be rewarded and much appreciated here!

(n)

SECRETARY/PA
£12,000 + BONUS

Super opening in a very fast moving computer sales organisation for a sec with 80wpm shorthand. Age 23–33 with WP experience. Very informal offices, but very busy admin support to a sales executive, organising travel, diary and meetings. Exc fringe benefits inc. BUPA + £270pa lunch allowance + bonus.

(l)

SECRETARY

Jackson Turner invite applications for the post of secretary to the service manager.

The successful applicant will be accurate in the usual office skills, will be dedicated, and able to work without supervision within the department. Previous experience as a secretary is not essential but secretarial training is desirable.

The use of English in written form and on the telephone is most important. Word processing and a current driving licence would be assets. Good employment conditions, including a subsidised canteen, and pension scheme.

(o)

33

The field is wide open!

(p)

Is there a good AUDIO SECRETARY out there?

Our planning Department deals with such things as Ethnic Minority Arts, liaison with Regional Arts Associations, Training and Education. Its manager needs a secretary to help her and is looking for someone (male or female) who is cheerful, able to cope with their own workload, can show some initiative and likes audio and copy typing, word processing and using the telephone!

The salary will be approximatley £8,500 per annum to start, plus free pension scheme and flexi-time.

(r)

INSTITUTE FOR FOREIGN STUDY

SECRETARIAL ASSISTANT £8,500 + BONUS + BENEFITS

A vacancy exists in our West End office, which provides academic support for American degree programmes operating in London.

Fast and accurate typing, administrative skills and education to GCE 'A' level are required.

(s)

Secretary

Advertising Agency – W1

A bright enthusiastic secretary is needed to work with a small, dynamic business development team, in a busy advertising agency.

If you have excellent organisational ability a good telephone manner and accurate typing skills and are eager to learn, we can offer you an exciting and interesting working environment.

(q)

AIRLINE SECRETARY

London Bridge

This interesting and varied position is at our Head Office which is located in a new prestige block five minutes from the station. The successful applicant will provide a secretarial service for the Administration section of Scheduled Services division which operates regular air services in the UK and Europe and carries in excess of 1 million passengers per annum.

The job will appeal to experienced secretaries over 21 with good typing and shorthand speeds who are also willing to undertake some audio work. Word processing equipment is in use and full training can be provided. Duties will include typing and distribution of weekly planning schedules, general correspondence, industry affairs and work related to tariffs.

We offer good conditions of employment including LVs, IFSTL and concessional travel.

Applications, giving details of age, experience and present salary should be addressed to:

The top

(t)

(u)

SECRETARY/PA TO MANAGING DIRECTOR

(v)

A vacancy for a confidential Secretary/Personal Assistant to the Managing Director. Applications are invited from experienced, mature secretaries who are seeking career advancement. As well as a high degree of secretarial skills, including word processing (Word Star Professional) and shorthand, the position calls for excellent organisational capability and the ability to work on your own initiative.

Salary will be negotiable, taking age and experience into account.

SECRETARY TO DIRECTOR OF FINANCE (HIGHER CLERICAL GRADE)

(w)

An efficient and resourceful person is required to provide the secretarial support to the Director of Finance and other Managers in the Finance Department. Applicants should have good audio-typing skills and word processing experience would be a definite advantage.

The successful applicant will have a mature and business-like approach to work which will involve contact with the most senior managers of the Authority. Personal attributes of integrity and discretion will be called for.

Hours of work: Full time - 37 hours per week
(Flexible working hours)

Salary: Up to £9,229 per annum plus proficiency allowances for certain secretarial qualifications

If you are interested and feel you have the skills that we are looking for, please telephone:

CHAPTER 2

Telecommunications

ANSWERING THE TELEPHONE

One of the important responsibilities of a secretary is to screen her employer from interruptions by telephone calls as far as possible. Obviously in some instances, the call has to be put through, but an experienced secretary can often deal with callers herself, be able to find someone else who can, or take a message and have the matter dealt with later on.

A secretary's own work is important and quite often pressurised; a telephone answering machine (see p. 50) will intercept calls during busy periods, by taking messages, but is unsatisfactory for callers requiring urgent or personal information. Also, it does not intercept internal telephone calls.

Many advertisements for office staff mention 'a good telephone manner' as one of their chief requirements, so it is obvious that it is rated very highly among secretarial qualifications. Answer the telephone 'with a smile in your voice' is a very good axiom, however tired or cross you may feel. A caller is unknown until he announces himself, and he may be someone very important or influential indeed.

General Guidelines

- *Answer* on the first ring, if at all possible.
- *Never* answer by saying 'Hello' – this tells the caller nothing and only wastes time.
- *Never* leave a telephone unattended. During your absence, make sure someone else will answer it.
- Answer an *outside* call by giving your firm's name, and the title of your employer – 'Good morning', (or good afternoon) GPR Developments Ltd, Sales Manager's secretary speaking. Answer an *internal* (inside) call by giving your own name, followed by 'Sales Manager's secretary speaking'.
- Find out the *name* of a caller, and use it at the first opportunity. You will recognise the voices on internal calls in many cases, but not all.
- *Conclude* a telephone call by saying 'Goodbye' followed by caller's name. Thank caller for ringing.

- If a call has to be *transferred*, pass on caller's name and his enquiry, so that he does not have to repeat himself.
- If you are *cut off* in the middle of a telephone conversation, replace the receiver and, if it was an incoming call, wait for *your caller* to dial again. If it was *your call,* you dial again, This avoids waste of time while callers find the line engaged if both are dialling again.
- When a caller has to be left while information is found, keep going back at short intervals to reassure him that he has not been forgotten.

Many expressions in common use in daily conversation are not acceptable on the phone: okey-doke, so long, ta-ta, hang about a bit, cheerio, see you, ok, and so on.

By the side of the telephone should always be: something to write *with* and something to write *on*. Better than a notepad is a pad of telephone message forms.

```
TELEPHONE MESSAGE

FOR Mr. P. Jenkins          FROM Mrs. P. Barker
DATE Jan. 25th 199-         TEL. NO. 436551    EXTN 23
TIME 10.30 hrs              COMPANY NAME Barker and Lane
                            ADDRESS Highfield Trading Estate
                                    Rudd stoke
URGENT/NON-URGENT

TAKEN BY P. Hill


    Mrs. Barker regrets that she cannot call
as arranged    (at 11.30 hrs today) as
she has been called away unexpectedly.

    She would be able to come on Friday
27 January at the same time. Would you
please telephone her office to confirm?

                                        P. Hill
```

A hand-written telephone message

38

TELEPHONE MESSAGE

FOR <u>Mr P Jenkins</u> FROM <u>Mrs P Barker</u>

DATE <u>25 January 199_</u> TEL. NO. <u>436551</u> EXTN <u>23</u>

TIME <u>1030</u> COMPANY NAME _____

ADDRESS <u>Barker and Lane</u>

URGENT/NON-URGENT <u>Highfield Trading Estate</u>

<u>Ruddstoke</u>

TAKEN BY <u>P Hill</u>

Mrs Barker regrets that she cannot call as arranged (at 1130 today) as she has been called away unexpectedly.

She would be able to come on Friday 27 January at the same time. Would you please telephone her office to confirm?

A typewritten telephone message

The headings on a printed telephone message form act as a reminder of questions which must be asked before the caller rings off. Messages should be written down at once and read back to the caller so that they can be checked, rather than trying to remember what has been said. A message pad with NCR sheets (no carbon required) (see p. 90) or interleaved with carbon provides a copy of a message for future reference, if necessary. A message should be passed on at once to the person for whom it is intended.

A telephone caller may not be willing to leave a message, in which case he (or she) should be asked:

- if he would like to ring back – ask what time,
- if he would like to be telephoned back – ask when it will be convenient.

In any case, he must be asked for his name, address (or his firm's name and address), telephone number and extension number. The extension number is the number of his internal phone and if it is known, the caller can ask for it and be connected immediately. It saves the operator's time. If caller's name is a fairly common one, such as Smith or Jones, his address will be essential to identify him. There are numerous Smiths in any telephone directory!

MAKING TELEPHONE CALLS

Unnecessary chat on the phone is a great time waster, and a call should be politely but firmly concluded when the conversation has achieved its purpose. You can always say that you have someone waiting to see you.

Keep your own calls to a *minimum* by jotting down the main points you wish to mention on a notepad before dialling – this also avoids making mistakes about information involving figures, for example.

Spell out names of people, cities, countries, trade names, etc. if caller has difficulty in hearing them. Speak slowly and clearly – *don't* shout. The telephonist's alphabet is useful.

Telephone Alphabet

A	Alfred	J	Jack	S	Samuel
B	Benjamin	K	King	T	Tommy
C	Charlie	L	London	U	Uncle
D	David	M	Mary	V	Victor
E	Edward	N	Nellie	W	William
F	Frederick	O	Oliver	X	X-ray
G	George	P	Peter	Y	Yellow
H	Harry	Q	Queen	Z	Zebra
I	Isaac	R	Robert		

This call logger monitors telephone calls by printing out a list of numbers called and the cost of each call

40

Find out what the company policy on private telephone calls is. Some firms require their employees to make a note of private calls. These should be restricted to short, urgent calls. The office is not the place to have lengthy conversations with friends.

STATEMENT OF PRIVATE TELEPHONE CALLS

Name _____

Department _____

Extension _____

Amount _____

Date _____

A form like this may be used to monitor private telephone calls

Less urgent calls should be made after 1300, when they will be cheaper. The other cheap period is before 0900. Many firms now operate flexible working hours and this means that telephoning before 0900 is worth remembering when planning to telephone these firms. The most expensive time for inland phone calls is between 0900 and 1300.

All inland calls

Charge rate period	Mon	Tue	Wed	Thur	Fri	Sat	Sun
6.00 pm–8.00 am	Cheap rate						
8.00 am–9.00 am	Standard rate						
9.00 am–1.00 pm	Peak rate						
1.00 pm–6.00 pm	Standard rate						

International dialled calls

Charge rate period	Mon	Tue	Wed	Thur	Fri	Sat	Sun
8.00 pm–8.00 am Does not apply to Charge Band 5B	Cheap rate						
8.00 am–8.00 pm	Standard rate						

Value Added Tax
Telephone **charges** are VAT exclusive and a sum for VAT is added to the bill at the appropriate rate.
To help you, call **costs** (to the customer) of all the examples of telephone calls shown include VAT at 15%.

Charge bands for telephone calls

Using a British Telecom operator increases the cost of a call – dial whenever possible. Avoid 'person-to-person' calls and transferred charge calls unless absolutely necessary – the extra charge for these is now quite high.

A database on a computer will be useful for frequently used telephone numbers.

SOURCES OF REFERENCE FOR TELEPHONING

The Phone Book

This is now the new name for a local Telephone Directory in most areas, and includes national and some international dialling codes. The latest British Telecom directory is available on microfiche and the complete UK set of alphabetical telephone directories, including telex numbers, fits in one small drawer file – saving 4.5 metres (15 feet) of shelf space. It can be automatically up-dated. It suits almost any type of microfilm viewer.

International dialling codes booklet

Contains a more comprehensive list of international codes than the *Phone Book* as well as information about time differences overseas.

Classified Trade Directory (Yellow Pages)

This provides a list of firms or individuals offering specific services.

World atlas

This helps to locate foreign cities and areas.

Index of frequently used numbers	This saves time looking up numbers, and should include extension numbers and people's titles (e.g. Technical Director, Area Manager) as well as names and initials, together with emergency numbers (see p. 46). This index can be on cards, in a box, or on a visible strip index (see p. 116). The latest telephones include a tape which stores 400 numbers which can be altered, added to or removed. Other latest developments in call-makers incorporate a memory, which will re-dial the last number called automatically.
Internal staff directory	Large firms have a directory of extension numbers, with departments listed alphabetically, giving staff extension numbers.
Fax directory	Many firms now have facsimile transmission machines (Fax for short) and a Fax number in addition to a telephone number (see p. 54).
Talking pages	There is a service in some areas (eventually to be extended to all) whereby the telephone operator will answer queries about names, addresses and telephone numbers of suppliers of goods or services. A special number has to be dialled. The service is charged for at local call rates.

TELEPHONE SERVICES

Alarm Call

When an early plane or train has to be caught, the telephone operator will ring at a pre-arranged time and continue to ring until the phone has been answered.

Person-to-person Call

There is no charge for this call until the person asked for actually speaks on the telephone, except an additional charge for the service by British Telecom. It avoids time being wasted looking for someone who may be out of his office.

Fixed Time Call

A fixed time call is a way of making sure that the person called is by the telephone when the caller rings. A fixed time call is especially useful for

overseas calls, to countries where the time is different from the time in the British Isles.

Message Call

A message is recorded and is delivered automatically to a given number at a specified time.

ADC Call

The caller may need to know how much a telephone call has cost, if for instance, she is telephoning from someone else's telephone. The call must be made through the operator (it cannot be dialled); the operator is then asked to ring back at the end of the call and let the caller know the cost. This is known as *advice of duration and charge.*

Transferred Charge Calls

Another name for a transferred charge call is a *reversed charge call.* This enables the caller to make a telephone call without payment, but first she must ask the operator to ring the person she wishes to speak to and ask if they are willing to pay for the call. Only when permission has been given will the operator connect the caller. This service is used in some firms by their representatives when they wish to telephone in whilst they are travelling around on firm's business. The switchboard operator would have a list of representatives and also keep a note of the transferred charge calls made.

Information Services

Timeline gives the time correct to one-twentieth of a second. *Traveline* provides travel information on rail, road, sea and air. *FT Cityline* keeps callers in touch with the stock market and other business news items. *Weatherline* gives local weather forecasts provided by the Meteorological Office. The numbers to dial are in the telephone directory. The services are available 24 hours a day, but are chargeable.

Freefone

Firms use this method to encourage customers to telephone them and ask for advertising material to be sent to them. A special Freefone number is published in their advertisements in newspapers and magazines, and all that the caller has to do is to ask the operator for the Freefone number. The cost of the call is added to the account of the firm.

Telephone Credit Cards

These are used by businessmen travelling around, who may need to telephone their offices frequently from public payphones.

Credit cards have a number on them, and it is this number which has to be given to the operator by the caller before he tells her what number he wants. The cost of the call goes on to the account corresponding to the credit card number. It is not necessary to use coins, but as all credit card calls have to go through the operator, they are more expensive.

Phonecards

Phonecards enable callers to make telephone calls from *some* public payphones without using coins. Payphones which take phonecards will *not* take coins. They can be distinguished from conventional payphones by a phonecard logo.

Phonecards can be bought from post offices, stations, garages, off-licences, newsagents and many other retail outlets, displaying the logo, for values of between £1 (10 units) and £20 (200 units).

The phonecard is inserted into the payphone and a digital display shows the amount of credit on the card. At the end of the call, the number of units remaining is shown, and the card is returned to the caller.

Phonecards can be used to call all telephone numbers on direct dialling and international direct dialling.

Telephone Charge Card

This is a credit card which can be used in special payphones throughout the UK to pay for calls.

Emergency Calls

There are *three* main emergency services:

- fire,
- police,
- ambulance

and *three* other emergency services:

- coastguard,
- cave or mountain rescue services,
- lifeboat.

To call any of the above services, dial 999. The operator will answer and ask which service you want. Then wait until the emergency service you have asked for speaks to you. They will want to know:

- The address of the person requiring help (not necessarily yourself).
- Directions to where they can be found (i.e. if they live in a very long road, it may be helpful to give a landmark such as a pub or church).

One emergency for which you do *not* dial 999 is if there is a smell of gas. In this case, the Gas Board operate a 24-hour service and their number is in the telephone directory under Gas. Make a note of it by the telephone, together with numbers for:

- water board (in case of leaking pipes),
- plumber,
- electricity board,
- nearest doctor,
- nearest hospital with casualty department,
- taxi rank,
- British Rail enquiries.

INTERNATIONAL TELEPHONE SERVICES

It is possible to dial direct by International Direct Dialling (IDD) to most overseas countries. A few international codes are given in the *Phone Book* (telephone directory); for a fuller list dial 100 and ask for Freefone BT1.

If IDD is not available, an international call should be made by dialling 153 and asking for 'International Operator' or 'Continental Service' (depending on where the country is).

When telephoning countries in Europe remember that their time is ahead of GMT (Greenwich Mean Time). It varies from country to country. Keep in mind, too, that in non-European countries farther afield (America, India,

Australia), time differences are much greater. You may not just be wasting your time when you ring in what could be the middle of their night, but, if it is to a home telephone number, you might be waking someone up! IDD leaflets give details of time differences.

Dialling International Calls on IDD

- Write down the *full* number before starting to dial.
- First dial the international code – 010.
- Then dial the country code.
- Follow this by dialling the area code.
- Finally dial the number of the person required.

If no country code is listed, it means that particular country is not on IDD and you will have to make your call via the international operator. Help can be given with any problems by dialling 155 for the International Operator.

Tones used in other countries are often different from those in the UK. More information about tones is given in the IDD leaflets.

Special Services Available by International Telephone

- Advice of duration and charge.
- Conference calls.
- Facsimile/Datel calls.
- Calls to ships at sea, including IMMARSAT (Maritime satellite).

47

- Person-to-person calls.
- Credit card calls.
- Transferred charge calls.

TELEPHONE EQUIPMENT

Loudspeaking Telephone

This has a loudspeaker incorporated into the normal telephone dialling arrangement, which can be switched on when a call is being made, so that both speakers in the telephone conversation can be heard by other people in the room. This is part of the external telephone system.

Intercom

Conversations between boss and secretary are relayed through a small loudspeaker. All that is necessary is to press a button. The latest type of intercom can be left on a desk or picked up and used as a telephone.

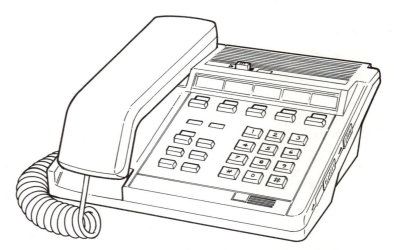

This telephone has both intercom and loudspeaking facilities

Radiophone

The radiophone involves taking a *telephone* with you and can be used in cars or boats for calls anywhere in the world. Calls from a radiophone are dialled in the normal way and incoming calls can be received. It is more expensive than the normal telephone service but is useful for business people such as sales representatives whose job involves a great deal of travelling, and who need to keep in touch with their firms. The latest developments have a small microphone above the windscreen and receiver via a loudspeaker, so that the driver does not have to take a hand from the steering wheel (which could be dangerous).

Cordless Telephone

Cordless telephones can be used anywhere up to a range of 100 metres (slightly less in built-up areas) and are ideal for people working on building sites, or in small businesses, such as garages, when having a portable telephone can save missing important enquiries and can allow the person to move about while speaking.

Tannoy or Public Address System

Loudspeakers are necessary in noisy areas, such as factories, to call people to the telephone, which is situated in a quieter part of the building.

Some of the equipment for a public address system is shown below (left to right: a microphone for making a call; a telephone for answering a tannoy call; and two types of wall-mountable loudspeakers).

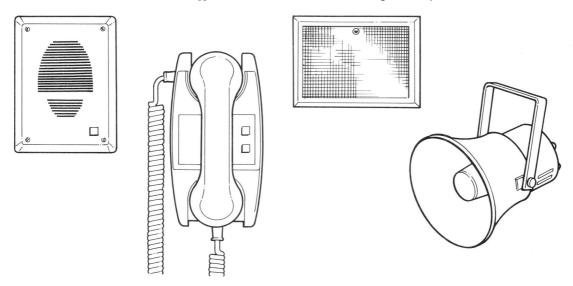

Flashing Lights

Where the ringing of a telephone disturbs people's concentration (where office workers may be spending most of their time on calculating figures, for example) different coloured lights, which flash to indicate that someone is wanted on the telephone, are a noiseless alternative.

Telephones on the Move

Pay-on-answer telephones are now available on inter-city trains to enable business people to make telephone calls while travelling. Soon, telephones will be available on planes. These will be especially useful on long distance air routes.

Radiopaging

People do move around – to meetings, to other parts of a large building, outside to other buildings – and it becomes very difficult for the switchboard operator to locate them. One way to make sure that managers and other staff who are frequently away from their own telephones can be contacted is by using a radiopager.

The radiopager involves carrying a small receiver which 'bleeps' when you are required to telephone your base. It is possible to have four different 'bleeps' so that the person carrying a receiver knows who to telephone. The alternative to a 'bleep' is a receiver which vibrates for use in areas where noise would be a nuisance (in a theatre or restaurant, for instance) or in noisy surroundings, such as airports, where the sound of a 'bleeper' would not be heard. Radiopaging is available all over the UK. The latest radiopagers have a print-out to enable users to record messages.

This pager is tailor-made for top pockets

Telephone Answering Machines

Busy secretaries find a telephone answering machine useful, as it enables them to concentrate on urgent work without being constantly interrupted by phone calls. The calls on the tape can be dealt with at a later, more convenient time – the message recorded may be one which asks caller to ring back at a later time.

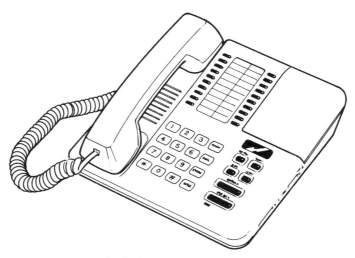

A telephone answering machine

A telephone answering machine can be left switched on to receive messages after the office is closed – very useful to one-person businesses.

A telephone answering machine incorporates a tape recorder, which plays a pre-recorded message (started by an incoming call), and then switches automatically to 'record', giving the caller a short time in which to give his or her name, address, telephone number and message. It is possible to link a telephone answering machine to a computer, which can display the number of messages recorded. With some types, the owner can phone in (using a code) and have his messages played back to him (useful for executives constantly on the move). The messages are erased if the code is repeated at the end of the call.

Telephone answering machines have the disadvantage of being impersonal and also many callers dislike using them because of the feeling that they may be cut off at any moment.

Switchboards

A private manual branch exchange is one where a switchboard operator deals with all incoming (external) calls, re-routing (connecting) them to the person who has been asked for. Employees' external (outgoing) calls are also connected by the switchboard operator. A private manual branch exchange is known as a PMBX.

An automatic exchange is the type which allows employees to dial calls direct without the operator's help. This is known as a PABX (private automatic branch exchange). Incoming calls are still routed by the switchboard operator. A disadvantage of a PABX is that an extension number may be engaged on an internal call, but the operator can break in and interrupt.

HOW A SWITCHBOARD OPERATOR SHOULD DEAL WITH CALLS

Answering an External (Outside) Call

Give the name of the firm, followed by 'good morning' or 'good afternoon'.

The caller then states who he (or she) wants (giving the extension number if known). If he does not know the extension number, the operator will look it up from the alphabetical list she has near at hand, and dial it. If it is answered, the caller is connected. If no one answers, she tells the caller, and asks him whether he would like her to try again or prefer to phone back later. If the caller decides to wait while she tries again, and there is a delay of some minutes, the operator frequently comes back to the caller saying 'still trying to connect you' so that he does not think he has been forgotten, or cut off.

Answering an Internal (Inside) Call

This will be someone working in the firm. The operator should reply 'switchboard' and deal with any queries promptly so that external callers are not held up.

TODAY'S SWITCHBOARDS

The latest range of switchboards offer even the smallest office the choice of facilities previously found only on large switchboards. These latest small switchboards are known as 'call connect' systems and take up less than 2 square metres for some systems. One switchboard automatically routes incoming calls to another extension (if one line is engaged) and repeats the last number dialled, so that if it was engaged, it can be tried again without redialling. Larger switchboards offer these facilities and also faster methods of handling calls, so that staff are not waiting for engaged numbers to be free, together with many other automatic services such as keeping a record of all calls (logging). British Telecom provide training on these switchboards after they have been installed, to make sure that the operators and other office staff get maximum benefit from new and rapidly changing technology.

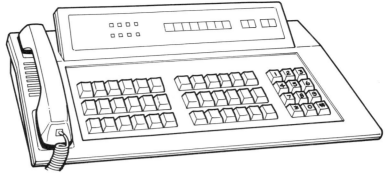

A modern switchboard

Internal Telephones

These are automatic – that is, employees are able to dial and obtain the connection to another office in the same firm. Some offices are supplied with an internal telephone and an external telephone, usually in different colours; a different ringing 'tone' is also a help in identifying which telephone is ringing, or, similarly, a flashing light.

OTHER FORMS OF TELECOMMUNICATION

Audio-conferencing

Confravision is a British Telecom service which links people or groups of people in different cities by television. There are Confravision studios in seven large cities in the UK. These can be booked for discussions to save the expense and time of travelling over long distances.

Confertel

Confertel is a service which links business people by telephone in international telephone meetings and uses specially developed equipment to ensure good quality lines, with operators trained to offer advice and help at any time. There is now a service linked to Confertel offering simultaneous translation of telephone conversations with non-English speakers.

Prestel

Prestel is the British viewdata system which links a specially adapted television screen or microcomputer over an ordinary telephone line to about 250 000 pages of information supplied by organisations who are in contact with the central Prestel computer. Users pay for their telephone calls and for each page they call up. The specially adapted television set either has a keypad or a keyboard for the user to select information. Messages may also be sent to other Prestel users via the Prestel computer. The immediate access available to information and current news is very useful in offices where constant reference is being made to facts.

The system allows ordering goods, or making hotel bookings, for example, as well as many other facilities. A wide range of businesses, such as travel agents, now find Prestel very useful.

Prestel Gateway links a Prestel terminal to other computers. This allows Prestel users to receive additional information and services, such as data from sales people travelling around.

A service which allows users to check their building society and bank account balances is *Homelink*. In some areas it is already possible to do the shopping by Homelink via supermarket computers, examining prices and selections of goods from the Prestel page on the television screen.

Teletext (Oracle and Ceefax)

Oracle and Ceefax are information services provided by television and are used mainly in homes. Teletext services are not to be confused with telex. Oracle is supplied by the IBA and Ceefax by the BBC. Television sets have to be specially adapted to receive Oracle or Ceefax and there is an extra charge.

Datel

Datel (a data transmission service) links computers either by telephone or a special data network. By Datel, firms can be linked to a central computer.

Facsimile Transmission (Fax)

Facsimile transmission (Fax for short) is the transmission of a document, picture or letter using the telephone system to reproduce an accurate copy of the original at the receiving end.

Fax works by scanning the original document on the transmitter and electronically encoding its image. The coded information is then sent down a standard telephone line. At the receiving end, another Fax machine decodes the message and prints out an exact 'facsimile' copy of the original document, in black and white. Some machines can print in colour.

Fax is faster than telex, transmits both words and pictures, and is as easy to use as an office photocopier.

British Telecom operates a Fax service for use by firms without their own facsimile transmitters (Bureaufax).

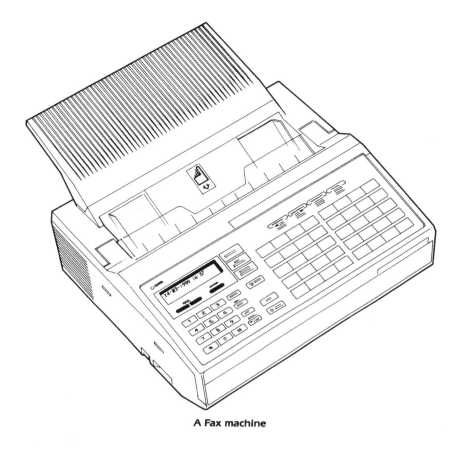

A Fax machine

The Post Office offers Intelpost, which gives a similar service, but the documents copied are delivered by post or collected.

It is possible to send documents by facsimile transmission to many parts of the world.

Senders (and recipients) of Fax have to have a special Fax telephone number. There is a directory of Fax numbers. Firms print their Fax numbers on their letterheading.

Some types of Fax machines may also be used as high-quality photocopiers. However, fax copies do fade eventually.

Computers and the Telephone

The ability to 'talk' to other computers and remote databases like Prestel is already standard on some personal microcomputers, and other manufacturers are beginning to offer the modem devices necessary to connect the computer to telephone lines as optional extras, usually in the form of a circuit board that plugs into a slot inside the computer.

At the same time, telephones are becoming more and more computer-like: the latest key telephone equipment being offered to small businesses positively bristles with microprocessors, giving fairly simple systems capabilities very much like those of a large branch exchange. The latest telephone handsets are light years ahead of even the recent dial-and-speak sets.

Existing personal computer owners can connect their sets with Prestel or other viewdata sets amazingly cheaply and modem prices have fallen dramatically, too. It is possible, for about £100, to buy a modem which will be adequate for use with the national electronic mail service, Telecom Gold, and for direct communication with other microprocessors.

With an ever higher proportion of telephone calls being placed by computers rather than people, the all-too-common irritation of wrong numbers may eventually disappear.

TELEPRINTERS AND TELEX

Telex and its Advantages

Telex enables someone to type a message to someone else without posting it. It is like sending a letter by telephone! The typist taps the keys on a teleprinter in London for instance and the message can be printed out in Birmingham or a message from Manchester can be received in Milan.

Telex messages are quick – an expert operator is able to transmit at about 50 words a minute. Telex messages are less likely to be misunderstood if in foreign languages, as translations can be made carefully from a written message. Technical information is also received without errors.

Letters may take days, especially those from foreign countries. Also, the sender of a letter does not know when the letter has been received, but with telex the automatic answerback code provides confirmation that the message has been received.

Telex messages give a record both for the sender and for the person receiving the message. As the operator types out the message he or she is sending, it is automatically printed by the teleprinter receiving it. Up to six copies can be produced at once, if required. Red print indicates outgoing messages. Incoming messages are printed in black.

Incoming telex messages can still be received even after the office is closed, at any time of the day or night, provided the power supply is left switched on and the teleprinter has a supply of paper left in it. This is especially useful for receiving messages from other parts of the world, where the time may be very different from the time in Britain.

Telex messages are less likely to be misunderstood . . .

Charges for telex calls are based on distance between telex subscribers and the length of the message (i.e. time taken to transmit the message). This is the way charges are calculated for telephone calls too.

The units which send and receive telex messages are called *teleprinters.* They are available for rental. Rental charges include the maintenance of the teleprinter and there is an extra charge for the connection of each new telex exchange line. Large cities have telex bureaux where messages may be sent by firms who do not have a teleprinter.

Telemessages (see p. 58) may be sent by telex.

Teleprinter Keyboard and Dialling Unit

The teleprinter keyboard is similar to that on a typewriter. What is printed by the operator on her machine is printed at the same time on another teleprinter at the other end of the line. Only capital letters are printed and there are certain special keys.

Reference Books

When you are operating a telex you will need the following books:

Telex Directory (UK)
International Telex Directory
Dictionary (telex messages are *written,* not spoken, so check up on your spelling!).

Telex Plus

Telex Plus is available to all telex users and saves the operator's time by sending the same message to up to 100 correspondents.

It stores the message and forwards it as soon as the lines are free, making repeated attempts to forward, if necessary. Customers are automatically notified when all Telex Plus messages have been delivered.

International Telex Calls

The international telex service is available to many countries throughout the world. It is possible to dial direct to New Zealand and to the United States of America, Canada and Europe.

Telex calls to other countries can be made through the London Telex switchboard operator, and international telex directories can be bought from the local Telephone Manager's office.

Latest Developments in Teleprinters

The latest teleprinters are equipped with:

- Visual display unit (VDU), which shows the characters typed on the keyboard, making editing of a message easy, before it is transmitted.
- Automatic calling, message editing and storage of messages.
- Storage facilities on floppy disks of around 20 pages of typescript.
- The facility to hold incoming messages in memory and re-transmit them.
- Automatic repeating of the same message to several different destinations.
- Storage in the memory for the most commonly used telex numbers – forming an internal telex directory.

It is possible to link computers throughout a firm to the teleprinters, and messages can be transmitted direct from the computers. This is having the effect of dispensing with the need for operators to sit all day by teleprinters – most office staff are able to send their own messages.

The appearance of teleprinters is changing. There is often now no dial – calls are selected from the keyboard – and the most comprehensive model now has a keyboard, printer and visual display unit (VDU) with a word processing facility for preparing and editing texts.

TELEMESSAGES

Telemessages are an electronic letter service, and may be sent by telephone (not phonecards), telex, or firm's computer terminal equipment.

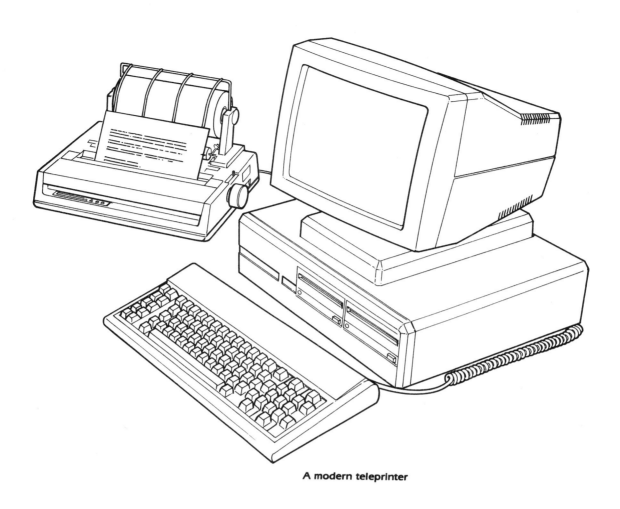

A modern teleprinter

Telemessages are delivered by the postman the day after sending, by the first post. There is no delivery on a Sunday.

Telemessages are delivered in a bright yellow envelope with three blue stripes across.

There are telemessage greetings cards available for special occasions such as weddings, christenings, anniversaries. There is an extra charge for these, but they are supplied free with every telemessage sent *before noon* on Mondays and Fridays.

To send by telephone – dial 100 (190 in London) and ask for 'Telemessage'.

To send by telex – consult your telex directory for the correct number to dial. Type TELEMESSAGE two lines down from your answerback number (see p. 56) followed by the address and your message.

The telemessage service operates to any address in the UK, including the Channel Islands and Isle of Man. Telemessages may also be sent to the USA. The American version of the telemessage is known as the 'mailgram'. The telemessage service will be extended to other countries in the near future.

The maximum number of words which can be sent by telemessage is 350 (the limitation is because telemessages are printed on sheets of A4 paper, which will enable 35 lines of text to be printed). Help from the telephone operator about the maximum number of words is available if required.

There is a specially reduced rate for telemessages which are sent to a number of different addresses with identical messages. Freefone 2741 gives the details (calls to be made during normal working hours). The service to ask for is Multiple Telemessage.

There is now a private inland telegram service called 'Couriergram', with a guaranteed two-hour delivery in the UK on weekdays, Sundays and bank holidays.

Sending a Telemessage

It is necessary to write out a telemessage first, before dictating it to the operator, when it is to be sent by telephone.

After drafting, count the number of words in the message to see if unnecessary words could be eliminated.

Finally, dial 100 (190 in London) and ask for 'Telemessage'. When the operator answers, dictate the name, address and message. You will be asked for your own telephone number, name and address. The cost of the telemessage will be added (plus VAT) to your telephone bill.

Telejet

This is a service for sending messages by phone, using a credit card number. The message is delivered personally within 5 hours, and may be accompanied by a suitable card (and present, if required) for extra cost. The service is available in England, Scotland or Wales.

International Telegrams

Telegrams may be sent overseas by dialling 190 and asking for 'International Telegrams'. They may be sent by telex, or telephone but not from post office counters. They are charged for according to distance sent and length of message so it is important that they are kept as brief as possible without losing the sense.

SECRETARIAL TIPS

1 If person required is not available, try (tactfully) to find out what a caller wants; this enables any necessary information to be acquired before he is contacted (or rings) again and saves a great deal of time.

2 Whenever time permits, type out a telephone message neatly before it is passed on.

3 Before making a phone call, as well as jotting down the main points beforehand, have any relevant files close at hand, in case further information is needed.

4 Write down a telephone number with which you are unfamiliar, including the dialling code, before making a phone call. This will avoid misdialling.

5 Remember that a telephone conversation has no written record – confirm anything important which has been said in writing (hotel bookings for example).

6 Local calls, made after 1300, are cheaper than sending a letter, provided they are kept short.

QUICK REVISION

1 By the side of the telephone should *always* be ....

2 If a telephone caller is unwilling to leave a message, he should be asked ....
....

3 Before letting a caller ring off, the following details should be asked for: ....
....

4 For spelling out awkward words and names use a ....

5 The most expensive time for making inland phone calls is between ....

6 The cheaper times are before 0900 and after ....

7 Preparations for making an important phone call: ....
....

8 Sources of information to be kept by the telephone: ....

9 A useful telephone service for business people who may have early trains or planes to catch is
....

10 Another useful service when making overseas phone calls to countries where the time is different from time in the UK is ....

11 An advice of duration and charge call (ADC) is made by .... followed by ....

12 It is possible to make a telephone call without coins by telephone credit cards, a freefone number, phone cards and ....

13 A call which avoids time-wasting when the person called may be away from his office is ....

14 In an emergency, after dialling 999 and asking for the emergency service required, you will have to tell the operator ....

15 Do not dial 999 for an emergency which involves ....

16 Other phone numbers which may be needed in a hurry are British Rail enquiries, taxi rank,

....

....

ASSIGNMENTS

1 Draw up 5 *brief* guidelines which you consider to be the most important for a new office junior who is inexperienced in using the telephone.

2 Explain what is meant by 'a good telephone manner' in advertisements for vacancies for office staff.

3 (a) Write out a script for a telephone call between a nervous junior and an external caller whose grasp of English is poor; the conversation should demonstrate how NOT to deal with difficult callers!
(b) Re-write the above with the caller dealt with efficiently.

4 Explain the differences (and similarities) between an alarm call, and a fixed time call.

5 What are the differences between a 'personal call' and a 'person-to-person' call?

6 Telephone credit cards and phone cards are two ways of using a payphone without using coins. Explain how each operates.

7 What emergency services would you need in the following circumstances:
(a) Kitten stuck up a tree in the firm's car park.
(b) A telephone caller who states 'there is a bomb in your building which will explode in 30 minutes'.
(c) Strong smell of gas in the building.
(d) Leaking pipe in the cloakroom.
(e) Building in darkness on a winter's morning.
(f) Dripping tap.

8 What points should be borne in mind when making a telephone call overseas?

9 Explain why a telex message has been described as 'sending a letter by telephone'?

10 Your employer is interested in installing equipment which will send technical information to Italy and Spain (telephone messages are being misunderstood). Set out the various advantages (and disadvantages, if any) of a teleprinter and a 'Fax' machine.

CHAPTER 3

Reception

DEALING WITH CALLERS

In a small firm, reception of visitors has to be combined with secretarial duties. In a large organisation there may be several receptionists looking after a reception area, ensuring that the reception desk is never left unattended. In other, medium-sized firms, the receptionist may operate a switchboard and a teleprinter too. The allocation of these responsibilities depends upon the type of organisation and the average number of visitors expected, but every office which has an appointments system (see p. 68) needs to delegate reception of visitors to certain members of staff.

The reception area and receptionist's desk should be near to the main entrance of a firm, so that callers are able to find it easily. The first impression a caller has of a firm is its reception area and even the very smallest office should arrange for a comfortable chair in which a visitor can sit and wait.

An example of a well-planned reception area

In a large firm, many amenities should be included – toilets, payphone, vending machines for refreshments, coin changing machine, stamp machine and a non-smoking area. Samples of firm's products (if appropriate) can be displayed in the reception area, and copies of house journals on low tables will give visitors information about the firm and the activities of their employees. Daily newspapers are also welcomed by waiting visitors.

Receptionists (not always female) must be well groomed, and have a calm and cheerful disposition. Tactfulness is of great importance, as not all visitors are easy to deal with; some may not have appointments and be unwilling to leave until they have seen the person they want. A knowledge of simple first aid is useful in the reception area for minor emergencies such as a nosebleed, blister or foreign body in an eye.

In addition to operating a switchboard and/or teleprinter, the receptionist may type, file, give out brochures and handbooks issued by the firm, open and arrange for distribution of mail, and help with making tea or coffee for visitors.

Visitors to a firm must never be kept waiting unnecessarily, but sometimes a delay occurs and the receptionist should go back to callers at short intervals to offer tea or coffee, and reassure them that they have not been forgotten.

There are two main categories of visitors – those with appointments and those without. Callers without appointments may be sales representatives hoping to see the chief buyer or someone in the Buying Department, customers with complaints about the firm's goods, or people enquiring about vacancies for jobs. Callers without appointments should be politely asked to write in for one. If they refuse to leave, the receptionist should phone the secretary of the person the caller is trying to see and ask her when a appointment can be made. As a final measure, if a caller becomes really awkward, the firm's security staff should be called to escort the caller out, but if the receptionist knows her job, this should rarely be necessary.

What to do if all else fails!

Regular callers who do *not* normally make appointments are:

- postmen or women,
- security van drivers delivering cash for wages,
- delivery people from other firms,
- private courier delivery people,
- British Rail (BR) delivery people,
- window cleaners, suppliers of pot plants, telephone disinfectant service staff,
- people delivering letters and parcels from other firms by hand.

THE RECEPTION AREA

Using a person's name is friendly and makes a caller feel welcome. The receptionist's name should be on a brooch pinned to her dress or on a stand in front of her, so that callers see it at a glance and can use it at once.

Many businessmen and women have business visiting cards and will give one to the receptionist. Business visiting cards have printed on them the caller's name and firm, the firm's address and telephone number, and occasionally the caller's home address and telephone number. Sometimes a card also gives information about the firm's products. The information on the business visiting card tells a receptionist all she needs to know about a caller, saves her asking a great many questions, and helps her to introduce the caller to members of staff. Usually, business visiting cards are left with the receptionist and if she files them away in alphabetical order of the firms' names, she is able to look up the relevant card the next time a caller comes and refer to it for information.

Derby and Drew

Office furniture

Office carpets

Fleet St.
London
EC4B 6PB

A. P. Rowson

071-611 4479

A business card

Filing a business card

THE RECEPTIONIST'S DESK

As well as an index of callers' cards, a receptionist will have:

- records of callers – callers' register and appointments book,
- a staff 'in' and 'out' book,
- a computer (this can take the place of an appointments book),
- plan of the firm on the wall behind her,
- organisation chart on the wall. This gives the names of the directors and executives of her firm.
- internal staff directory.

DATE	NAME	DEPT	TIME OUT	TIME IN	REASON

Staff 'in' and 'out' book

Date:			
Name of caller	Firm	Time of arrival	To see

Visitors' book

Date	Name of caller	Caller's firm or home address	Time of arrival	Seen by	Action taken

Another example of a visitors' book

SECURITY AND RECEPTION

Visitors must always be supervised, for security reasons, as well as out of politeness. A man in overalls wandering around *could* be a workman, but could just as easily be a potential thief or someone who wants to acquire confidential information. No stranger should ever be in a position where he has wandered into a firm and walked around it alone. A badge issued to visitors showing their name and date, ensures them temporary authorisation and must be handed back as they leave. Closed-circuit TV cameras are also useful.

THE SECRETARY AND RECEPTION

Information for entries in the appointments book should be given to the receptionist by the secretaries in a large firm, as soon as the appointment has been confirmed – certainly no later than early in the morning of the day on which the visitor is expected. On arrival, the secretary is informed, and either goes to reception to escort the visitor to her boss at once, or, asks if the receptionist would see that he waits in the reception area for a few moments. Alternatively, the secretary's junior assistant may be asked to escort the caller to her boss. As the caller leaves, he is escorted back to the reception desk, handing over his badge to the receptionist, who has been informed of his departure by a telephone call so that she will know he must be seen to leave the building.

Introducing Visitors to the Office

Some callers will be known to your boss, so their arrival can be announced on the intercom (see p. 48) or internal telephone and they can be asked to go in when you have been told it is convenient. Visitors who are strangers should be introduced. The correct way to do this is to precede the caller through the door, stand on one side, and say 'This is Mr Brown, from A. L. Carter & Co. Ltd' and then leave your boss's room. It may happen that you have to introduce two callers who have not met before.

There are some simple rules about this:

- Introduce a man to a woman – Mrs Jones, may I introduce Mr Green?
- Introduce an obviously younger woman to the older one. Make sure you know their titles (Mrs, Miss, Ms). This can be tricky for obvious reasons – all your tact will be required!
- Introduce an obviously younger man to the older one.
- Introduce titled people in order of rank – look this up beforehand in *Black's Titles and Forms of Address* (see p. 124).

Take care when making an introduction

If you are introduced to someone, shake hands and say 'How do you do'.

The person to whom you are introduced will also reply 'How do you do' but does not expect an answer. *Do not say* 'Pleased to meet you'.

Reception in a Small Firm

Where a firm is too small to justify employing a receptionist in a separate reception area, receiving visitors may be included in the duties of a secretary. It is important to attend to callers promptly, pleasantly and politely. Anyone kept waiting in a draughty lobby without a chair can be forgiven for departing forthwith.

Guidelines for Receiving Visitors

- A visitor's bell just inside the main entrance with a notice 'Please ring for attention and take a seat while you wait' allows a visitor to announce his presence at once.

- There should be several chairs nearby.
- A telephone extension in the lobby is useful as a short call to the secretary of the person the caller wishes to see avoids unnecessary waiting.
- Callers should be greeted by 'Good morning/afternoon. May I help you?' followed by: 'What is your name, please; who would you like to see; have you an appointment?' If the answer to the last question is 'Yes' then a telephone call can be made to check that the person caller wishes to see is free and the caller escorted to the appropriate office.
- If the answer is 'No' then a polite suggestion can be made that the caller could make an appointment and call again.

RECEPTION REFERENCE BOOKS

Many callers at a firm will be strangers to the area and may ask about suitable hotels, restaurants, entertainments and where to find other firms. The following would be useful.

Sources of Reference for Reception

AA or RAC handbook	contains information about hotels, garages, market days and early closing days in the UK, as well as mileage charts, and plans of city centres.
Post Office Guide	Foreign visitors may ask about postage rates to overseas countries and other post office services.
Local maps and guide books	for places of interest in the locality.
A–Z Street Atlas	gives detailed street maps of most large cities, together with indexes of hospitals, police stations, railway stations and post offices. Along main streets, house numbers are given, also.
Phone book	
IDD booklet	for details of International Direct Dialling.
Yellow Pages	
Thomson Local Directory	
Trade directories	relevant to the business of the firm.
Firm's House Journal	
Entertainments guide for the area	
Local newspapers	showing 'what's on'.
Pub food and restaurant guides	

SECRETARIAL TIPS

1 A card index box is useful for filing business visiting cards. They should be glued or stapled to an index card, which makes them easier to handle and find. Business visiting cards form a useful record of callers and can be referred to for names and addresses for sending out advertising material.

2 Normally, your boss would not want to be interrupted while he has a caller with him, but occasionally it is necessary. Write the message down, mark it *urgent*, go quietly into his office (secretaries are not expected to knock on the door) and place it in front of him so that he cannot miss it. It is up to him then to take any action he thinks necessary.

3 Avoid answering questions from callers about the firm's business. There *are* such individuals as industrial spies and they are well trained to ask apparently trivial questions which may reveal vital information inadvertently.

4 Unclaimed lost property left behind by visitors without any identification should be handed over to the police (if valuable) or to a charity, if not, after a certain period of time. Six months is a reasonable period.

5 An internal staff directory, which lists all names and titles of staff, together with their extension numbers, is a useful help to remembering names when starting work in a large organisation.

QUICK REVISION

1 A firm's reception area should be near the main entrance and can be used to publicise the firm and its products by displaying: (a) .... (b) ....

2 A receptionist's duties may include operating a switchboard and teleprinter as well as ....

3 A receptionist's desk will have records of callers ....

4 A record of the movements of staff may be kept in a ....

5 An organisation chart gives ....

6 Security in connection with visitors to a firm can be ensured by ....

7 When is information about appointments given to a receptionist by secretaries? ....

8 Business visiting cards should be kept and can be referred to as a useful source of names and addresses for ....

9 If an interruption is unavoidable when your boss is engaged you should ....

10 Deal with unidentifiable items left behind by visitors by .... or ....

ASSIGNMENTS

1 Your firm is expanding and plans to have a reception area with a full-time receptionist to look after visitors. Draw up a list of amenities for the convenience and comfort of any visitors who may have to wait.

2 Draft an advertisement for a receptionist, listing qualities she should have, and qualifications (she will have a switchboard to look after and there will be typing and filing to do).

3 You work in a small firm and deal with callers as part of your job as a secretary. Several callers arrive at the same time, and while you are dealing with them, the telephone rings. What should be said to the waiting callers, and what are your priorities?

4 On a piece of card or sheet of paper, make yourself the following reminder list:

> *Remember this*
>
> **R**esponsible
> **E**fficient
> **C**aring
> **E**ngaging
> **P**leasant
> **T**actful
> **I**nterested
> **O**bservant
> **N**eat
> **I**ntelligent
> **S**miling
> **T**rustworthy

CHAPTER 4

Office Machinery

TYPEWRITERS

There are three kinds of typewriter in general use in offices – manual, electric and electronic. Manual typewriters are cheaper than electronic typewriters and they need no power point. Electronic typewriters are now replacing electric typewriters in most offices. The electronic typewriter is almost identical in operation to an electric typewriter with the addition of a small memory which is used to enable automatic correction. The typing element on an electronic typewriter is shaped like a daisy – there are no typebars or typeface. 'Daisywheels' are interchangeable to give different pitch and characters.

Memory Typewriter

This can store up to 200,000 characters (about 200 pages of A4 typing). The characters are not just the letters printed on the paper, but also include instructions to the machine regarding line spacing, headings, etc. A copy of each letter or document stored in the memory must be kept in a folder so that it is possible to refer to them for reference and retyping when required.

Supplies for the Typewriter

Ribbons

Typewriter ribbons are made of nylon, silk, cotton, or carbon. Nylon and silk ribbons produce work of very good appearance – the finer the fabric, the sharper the imprint. Carbon ribbons produce the best imprint. Unfortunately, they can be used once only and so are very expensive. Two-colour nylon and silk ribbons are available (called bi-chrome), usually red and black, and correcting ribbons, which switch from normal black to white, so that the error is typed over in white, made invisible and the correction typed over again in black. Lift-off ribbons can be used on all self-correcting typewriters (electric and electronic) that have provision for fitting the tapes, but they are suitable only for correcting errors made with carbon ribbons.

Copyholders

Many typists are trained to stand their textbooks and notebooks upright on copyholders and prefer to continue to use them in the office. Complicated work is assisted by accurate line-by-line reading and some copyholders are electrically operated by means of a foot-controlled switch.

Using an illuminated copyholder

Continuous Stationery Attachment

This is fitted to the back of a typewriter (see p. 77) and enables the forms (which are in sets with interleaved carbon or NCR perforated between each set) to be fed into the machine and torn off as completed. A continuous stationery attachment saves the typist's time as each set of documents is ready in the typewriter when the previous one has been completed.

Continuous stationery may consist of perforated labels or letterheading for use on computer printers (see p. 90).

Typist's Accessories

- Erasers: These are available in many shapes and sizes, from the pencil type, which can be sharpened to keep a fine erasing point, to the larger rectangular one which has a soft pencil rubber and a hard typewriter rubber combined.
- Eraser shields: These are made of clear plastic and are placed over the word to be corrected so that only the letters to be replaced are erased.

A typewriter with a continuous stationery attachment

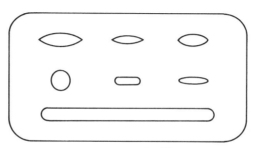

An eraser shield

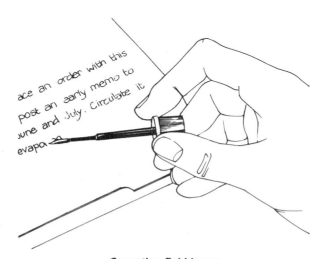

Correcting fluid in use

- Liquid corrective: These are available in many colours (and several kinds of dispensers) so that the colour of the letterheading and/or typing paper can be exactly matched. The error is 'painted' over, allowed to dry and then retyped. The carbon copy must, of course, be corrected also.

- Backing sheets: These can be supplied with scales showing the typing lines and inches along the top. They help to show the typist when she is nearing the bottom of her page. Backing sheets also protect the platen (roller) from wear and tear and improve the appearance of the work. The 'fold over' top of a backing sheet helps to keep carbons and carbon copies level when the typist is feeding them into her machine.

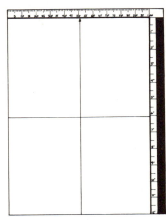

A scaled backing sheet

The Care of the Typewriter

A typewriter is an expensive and complex piece of machinery and should be looked after by the typist, whether it is her own portable, which she uses at home, or an electric typewriter she uses in an office.

Here are some guidelines:

- Switch off and unplug an electric or electronic typewriter at the end of the day. Switch off when not in use, during the day.

- *Always* cover a typewriter after use, to keep out the dust.

- Remove dust daily (preferably first thing in the morning) especially underneath, because this rises into the machine and clogs it.

- Rub out carefully on manual and electric machines, moving the carriage (using the margin release) so that the bits of rubber dust fall on to the desk and not into the type basket. *Do not rub out* if using an electronic machine – use the lift-off corrective ribbon or, remove typing from machine, paint over liquid corrective, allow to dry and retype.

- Use a backing sheet when single copies are being typed – this improves the look of the typing and protects the platen from wear and tear.

- To move a typewriter, *lift from underneath,* not by the carriage, and move both margins to the centre so that the carriage will not slide along.

- Never leave a typewriter near the edge of the desk, where it could be accidentally knocked off by a passer-by.

- Never leave a typewriter near a hot radiator – this will dry out the oil in the machine.

- Clean the typeface on a manual or electric typewriter with a stiff brush and white spirit, once a week. This will remove the surplus ink which will eventually clog the typeface. On an electronic typewriter, use specially impregnated cleaning paper. Clean finger marks off the machine with spirit and dust with a soft brush where rubber dust has collected on a manual or electric machine. Wipe the platen with a duster dampened with spirit.

- *Do not oil* a typewriter – leave this to a trained mechanic. Surplus oil in a machine can ruin typing and is difficult to get rid of.

- Always call in a trained mechanic to repair faults – *do not* try to mend them yourself.

AUDIO-TYPING EQUIPMENT

One area in which the use of two pieces of equipment is combined is that of audio-typing. The typist listens through headphones to a pre-recorded cassette or tape and types what she hears, either on to a typewriter or a computer with a word processing program (see p. 79). She can stop or start the recording by the use of a pedal, thus leaving her hands free for typing. A competent audio-typist develops a technique which allows her to listen to

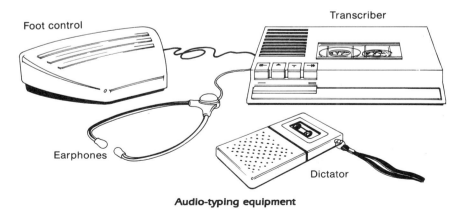

Foot control

Transcriber

Earphones

Dictator

Audio-typing equipment

quite long phrases, and type them back very quickly. She must also have a very good standard of English, as she has no 'copy' to look at. Her spelling and punctuation have to be very accurate indeed.

Recording media used on dictating machines may be: belts or sleeves, tapes, cassettes, sheets, wire, discs.

Magnetic media can be re-used. Non-magnetic media is used once only and then discarded. It is cheaper than magnetic to buy, but more expensive in the long term.

Advantages of Audio-Typing

The workload can be spread among several audio-typists

Cassettes, sleeves, tapes, etc. can be posted

Time is saved while a secretary is typing from one audio machine and her boss is dictating on to another.

Disadvantages of Audio-Typing

Audio-typing requires intense concentration and is tiring for long periods

The dictator's voice may be indistinct and difficult to hear

A great deal of background noise is often recorded also – many rooms in firms are far from sound-proof

Loss of personal contact between boss and typist or secretary

Recording media is difficult to keep entirely confidential – copies are easily 'dubbed'

Tapes are cleared when finished (if magnetic) and all records are lost – shorthand notes could be referred to later, long after the notes have been transcribed, if necessary.

Centralised Audio-typing

With centralised audio-typing several dictating machines are located in one room (often part of the typing pool; see p. 12). The manager dictates his correspondence on to tape in his office. The tapes are then taken to the central audio-typing unit by messengers.

Bank System

In a bank system the manager has a microphone only in his office (sometimes like a telephone) and when he wants to dictate he dials a code and starts dictating after receiving a signal to say the machine is free. The tape is then taken to an audio-typist to be transcribed.

Tandem System

Yet another arrangement is the tandem system. Each typist has two dictating machines and can type from one while the other is available to record dictation. If she has any queries, she can telephone the person dictating to ask him what he said or even play back part of the tape to him, so that he can listen and explain. The 'tandem' system is used by many firms because it means the typist has some contact with the person dictating and feels the work is less impersonal.

A dictating machine cannot take over the role of the secretary, who is able to think for herself and use her own initiative. Ideally, a good secretary should be able to write shorthand *and* use audio-typing equipment.

WORD PROCESSING

Word processing is the ability to correct text and move it around on a word processor, or computer with a word processing program (the software), before printing. Word processing is of enormous advantage to anyone who puts words on paper, in particular secretaries, and saves all the drudgery of re-typing which used to be an inevitable part of their jobs.

Word processing allows the typist to see her work on the screen (VDU) in front of her, read it and correct it before it is printed. Word processing also enables the typist to delete, re-arrange sentences, change paragraphs around or change the layout of whatever is on the screen. Typing can also be 'justified' (the right-hand margin is printed exactly even in the same way as the left). Word processing produces all the repetitive work of typists and secretaries such as circulars, reports, minutes, legal documents, much faster than they can. The work produced is of sufficiently high quality as to be indistinguishable from individually typed work.

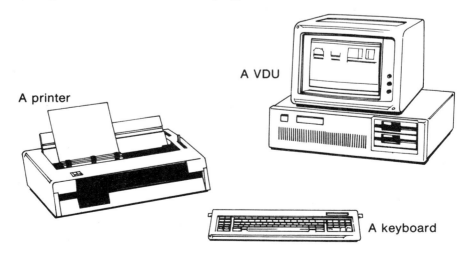

A printer

A VDU

A keyboard

All the work typed may be stored in the memory of the computer, which is a useful facility for such documents as form letters (see p. 241). Many word processing programs provide a check on spelling, and contain a dictionary to which any new words are added as they are used.

Word processing has had a great effect on the number of copy-typists employed by all types of firms, especially the very large organisations, because there is no longer the need to re-type whole documents from corrected drafts. The original draft is recalled from the memory of the word processing program, altered on the screen, and reprinted – a matter of minutes when previously it could have taken hours. Now that computers with word processing programs have come down so dramatically in price, word processing is becoming much more commonplace in offices.

Printers

The printing of the work which has appeared on the screen is done by a printer. The quality of the work produced by word processing depends on the printhead used, and the choice of printer is therefore very important.

The printer is similar to a typewriter but without a keyboard. It receives instructions from the typist through the computer about when to start printing, the number of copies of each page and when to stop.

A dot matrix printhead forms characters by a series of dots, and although very fast, does not produce work of a quality sufficiently high for letter word processing, although improvements are being made.

The daisy wheel printhead produces work similar to typing and is the one most used in offices for word processing. Daisy wheels are easily and quickly changed when different typefaces are needed, but have the disadvantage of being noisy. Daisywheel printheads are also slower than the two other types of printheads (see below).

Another type of printhead, which is quieter, quicker and very good quality is the laser. It makes no more noise than an office copier, and is several times faster than a daisy wheel, but it is expensive.

Ink jet printheads are also silent and fast; their main advantage is the very high-quality printing they produce, as there is no typeface to strike the paper – characters are produced by forcing ink at high speed through an electrostatic field. The lastest ink jet printheads can also produce work in many different colours.

A daisy wheel

VDU HEALTH AND SAFETY

Very few offices in the UK are without visual display units (VDUs) and most modern units do not present any health hazards to the health of women (even when pregnant) or men. A great deal of research has been carried out all over the world in the last 10 years to establish possible links between using VDUs and health problems, and none have been proven. However, although the VDU itself is innocent, the environment in which it is used and the way users sit may not be, especially if the VDU is used for long periods of time. Good ergonomics can eliminate headaches, stiff necks, backache and eyestrain – the problems from which some VDU operators do suffer.

The first essential is an armless swivel chair with a stable five-leg base, and an adjustable back and height.

Guidelines for VDU Operators

- The height of the screen should be adjusted to make eyes level with the top of the screen when sitting upright looking straight ahead, so that when reading data on the screen, only the eyes have dropped and *not* the head. If the head drops, this can cause neckache and stiff shoulders.
- The many wearers of glasses may need a special pair for VDU work, particularly the short-sighted, because of the distance between them and the screen. An optician will advise about this.
- The office lighting should not be so bright that it causes reflections on the screen and direct light from windows should be avoided. Screens should be at right angles to windows and not facing or backing on to them.
- A copyholder (see p. 74) will be helpful for copying from other documents on to a VDU – it will keep the documents at the right angle to the eyes and in the same plane as the screen.

Ideal Positioning of a VDU

Study this illustration in conjunction with the points listed on p. 83.

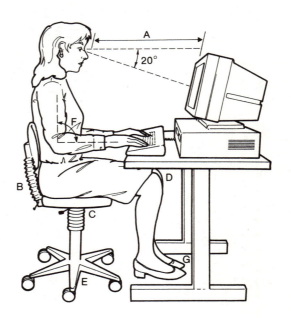

- 350mm to 600mm distance. Eyes downcast at 15 degrees to 20 degrees (see A).
- Adjustable backrest holding back up straight (B).
- Adjustable height of seat to give good forearm position and to create clearance for knees under desk (C).
- Desk height to be adjusted from seating position (D).
- Stable five leg 'star' base on castors (E).
- Elbows approximately 90 degrees forearm parallel to ground (F).
- Feet flat on floor or on a footrest, with the thighs supported by chair seat (G).

COMPUTERS AND PRINTERS

Computers are electronic machines which can:

- store information. This information is called data.
- sort out the data and, if required, perform calculations. This is called data processing.

In business organisations the computer may be used for many purposes including:

- word processing
- diaries
- receptionist's records
- personnel records
- electronic mail
- payroll calculations
- stock control
- accountancy
- analysis of sales information
- desk-top publishing (high quality word processing suitable for photographic reproduction in publications).

Other uses of computers include navigation of ships and aircraft, bar code readers and information analysis at supermarket checkouts.

Types of Computer

There are three types of computer:

- Mainframes are large computers which can support many terminals and perform complex high-speed calculations. They would probably be used by organisations such as banks, insurance companies, the Inland Revenue and the AA or RAC.

- Minicomputers, smaller than mainframes, usually work less quickly with fewer terminals.
- Microcomputers are small independent computers which can perform a comprehensive range of operations. They are now to be found on many desktops in offices. Microcomputers can be linked together to form a network. This enables a number of individual users to share software programs, and data. The network will often be linked to a high-quality printer (see p. 80) so that all users are able to benefit from one expensive item.

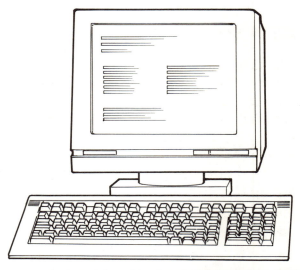

A computer terminal consisting of keyboard and visual display unit (VDU)

Computer Hardware

The main features of a computer are:

- The input, where information is put into the computer. This may be typed in at a keyboard, or inserted by magnetic tape, magnetic disc, or other devices such as bar code readers.
- The central processing unit, the core of the computer, which performs calculations and manipulates data.
- The memory, which is the active storage of the computer and holds the operating program and data being used by the program.

- The output, where information comes out of the computer. It may appear on the screen of a VDU, be printed out on paper, or be transferred electronically to provide instructions to other equipment.
- The data store, where information is stored on magnetic tape or disc for the computer to use when necessary. Disks or tapes can be changed when the computer is required to perform a different job with another set of information. There are two types of disk – a hard disk which is usually built into the computer and can store a large quantity of data and a floppy disk which can be removed from the computer and stored elsewhere.
- Peripherals, or other devices which are linked to the computer to help it operate, such as a printer, modem, bar code reader, or VDU.

Computer Software

Once a computer has been assembled from electronic components, it is unable to perform any task until it is given a set of instructions to follow. These instructions, which have to be loaded into the computer's memory, are known as software. Software programs used most frequently in offices today are:

- word processing,
- spreadsheets,
- databases,
- electronic mail (see p. 174).

A *database* can be regarded as being a large store of information – the computer version of a filing cabinet. The computer can retrieve and sort selected sections of the database. Mail order companies may use a database to select special categories of customers to target a sales campaign.

A *spreadsheet* is a large electronic sheet of paper divided into vertical columns and horizontal rows. Numbers can be entered in boxes at the intersection of a column and row. Calculations can then be defined easily for rows or columns. The major benefit is that users can quickly design their own spreadsheet to perform a large number of complex calculations. Spreadsheets can be used in conjunction with databases and information can be formatted through the word processing program. Spreadsheets can also be used to plot charts and graphs (see pp. 129–136).

Computer Supplies

Paper

The most commonly used output from a computer is printed *hard copy*, so paper is an important 'consumable supply'. Paper can be in sheets similar to ordinary typing paper, or continuous stationery (see p. 74). Paper must be kept flat and uncreased, especially if separate sheets are used, otherwise it will not feed singly through the sheet feeder. It is also important to 'fan' the paper before placing it in the sheet feeder, to make sure the sheets are not sticking together.

Ribbons

Fabric ribbons can be used in the same way as fabric ribbons on a typewriter – until the ink has started to fade and the copy is not clear. Fabric ribbons are used on computers with dot matrix printers (see p. 81) as they are cheaper and so more economical when large quantities of work have to be printed. Plastic film ribbons (otherwise known as carbon ribbons) are supplied in cartridges which can be changed very easily. Carbon ribbons are used once only and then discarded, so they are obviously expensive and used for high-quality word processing.

Printheads

Daisy wheel printheads are delicate (especially the plastic ones) and easily damaged, so spare ones should be safely stored in boxes and labelled for easy identification. Additional daisy wheels may be needed to change the pitch or style of the typeface.

Day-to-day Care of Computers and Printers

It is important to look after a computer and printer as follows:

- Avoid switching computers on and off while programs are running, otherwise data on disk may be 'corrupted' (spoilt) and made useless.
- Close computer down correctly before finally switching off.
- Dust covers should be used for computers and printers whenever they are not in use.
- Screens should be dusted daily with a dust-free cloth (a dry wash-leather is ideal) to clean off fingerprints. The other surfaces of the computer should be dusted frequently.

Care of Disks

- Always file disks upright in the special boxes. Note the disk contents on the label.
- Do not expose disks to strong magnetic fields – these may occur near telephones, electrical equipment, paperclip holders with magnets. A magnetic field may destroy the information on the disk.
- Do not leave disks lying in sunlight as this could warp them and make them useless.
- Never touch the surface of a disk, or allow liquids, dust or cigarette ash to come into contact with it.

- All data on a computer which is important should be copied on to a 'back-up' disk at the end of each working day, and stored separately, in case information is accidentally wiped off the computer or corrupted.

Security of Computers

It is becoming increasingly important to make computers thief-proof, because of the value of the data stored in them. Hours of work may have been devoted to entering complex information on to a computer and this cannot be easily or quickly replaced. There are separate covers which can be locked over a computer keyboard so that when it is not in use it cannot be tampered with. It also protects the keyboard against dust and spillages. When the keyboard is opened, it can be used as a copyholder.

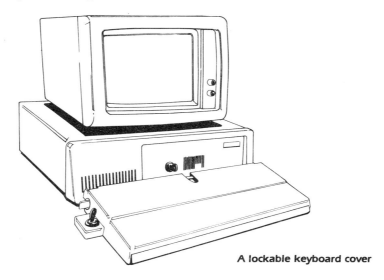

A lockable keyboard cover

Special locks are available which can link computers, printers, office copiers, and typewriters together with steel plates and cables.

There are also fireproof computer cabinets available, which protect the computer and its data in the event of fire.

CALCULATORS

Machines for adding have been used since the seventeenth century. One of the first machines capable of dealing with money columns was the Burroughs, produced in 1888. The cash registers largely in use until a few years ago were a development along the same lines. Modern calculators which carry out very complex mathematical calculations, as well as simple addition, subtraction and multiplication, have become smaller and cheaper due to the development of the 'silicon chip'. Pocket calculators are used everywhere today – in schools, colleges, offices, shops and the home. The slimmest pocket calculator is no larger than a pocket diary, and there is even one with an alarm and a clock which prints a message when the alarm rings, to remind the person awoken where he has to go!

In offices, it is often useful to have a slightly larger, heavy-duty calculator to stand on a desk. It is also necessary when working with figures to have a record of the total, and some calculators print-out the calculation in addition to showing the answer in the display unit.

The larger calculators can be plugged into the mains, or operated from batteries, some of which are rechargeable by being left plugged in overnight.

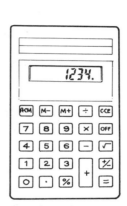

A pocket calculator

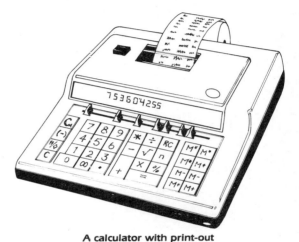

A calculator with print-out

THE DATA PROTECTION ACT

In 1984, the Data Protection Act became law; its purpose is to protect the use of information about individuals on computers and word processors, and to enforce a set of rules for the processing of such information. The Data Protection Act gives new rights to individuals, and brings obligations for computer users. An important obligation is to register details of the personal information kept on electronic files. This includes the users of computer bureaux. A computer bureau is an organisation or individual who processes data or allows a data user to use his equipment.

The three categories of *unconditional* exemption from requirements laid down by the Act are:

- Individuals keeping personal details on a computer for personal, family, household or recreational purposes.
- Personal data which the user is required by law to make public.
- Personal data which has to be exempt in the interests of national security.

The following *may* be exempt: firms keeping lists of individuals for accounts and payroll only, providing the data are not used for any other purposes (e.g. analysis of absenteeism, or mailing advertising material). The moment the information on the computer is used for any other purposes, it has to be registered.

There are other conditional exemptions regarding the detection of crime and the collection of tax, which do not apply to business firms or individuals.

If there is any doubt at all about whether a person (or firm) is exempt, it is advisable to register.

Individuals will be able to obtain information held about them by data users from the register, which will be made available for public inspection. They will be able to see what types of personal information are held by data users and also how they are used, obtained and disclosed. Since August 1986, local libraries have had the list of registered computer users showing what sort of information is there, where the data came from and what is being done with the files.

The registrar has the power to investigate whether a firm is registered or not; if it should be registered and is not, there are severe legal penalties. The higher courts have the right to impose unlimited fines, and can demand the removal of the offending programs, which could have a disastrous effect on a firm. The full powers of the registrar came into effect on 11 November 1987.

In addition to the registrar's powers, individuals have the right to sue if they have good cause to think personal information about them on a computer is being used unlawfully.

COPYING AND DUPLICATING

Carbon Copies

Most firms today use what is known as 'long-life' carbon paper which is plastic-coated and is clean, easy to handle and less likely to curl or crease. It is this type of carbon paper which will be referred to from now on. Carbon paper is available in a variety of strong colours – red, black, blue, purple and green. It is often useful for identification purposes to send a certain colour to a particular department, or person.

Care of Carbon Paper

Carbon paper should be stored flat, preferably in a box, away from radiators in a cool place.

Creased carbon paper produces 'trees' on the carbon copies. A 'treed' carbon copy is the sign of a careless typist.

A carbon copy with 'trees'

Careful erasing prolongs the life of carbon paper. Rubber dust should be brushed off the carbon paper after erasing, away from the type basket on to the desk. The typewriter carriage on electric or manual machines should be moved as far as possible to left or right before rubbing out.

One-time Carbons

These are a thin, inexpensive type of carbon paper, often used for interleaving documents supplied in sets – teleprinter rolls, computer stationery, invoices, etc. and after removal from the documents are scrapped. One-time carbon saves the typist inserting carbons, although she still has to take them out. Another use for 'one-time' carbons is with ink stencils.

Continuous Stationery

This consists of sets of documents which are fed in from a continuous roll attached to a typewriter by a special attachment (see pp. 74 and 75). After each document has been typed, it can be torn off the roll by means of perforations, and the next document is brought into the machine, ready for typing. Continuous stationery increases the speed with which the typist produces the documents – inserting carbons, placing the 'set' in the typewriter and removing the carbons often takes far more time than actually typing the information on the documents.

Continuous stationery may be interleaved with 'one-time' carbons or NCR paper (see below).

Continuous stationery can also consist of 'peel-off' labels on a perforated sheet, or letterheading for use on a computer printer.

NCR – No Carbon Required

NCR when used in connection with making copies means 'no carbon required'. NCR paper produces copies by the use of chemicals, either on the back of the paper, or on the back and the front. NCR paper is supplied in sets, lightly attached at the top and thus saves the typist inserting and removing carbons. NCR paper will produce about five clear, readable copies. It is used for invoices, orders, statements, telex messages, computer print-outs.

Office Copiers

Using carbon paper means that copies are made at the same time that the original is typed. Photocopiers exactly copy an original *after* it has been typed. The two types of photocopiers in general use in offices today are:

- Those which require specially treated paper – the copies are more expensive to produce but the equipment is inexpensive.
- Those which copy on to plain paper – the copies are inexpensive but the equipment is much more expensive than that in above.

Plain paper copiers use the electrostatic system which produces a dry copy every half second on plain bond paper. There are now photocopiers available that can produce coloured copies.

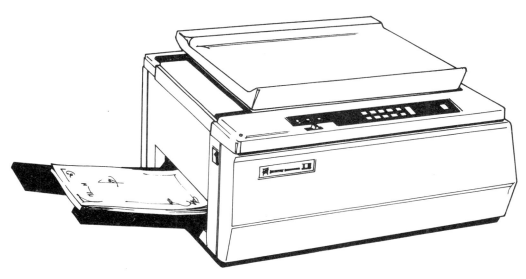

Guidelines for Making Photocopies

Modern photocopiers are simple to use, provided a little care is taken over positioning the 'master' copy – the one from which all the copies are to be made. Make sure that it is within the frame indicated on the photocopier, and placed square inside this, otherwise the copies will not be centrally placed on the paper, and even, in some cases, will have tops, bottoms or one side cut off completely, making the copy useless.

Safety

If a photocopier is not working (check that it is plugged in and switched on first, of course), phone for a mechanic from the firm who supplied it. *Do not attempt to put it right yourself!*

Don't use equipment marked 'Out of order'!

Enlarging and reducing documents and drawings can be carried out by some photocopiers, and copies can be made on both sides of the paper. Plain paper copies can be made from microfilm (see pp. 117–18). Transparencies for an overhead projector and 35mm colour slides can also be produced by the most up-to-date photocopiers.

Far from becoming obsolete, as had been predicted after the arrival of the electronic age in the office, photocopiers are likely to remain indispensable in offices and educational establishments for many years to come.

Heat Transfer Copying

Heat transfer copying (also known as 'thermography') will not copy ballpoint ink – only inks which have a carbon content (fibre-tipped pens, typewriter ribbon, indian ink) or lead pencil. Copies tend to fade after a time and are, therefore, useful for internal work only. A heat (thermal) copier will also make a master for a spirit duplicator or dyeline copier, an ink stencil for an ink duplicator and transparency for an overhead projector. Special paper is needed for heat transfer copies, which is expensive. A thermal copier will also 'laminate', that is, coat sheets with a thin film of plastic to protect from dust.

92

Duplicating

The word 'duplicating' refers to the production of a large number of copies. Plain paper (electrostatic) copiers both duplicate and copy, because they produce, very quickly, as many or as few copies as required.

Spirit Duplicating

This is a method which produces many copies from a master sheet and gets its name from the spirit which is fed into the duplicator and washes off a little of the carbon at the back of the master sheet to print each copy. It is not suitable for documents which are to be sent out of a firm (external use) because the copies are not of sufficiently high quality. They are in fact 'carbon' copies, although the carbon (hectograph carbon) which produces them is of a different type to that used in typewriters.

Masters for a spirit duplicator can be made by a thermal copier (see p. 92).

Spirit duplicating is particularly suitable for diagrams, maps and job cards where colour is advantageous.

Ink Duplicating

Ink duplicating is often referred to as 'stencil duplicating' because the ink in the duplicator goes through the spaces made on the 'stencil' by the typewriter keys.

About 5000 good clear copies can be obtained from one ink stencil if it is handled carefully. Colour can be introduced by changing the duplicator drum and ink.

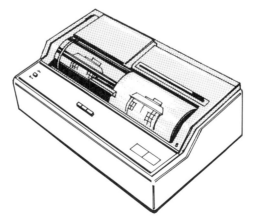

An electronic scanner for making ink duplicator stencils

An electronic scanner will make stencils for an ink duplicator as also will a thermal copier (see p. 92).

Both ink and spirit duplicating are being used less and less in offices today, because of computers with word processing programs (see pp. 79–80).

Offset-litho Duplicating

Offset duplicating (or simply 'offset') involves taking an impression first on a rubber cylinder and from the rubber cylinder printing on to paper. This gives a clearer, smudge-free impression and produces high-quality work which is like printing. 'Litho' is the abbreviated form of 'lithography' which means literally 'printing by stone'. Printing by stone is a process using grease and water that was discovered about 200 years ago. This principle of oil and water not mixing is still used in offset-lithography, but today thin metal or paper plates are used instead of stone for the master copy.

Reprography and Office Machinery

Computers

An image scanner (see below) can read text documents or graphic images and process into a computer for printing, or into a facsimile machine for transmitting.

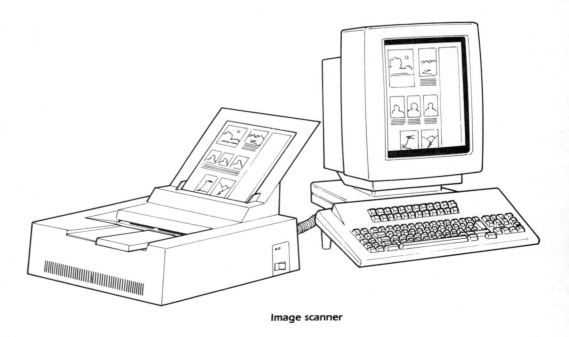

Image scanner

SECRETARIAL TIPS

1 When the centre of A4 carbon is no longer producing good clear copies, it should be cut in half (to give two sheets of A5). This will redistribute the wear.

2 Cut away the top left or right-hand corner of carbon paper – this enables it to be shaken out while the copies are held between thumb and first finger.

3 Copies produced by spirit duplicating are on smooth, non-absorbent paper and are thus suitable for forms which will be completed with ballpoint pen.

4 If an ink stencil is complicated, type a draft on plain paper first.

5 The fastest, most accurate copies are produced by a photocopier from a word processed master copy.

6 There is a special corrective fluid which should be used for errors on photocopies. Ordinary corrective fluid will leave grey marks.

QUICK REVISION

1 Audio-typing equipment consists of 4 components: ....

2 Strain caused by working at VDU screens can be reduced by ....

3 The most frequently used computer programs in offices today are ....

4 Three guidelines for the day-to-day care of computers and printers are ....

5 Three ways of safeguarding the valuable data on a computer are ....

6 The purpose of the Data Protection Act is to ....

7 The three categories of exemption from the Data Protection Act are ....

8 The two main types of office copiers are ....

9 Although spirit duplicating is unsuitable for external work, it has the advantage of ....

10 Both ink and spirit duplicating are being used less and less in offices today because of ....

11 If many hundreds of thousands of good quality copies are needed, the equipment to produce them is ....

ASSIGNMENTS

1 Set out the advantages and/or disadvantages of replacing your ink duplicator with either a plain paper copier or a computer with a word processing program. Your ink duplicator turns out hundreds of copies daily for distribution to many branches.

2 Give guidelines for all users of computers on the care of disks, paper for the printer, and daisywheel printheads.

CHAPTER 5

Retrieval and Storage of Information

REASONS AND GENERAL RULES FOR FILING

The storage of documents (filing) is carried out so that they can be found when they are wanted. There is no other reason for keeping papers. Therefore the system of filing must be easy to understand by anyone who needs access to it. The cleverest way of filing is useless if no one else except the person filing understands it!

In large firms there may be a central filing system into which all documents are stored, with individual personalised filing by secretaries of their employers' papers. In a small firm, the secretary will be responsible for most of the filing of her employer's papers, although this is a job which is often delegated to a junior.

The reason for filing!

Filing should be done as frequently as possible – several times a day, if time allows. It is time-consuming to locate one particular document if it is in a heap of papers in no particular order awaiting filing.

The filing point is the name under which the paper will be filed.

The most important part of the entire filing process is placing the papers in the right file.

Papers are filed mainly to allow access to them later, but also to keep them uncreased and clean. Place them flat and square in the file with the *latest* paper on top. Papers are filed in date (chronological) order, so the oldest paper is at the back of the file.

What Sort of Papers are Filed?

A large part of filing consists of letters which have come into the firm, and carbon copies of letters which have been sent out. Carbon copies do not need release symbols (see p. 102), and are quickly recognisable as they are often on coloured 'flimsy' (bank) paper, but also there is no printed name of a firm at the top. The other type of business letter received by firms is a personal one sent from a private individual to a firm. There would be no printed name at the top of a personal business letter – instead there would be

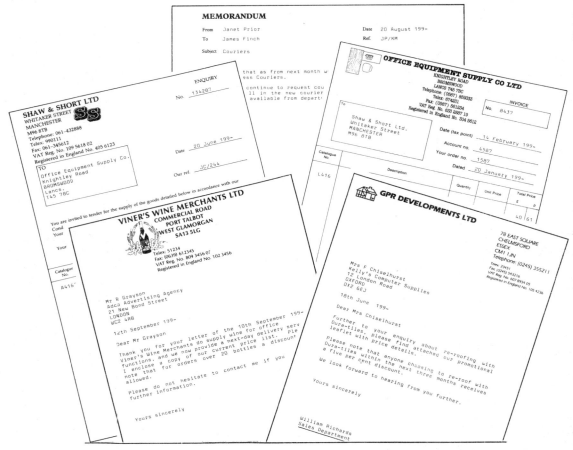

What sort of papers are filed?

a private address, either typed or written. Personal business letters would still need a release symbol, if a firm has a system of these. As well as letters, other papers to be filed would include memos, quotations, invoices, orders, credit and debit notes, and reports. Invoices and orders are numbered, so will be filed in order of number (numerically). Letter are usually filed alphabetically, in order of the name of the sender.

Miscellaneous File

A miscellaneous file is used for storing papers when there is no file for them (when no correspondence has been carried out previously). When four or five papers have been received or sent out, an individual folder should be made out. Do not allow miscellaneous files to become bulkier than other files; sort out the papers in them from time to time – it is possible some can be discarded. A convenient place for a miscellaneous file is at the front of each division of the alphabet in the filing cabinet. Papers are placed in alphabetical order in a miscellaneous file.

Lending of Files and Papers

A complete file borrowed should be replaced by an empty folder, ruled up and headed, known as an 'absent wallet' and marked 'OUT'. The wallet folder can then be used for filing papers during the borrowed file's absence.

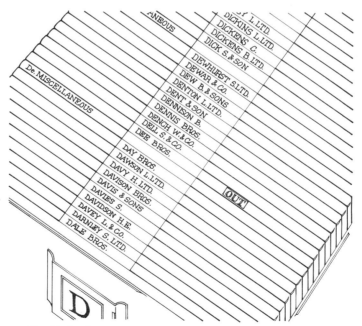

The file for Dee Bros has been borrowed and is marked 'Out'

One single paper taken out of a file should be replaced by an 'out' card:

Name of document	Borrower	Department	Date borrowed	OUT Date returned

An 'out' card

Cross-referencing

Firms sometimes change their names, because of mergers or take-overs. People change their names, especially women when they get married. Anyone looking in files under the old name has to be directed to the new name by means of a 'cross-reference'. A sheet is made out as below and placed in the files under the *old* name:

CROSS-REFERENCE SHEET

FOR CORRESPONDENCE FOR:
Waring and Simpson Ltd

SEE:
Swift Engineering Company Ltd

Cross-referencing can also be used for letters dealing with two topics (e.g. a customer sends a cheque paying for goods and in the same letter makes a complaint). File a photocopy under 'Payments and Complaints'.

Pending Papers

Some papers have to be kept available, out of the filing system, while they await further information. A box or lever-arch file is useful for pending papers, as is a ring binder or a concertina file.

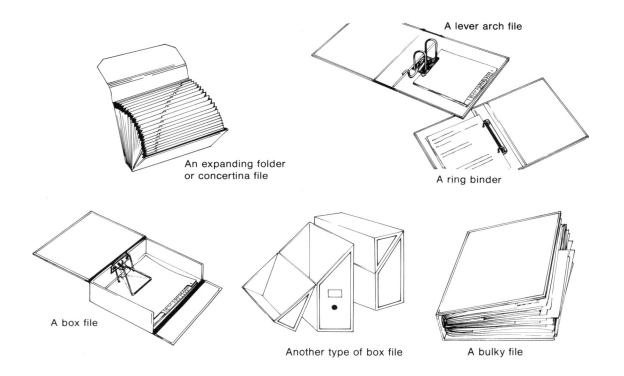

An expanding folder
or concertina file

A lever arch file

A ring binder

A box file

Another type of box file

A bulky file

Filing Bulky Items

Many offices collect bulky reports or technical journals. These can be stored in magazine files.

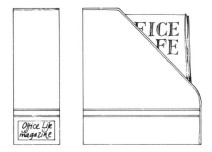

Front and side views of a magazine file

General Rules for Filing

There are several systems of filing, but whichever system is used in a firm, dealing with the filing should be approached in the same way.

- Pre-sort the papers, removing paper clips and pins and replacing them with staples. Place them into the order in which they will be filed. A desk-top sorter is useful for this. It is divided into sections labelled alphabetically and papers are placed behind flaps in their right section.

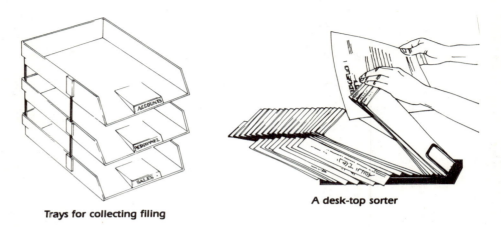

Trays for collecting filing

A desk-top sorter

- Check for 'release symbols' if the firm uses them. A release symbol may be just a line across the paper, a large 'F' for file or *'file'* stamped on as an instruction. Any document without a release symbol should be placed in a tray labelled 'queries' for confirmation later.

- While looking for release symbols, the filing 'point' should be circled or underlined.

- The filing point is the name under which the paper will be filed.

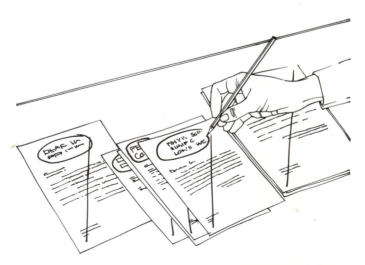

A filing clerk circling 'filing point' while pre-sorting the filing

Old Files

Eventually, some files become too packed with papers and have to be 'thinned' out. The oldest papers should be taken from the back of the file and transferred to files which are stored out of the way of the current filing system. As they may still be needed for reference, they should be clearly labelled and dated, with a note of which papers have been removed placed in the current file.

These out-of-date files are known as 'dead' files or 'transfer' files.

As papers cannot be kept forever, they are eventually destroyed and the most efficient way is to 'shred' them in a paper shredder.

The end of the filing system – but only after official instructions! No papers should ever be destroyed without permission to do so from a responsible person in a firm

The shredded paper can then be used by the packing department – a very practical piece of recycling.

As well as making useful packaging, shredded papers cannot be read by anyone who may be looking for confidential information.

FOLDERS AND FILING CABINETS

Storing Large Documents

Maps, photographs, drawings and charts must be kept flat – if folded they will crack along the folds, and if rolled, they will be difficult to keep flat when they are taken out to be used. A horizontal plan chest with wide, shallow drawers is one way to store large documents.

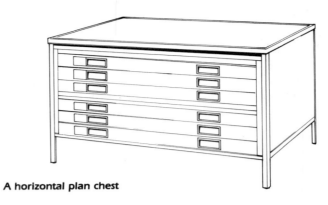

A horizontal plan chest

A suspension plan chest can also be used. The documents are suspended from rods in a chest deep enough to hold them. Alternatively, microfilming can be used to file very large documents (see p. 117).

A vertical suspension plan chest

Folders

Papers are usually kept in folders.

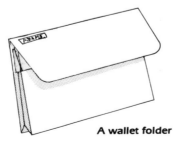

A wallet folder

A manilla folder

A folder with a metal clasp

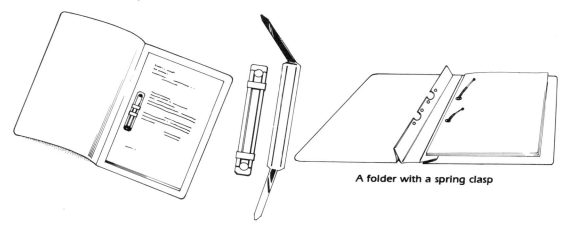

A folder with a spring clasp

Labelling Files

Labels for files can be flat, on the top edges of the pockets, or on projecting tabs 'staggered' so that they can all be seen easily. These are known as guide tabs. Colour is useful to help to find files quickly.

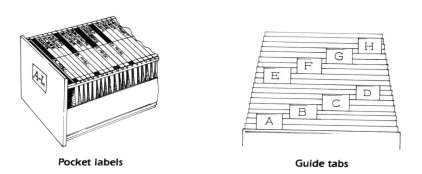

Pocket labels

Guide tabs

Useful Filing Accessories

Labels – for labelling files.

A hole punch and reinforcing washers for strengthening perforations.

Treasury tags for holding papers together loosely so that they can be turned over for reading easily.

Bulldog clips – springs for holding papers firmly.

A paper trimmer or guillotine.

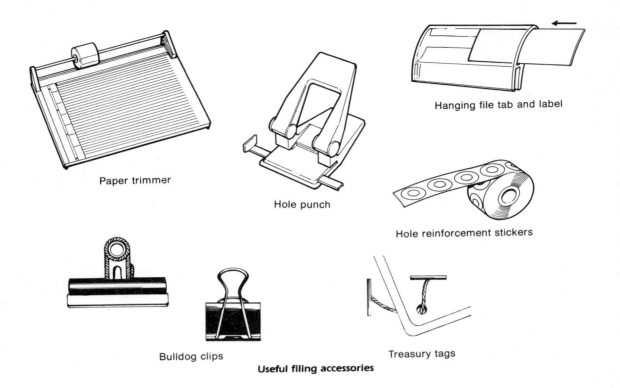

Paper trimmer

Hole punch

Hanging file tab and label

Hole reinforcement stickers

Bulldog clips

Treasury tags

Useful filing accessories

Vertical Suspension Filing Cabinets

Files are conveniently sorted in deep drawers in two, three, or four-drawer cabinets. Files stand upright in the drawers and should be supported and held by pockets linked together. These pockets 'suspend' the files and prevent them from slipping to the bottom of the filing cabinet drawer. The correct name for this type of filing is vertical suspension filing. The weight of the files is taken by the rails, thus keeping the files in perfect shape.

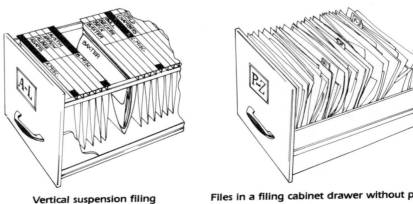

Vertical suspension filing

Files in a filing cabinet drawer without pockets

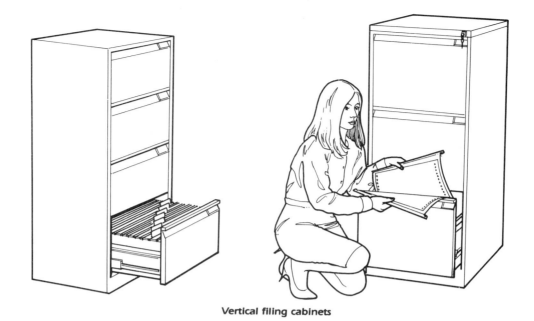

Vertical filing cabinets

Lateral Filing Cabinets

These take up less floor space than vertical suspension filing cabinets, as there are no drawers to be opened – the files are arranged side by side, like books on a shelf. Lateral filing cupboards can be extended upward towards the ceiling, but a safe means of reaching the top shelves will be essential. Pockets in lateral filing cupboards are suspended in a similar manner to those in vertical suspension filing cabinets.

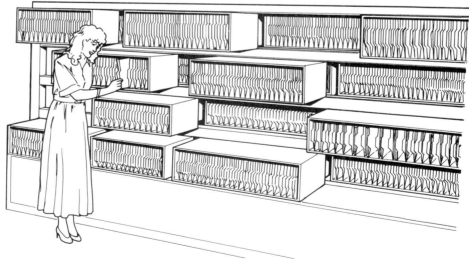

A sophisticated lateral filing system with horizontally sliding modules

SAFETY

Standing on a chair to reach the top shelf is dangerous!

Low filing stool

A suitable step ladder avoids accidents caused by standing on chairs or other makeshift objects. A low stool on castors saves an aching back while filing in the bottom drawers of filing cabinets and is easy to move around.

Vertical suspension filing cabinet drawers should always be closed after use.

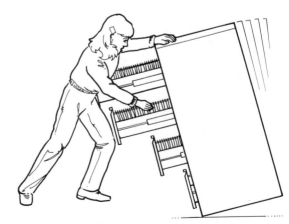

Situations to avoid!

Filing cabinets should not be placed behind doors

Security of Filing Systems

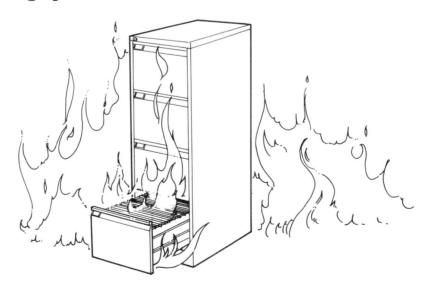

Special fireproof filing cabinets are available. All filing cabinets containing confidential information should be locked whenever the office is left unoccupied, and at the end of each day.

CLASSIFYING FILING

Classifying filing means the system by which papers are stored. Filing in alphabetical order is the simplest, and is the most widely used. It has one disadvantage – some letters (e.g. X and Z) will hardly be used at all and C or B may become overcrowded.

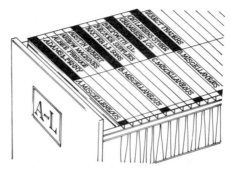

The top drawer in a filing cabinet, with the files arranged in alphabetical order of surnames or firms' names

Obviously, everyone knows the alphabet, but some guidelines are necessary to operate an alphabetical system efficiently.

Surnames

Use surnames as filing points. When there are identical surnames, file by forenames, or initial, if full first name is not known. If there are identical first names and surnames, file in alphabetical order of towns in which people live.

BROWN	Carole F	
BROWN	Carole Joanne	
BROWN	Carole W	
MARCH	Roy	Birmingham
MARCH	Roy	Huddersfield
MARCH	Roy	Worcester

File names with prefixes such as van, de la, O' under the prefix (i.e. the prefix and the word is treated as part of the surname).

DE BRAY	Martha
DE LA PARKE	Laurence
O'TOURKE	Patrick
VAN DE VEMEER	Vera

File surnames beginning with St as if it were spelt Saint.

ST GABRIEL
ST JOHN ERVINE
ST PHILIP

File all Scottish names beginning with Mc, Mac or M' as if they were all spelt Mac. Some Irish names begin with M', Mac or Mc, too.

McBETH	Thomas
M'BRIDE	Martha
McHENRY	Ian
MACKENZIE	Henry
MACMASTERS	Janet
McPHERSON	Martin

File a name such as 'Brown' before a similar one such as 'Browne' – i.e. the filing rule is 'short before long'.

MARCH	Andrew
MARCHE	Andrew
MARCHMONT	Andrew

Short before long!

Ignore altogether (from the point of view of filing)

- initials,
- titles,
- degrees (letters after a name),
- hyphens (file under the first part of the name).

BROWN	Lady Jane
CARTER-BROWN	James
REDD	Lord George
SILVER	Dr Mark
TAYLOR-JACKSON	Richard
WHITE	Dame Elizabeth

'The' and 'A' in names of firms:
 The O'Brien Steel Works Limited
file as: O'BRIEN Steel Works Limited (The)
 A modern Printing Company
file as: MODERN Printing Company (A)

Forenames in names of firms:
 Ernest G. Williams & Co. Ltd
file as: WILLIAMS Ernest G. & Co. Ltd

When the registered name of the firm includes two surnames, file under the
first: Hickson & Garrett Ltd
file as: HICKSON & Garrett Ltd

File any firm's name which includes a number as if the number were spelt in
full: The 45 Club
file as: FORTY-FIVE Club (The)

When it is not known what the initials represent in the name of a firm, file
their names before firms whose names are written in full:
 LKJ ENGINEERING Ltd
 LAMB'S Furniture Co. Ltd

When it is known what the initials represent, file normally:
 ICI Ltd   file under: IMPERIAL Chemical Industries
 RAC   file under: ROYAL Automobile Club
 BBC   file under: British Broadcasting Corporation

Numerical Filing

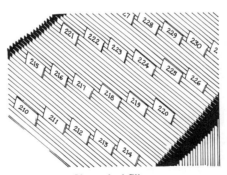

Numerical filing

This uses numbers instead of letters to divide the filing pockets of a filing
cabinet, and the documents filed are either numbered (invoices, orders,
quotations) or are given a number on receipt. A numerical system is easy to
add to (each new file is given the next number and added to the end of the
existing files). Numerical filing is especially useful in insurance companies,
building societies and hospitals. Numbers are difficult to remember,

112

however, and an alphabetical index of all the numbers has to be kept, with the numbers of the files against each name. This is another example of 'cross-referencing' – see p. 100. Many firms today would use a database program on a computer for this purpose (see p. 85).

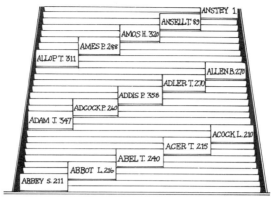

An alphabetical card index for numerical filing system

Chronological Filing

This is filing in date order. Most papers are placed in files in date order with the latest paper on top. The exception is numerical filing. Chronological filing is seldom used as a filing system on its own.

Geographical Filing

This is filing in alphabetical order of areas – towns, counties, countries or continents. Many organisations find geographical filing useful – travel agents, gas and electricity boards and export and sales departments in large firms.

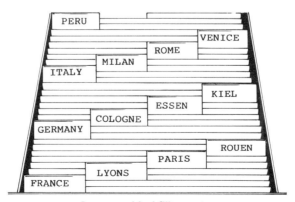

A geographical filing system

Subject Filing

Papers are filed in alphabetical order of topic. It is especially useful for filing personal papers.

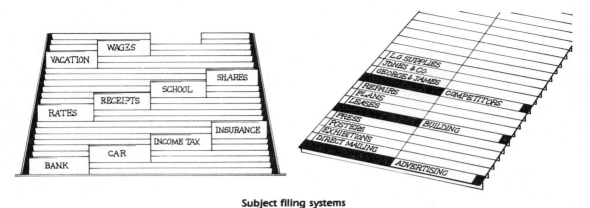

Subject filing systems

Cross-referencing is useful with subject filing. Examples:

- for salaries, see 'Wages',
- for PAYE, see 'Income tax'.

Terminal Digit Filing

Terminal digit filing is used where there is a very large number of files (hospitals, building societies, insurance companies). In a terminal digit system numbers are divided into pairs and read from right to left. In the numerical system, they are read normally, from left to right.

For example, in the number 987654, 54 would be the 'terminal digit' and could mean the drawer number, 76 the file number and 98 the place of the document in file 987654. Terminal digit filing has a high degree of accuracy, can be varied to suit different requirements and distributes the filing more evenly but it is more difficult to learn and operate than the normal numerical filing and still requires an alphabetical index.

INDEXING

Indexes are needed in offices for many reasons:

- Frequently used telephone numbers.
- Internal telephone numbers.
- Callers' business visiting cards.
- Alphabetical index for a numerical filing system (see p. 113).

All the items could be written in a book with indexed pages, but eventually the pages become full, or alterations have to be made. A loose-leaf book is a better idea, and enables the information to be typed in. A card index allows additions and alterations to be carried out easily and the cards can be stored in boxes with lids or small drawers. A rotary card index stores more cards in a smaller space than that taken up by boxes or drawers and all the cards are within easy reach (see illustration below).

MERCANTILE CREDIT Co. Ltd	071–242 98911
NEWTON & PARKINS Ltd	0227 64698
ORFORD Consultants	0223 354496
PALMER A. F. & Co. Ltd	0202 20696
QUEENSFERRY BUILDING SOCIETY	0705 820331
ROWLAND GEORGE and Partners	0702 34219
SCISSORS Hairdressing Salon	0382 36233
THOMPSON & MORGAN Ltd	0473 219478
UCL ENGINEERING Co Ltd	0232 46566
WAINWRIGHT SECRETARIAL AGENCY	0222 13697

A telephone index

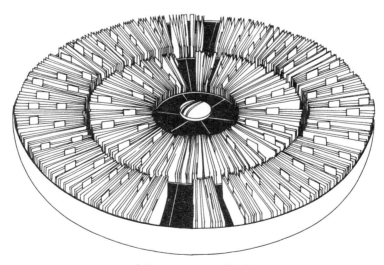

A large rotary card index

Visible edge cards is a method of storing cards in a shallow drawer or tray so that the edges overlap – there is not the danger of the cards falling out as there is with loose index cards in a box.

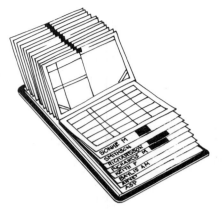

Visible edge cards in shallow drawers

Visible edge cards in a tray

Filing for Special Needs

Other items as well as documents have to be filed in offices today:

- *Disks for computers* — should be labelled and stored in racks and placed in lockable boxes.

- *Computer print-outs* — are too large for A4 folders, and should be in folders suspended from a frame as opposite.

- *Microfiche, aperture cards, microfilms* — microfilm reels should be stored in round containers (see p. 119).
  Aperture cards and microfiche can be stored in special cabinets.

- *Photographs, negatives and transparencies* — filed in transparent wallets, so that they can be used without being finger-marked.

- *Minutes of meetings* — see pp. 290–1.

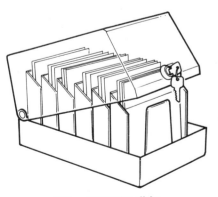

Filing computer disks

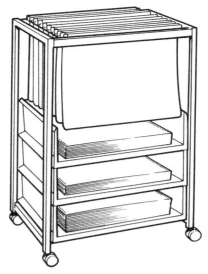

Filing computer print-outs

MICROFILMING

An alternative to plan chests for very large documents is to reduce them in size by a process known as microfilming.

Microfilming reduces documents to the size of a postage stamp. Eight thousand A4-sized documents will go on to a roll of microfilm 30 metres (100 feet) long. A single storage cabinet 1.3 metres (4½ feet) high will hold microfilms of one and a half million documents.

Microfilm is available in several forms. The following are convenient for filing:

- *Microfiche* – a sheet of film which holds 98 micro-images. A micro-image is an A4-sized document reduced in size 24 times.

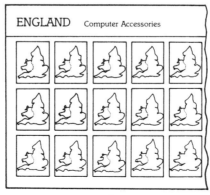

Microfiche

117

- *Aperture cards* have pieces of microfilm inset into them. They are usually punched cards for use in computers or punched card installations.

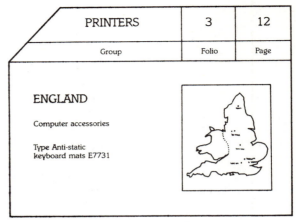

PRINTERS	3	12
Group	Folio	Page

ENGLAND

Computer accessories

Type Anti-static
keyboard mats E7731

Aperture card

Jacketing

Microfilm can be stored in a special protective transparent wallet or envelope, but it is difficult to remove the microfilms from this protective covering. This way of storing microfilms is known as microfilm 'jackets'. It has the advantage of making it almost impossible to lose a microfilmed document.

Microfilm on spools or reels is not suitable for filing and has to be stored in specially designed microfilm cabinets.

A reel of microfilm

Microfilm cassettes or cartridges are easier to handle and less likely to be damaged than reel film but are more expensive. Reel, cassette and cartridge films all suffer from the same disadvantage – it is difficult to locate any one particular section which may be required quickly.

Equipment

The following equipment is required for microfilming:

● camera,
● platform,
● jacketing machine,
● reader or reader/printer.

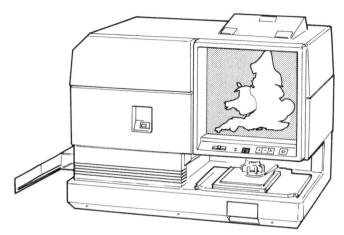

Viewing: enlarging on to screeen for reading off

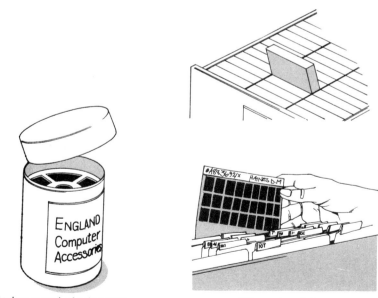

Storing a reel of microfilm   Filing microfiche

Storage: microfiling take under 2 per cent of normal file space

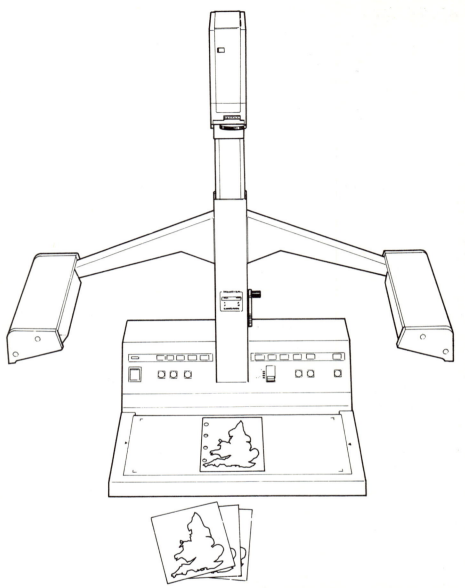

A microfilm camera and print from microfilm. Any number of copies can be made. Negatives are stored for future use

Microfilm can be produced directly from computer output, without any intermediate paper copy. This is known as COM, computer output on microfilm.

Firms use microfilming in many ways, including:

- for ordinary documents, to save filing space,
- for storing extra copies in case of fire,

- for large documents – maps, plans, photographs – to save space taken up by plan chests.

Libraries also use microfilming for back numbers of magazines and newspapers and to microfilm copies of thick, heavy books, so that they do not have the problem of carrying them from room to room.

Telephone and postcode directories for the whole of the UK are available on microfiche.

Museums microfilm very old and valuable papers so that the originals need not be handled.

The other advantages of microfilming are, in addition to space saving:

- postage is cheaper than postage for originals, especially airmail,
- duplicate copies of documents can be filed so that they are available in case of damage to originals by fire.

Apart from the cost of the equipment, the disadvantages are:

- a reader is needed to be able to see the documents,
- any particular section on reel or cassette is not easy to locate quickly when needed.

THE FILING CLERK AND SUPERVISOR

The Filing Clerk's Job

- Collection of papers.
- Pre-sorting – checking for release symbols – noting filing point. Queries placed on one side for checking later.
- Placing papers in correct file, latest paper on top.
- Lending files or papers only when record of borrower has been correctly completed.
- Completing cross-reference sheets for any files where names have been changed.
- Organising miscellaneous files for single papers which have to be filed until four or five have been received from the same firm.
- Filing as frequently as possible – preferably several times a day.

The Supervisor's Job

- Arranging for 'dead' files to be made, so that bulky files are thinned out.
- Obtaining instructions from a responsible member of the firm for papers no longer required to be shredded.

QUICK REVISION

1 The main reason for filing is ....

2 Three general rules for preparing to file are ....
....

3 A complete file borrowed should be replaced by an ....

4 A single document borrowed should be replaced by an ....

5 When there has been a change of name, this should be indicated in a filing system by a ....

6 Papers which cannot be filed because they are still being dealt with should be filed in a ....

7 Bulky files must be thinned out and the oldest papers ....

8 Shredding papers is the most efficient way of finally disposing of papers because ....

9 Three ways of storing large documents are ....
....

10 Four safety rules to be followed when filing ....
....

11 Centralised filing has three advantages: ....
....

12 and three disadvantages: ....

13 Departmental filing keeps files close at hand but has two disadvantages: ....
....

ASSIGNMENTS

1 Referring to the alphabetical filing rules on pp. 110–12 re-arrange the following list of names in the correct alphabetical order, typing (or writing) the filing point first, in upper case (capital letters).

```
O'BRIEN STEELWORKS LTD The
MODERN PRINTING COMPANY A
HICKSON AND GARRETT LTD
WILLIAMS ERNEST G & CO LTD
WTC TRANSPORT CO LTD
MIDLANDS DUPLICATING CO LTD The
OFFICE EQUIPMENT SUPPLY CO LTD
SHAW & SHORT LTD
CARTER A L & CO LTD
RAC
LAMB'S FURNITURE CO LTD
BRICKFIELD BUILDING SOCIETY
```

BARWEST BANK PLC
LKJ ENGINEERING LTD

2 Re-arrange the following, more complex list, alphabetically:

WINTER SUPPER FRIDAY 5 DECEMBER 199- GUEST LIST
Mr and Mrs Kenneth Richardson
Ms Sarah Walker
Mrs Diane Wootton-Jones
Miss Jenny Clark
Mr and Mrs Trevor Kilgallen
Mrs Linda Double
Ms Alison Houghton
Mr and Mrs Peter Smith
Mr and Mrs Arnold Hemming
Miss Helena Green
Mrs Lucia Frascina
Mr and Mrs Michael Snoswell
Miss Katharine Foster
Mr and Mrs Martin Mason
Mr and Mrs Tom Rudge
Mr John Pearson
Mr Keven Ashton
Mr and Mrs Ralph Moulson
Ms Kay Theobald
Mr Alan Baldwin
Mr and Mrs Robert Howes
Mr and Mrs Charles Payne
Mr Geoffrey Blackburn
Ms Claire Corbett
Miss Rebecca Black
Mr and Mrs Olav Wyspianska
Ms Elizabeth Gwynne

3 Compare card indexes and visible edge cards.

4 Explain the use of microfilming (a) by firms and (b) by other organisations.

5 You have asked your boss for another filing cabinet. He has replied that he has noticed that the bottom drawer of the existing one is only half-full. Will you (a) insist on another cabinet or (b) take steps to make better use of the spare space. If so, how?

6 Write a report on the filing system which you have inherited from your predecessor, who used subject filing. Your firm deals in cosmetics supplied widely all over the British Isles and the filing is organised under different types of cosmetics. Describe an alternative system which could be used and its possible advantages.

CHAPTER 6

Sources of Information

GENERAL REFERENCE BOOKS

Some reference books which secretaries need regularly are:

Dictionary	*Concise Oxford, Chambers 20th Century Dictionary,* or *Collins Dictionary of the English Language* are all comprehensive dictionaries, which as well as spelling and definitions, give pronunciation, abbreviations, hyphenation, foreign words and phrases, and correct ways to address titled people. Smaller dictionaries do not.
Roget's Thesaurus	('thesaurus' means 'treasury') gives a greater selection of synonyms than a dictionary.
Fowler's Modern English Usage	helps with difficult points of grammar.
Black's Titles and Forms of Address	gives correct ways of addressing all titled people, both verbally and in written communications.
Atlas	for information about climate, products, population, terrain, boundaries and principal cities.
AA and *RAC Handbooks*	for information about hotels, ferries, etc.
Pears Cyclopaedia	is a small one-volume encyclopaedia published annually so is more up-to-date than the larger multi-volume encyclopaedias. It is divided under 3 main headings – everyday information; events; home and personal.
Whitaker's Almanack	is a general reference book published annually, containing a remarkable wealth of information about every country in the world, as well as the Royal Family and members of the peerage, the House of Commons, the Law Courts and the police and armed forces.
Post Office Guide	contains information about all Post Office services (see p. 161).

Useful reference books

Additional reference books may be needed from time to time. Elsewhere in this book are sources of reference on:

- Travel (pp. 313–14)
- Mail room (p. 157)
- Telephone and telex (pp. 42–3, 57)
- Reception (p. 70)

REFERENCE BOOKS ABOUT PEOPLE

Who's Who is a biographical dictionary published annually, which gives a brief biography of famous people living today. It recognises distinction and influence, with emphasis on careers. Entries are invited from well-known people, who can refuse if they wish. It is updated each October, and contains 28 000 biographies. There are many other forms of *Who's Who* – famous foreign people are listed in *The International Who's Who*; famous people who have died are transferred to *Who Was Who*, which is divided into 10-year periods from 1897.

Chambers *Biographical Dictionary* gives details of famous British people both living and dead and the *International Dictionary of Biography* deals with internationally famous people.

Details of people who are titled (not necessarily famous) can be found in *Debrett's Peerage and Baronetage*, which also gives the correct forms of addressing titled people and an order of precedence.

Lists of doctors are in the *Medical Register*; of dentists in the *Dentists' Register*; of solicitors in the *Solicitors' and Barristers' Register*; of Members of Parliament in the *Times Guide to the House of Commons*; clergymen of the Church of England in *Crockford's Clerical Directory*.

REFERENCE BOOKS ABOUT FIRMS AND ORGANISATIONS

Who Owns Whom gives the names of parent companies with full names, addresses and classification with subsidiaries and associate companies.

UK Kompass is a register of British industry and commerce – it has also European volumes.

Ryland's Directory lists brand names and trade marks in the UK.

The Shorter ASLIB Directory of Information Sources in the UK deals with published information about 2000 organisations – educational, political, agricultural, commercial, industrial, travel and tourism. It lists UK embassies of overseas countries. It also has an abbreviations index. ASLIB stands for Association of Special Libraries and Information Bureaux.

Kelly's Manufacturers' and Merchants Directory lists manufacturers and service firms, with trade descriptions, addresses, telephone, telex and Fax numbers.

OTHER USEFUL REFERENCE BOOKS

Willings Press Guide contains a list of all British and principal European periodicals and newspapers, together with the addresses and telephone numbers of the publishing offices.

Keesings Contemporary Archives contains information on current events, up-dated each week.

Year Books give full details of trades and industries, and of professional organisations such as the Stock Exchange.

Croner's Reference Book for Employers gives information on legislation relating to employees in factories, offices and shops. The information is updated monthly. *Croner's Reference Book for Small Businesses* and *Croner's Reference Book for Exporters* may also be useful.

Many reference books are expensive, and it is not worth spending money on them if they are used only occasionally. Public libraries have a selection of reference books in a separate section. They are not always up-to-date, and it is important that the facts obtained are the most recent, otherwise they are worse than useless, they are misleading. The librarian will help if you have difficulty in finding the reference book you need.

OTHER SOURCES OF INFORMATION

When facts are needed quickly, a telephone call to one of the national newspapers' information bureaux will bring an immediate answer. The *Daily Telegraph* charges £2.85 plus VAT for a 5-minute call.

Libraries in large cities have information desks and will be ready to help through their online computer search service.

Business Statistics Office reference library in Newport, Gwent, is a Government statistical service and can provide official statistics covering almost every aspect of the UK's commercial, industrial, financial and social life.

Prestel is a two-way computerised service which gives useful information on a television screen to anyone who has a modified set and a telephone. Prestel supplies news and information from an enormous library.

Teletext (Ceefax and *Oracle)* provide information on news and current affairs on television screens, on specially adapted sets.

SECRETARIAL TIPS

1 The ordinary comprehensive desk diary has a great deal of useful information in it – UK customs airports, flights within the UK showing shuttle services not requiring booking, world time zones (see p. 307), details about EEC countries, IDD codes (see pp. 46–7) religious festivals and public holidays internationally as well as world maps.

2 When using a reference book, check the contents page first, to make sure that it deals with the information you want, then refer to the index, remembering that the item you are looking for may be indexed under a different word with the same meaning.

3 Make sure the reference book is up-to-date, if you are dealing with a query on current events. Your public library will have a list of libraries where the latest reference books are available.

4 A secretary's handbook is a useful source of concise information (this must also be up-to-date). *Chambers Office Oracle* is one and the *PA's Handbook* by Moncrieff and Sharp is another.

5 In a more expensive category, but very useful if frequent research into facts is carried out, is *The Office Companion,* which is up-dated every three months by means of loose-leaf pages and also has blank pages for individual notes. *The Office Companion* is published by Kluwer Publishing Limited.

6 When looking up information in a reference book, place slips of paper in between the pages which you want to go back to as you work through the book. This makes it much easier to go back and recheck. Many reference books have over 1000 pages!

7 Names and addresses of people not on the telephone may be found on electoral rolls – many public libraries have copies of these. In London *only,* there is a directory of streets and the occupiers of all properties – *Kelly's Post Office Street Directory.*

8 There are word processing programs available which include a 'thesaurus' – a useful addition to the spelling check provided by most word processing programs.

9 A Local Chamber of Commerce is helpful for business advice and information.

QUICK REVISION

In which reference book(s) would you look to find information on the following?

1 Several meanings for the same word (synonyms)   ....

2 Whether an apostrophe is before or after the letter 's' in a word   ....

3 Name and address of an hotel in Cardiff   ....

4 The climate in Finland   ....

5 The correct way to address a letter to the Prime Minister   ....

6 The Queen's Household   ....

7 The 1984 miners' strike   ....

8 Prohibited materials by post to the United Arab Emirates   ....

9 Details of Sir Lawrence Williams   ....

10 Lists of Members of Parliament   ....

11 Details about a clergyman of the Church of England   ....

12 Information about a doctor   ....

13 Details about a famous living Italian opera singer   ....

14 An order of precedence for titled people attending a formal banquet   ....

15 The meaning of an abbreviation which is not in the dictionary   ....

16 Names of all the newspapers published in Zurich   ....

17 Details of the owners of a large departmental store and its subsidiaries   ....

18 Information on a point of legislation regarding employees   ....

ASSIGNMENTS

You have been asked for the following information:

1 A list of local newspapers, with addresses and telephone numbers of their offices, in Newcastle-upon-Tyne.

2 Names of 3 hotels (not too near the city centre) in Newcastle-upon-Tyne.

3 Names and addresses of two self-drive car hire firms in Newcastle-upon-Tyne.

4 Details of domestic flights from Newcastle airport.

5 The address, and telephone number of Watson Norie Ltd, in Newcastle-upon-Tyne, and where other branches are situated, together with names of subsidiary and/or associate companies.

CHAPTER 7

Visual Aids

One picture is worth a thousand words (according to Confucius, an ancient Chinese philosopher) but it is possible to portray only statistics by means of charts and graphs.

In any organisation, small or large, much information is required not only to control the business but also to keep employees and/or the public shareholders informed of the organisation's progress. Much of this information may be in the form of words or figures, such as a balance sheet or profit and loss account.

Information is absorbed more quickly by means of a picture or diagram, which generally means changing lists or pages of figures into a display, so that the significance of 'trends' – a statistical term meaning 'the way things are moving' – is seen at a glance. Many people are not too concerned about detail but want a general impression. A local authority may indicate the sources of its income by a pile of coins, with the pile marked off at various points to show how much is raised by community charges, rent, central government grants, etc. The same type of chart can be used to show how the money is spent – housing, education, social services, etc.

CHARTS AND GRAPHS

Pie Charts

One common way of presenting information is by means of a pie chart, so called because it presents information by means of slices of a circle. Below is the total production of a china factory in a certain period:

cups	16,000
saucers	12,000
plates	12,000
dishes	8,000
total	48,000

The fraction and percentage of each item is:

		Fraction	Percentage (%)
cups	16,000	1/3	33.3
saucers	12,000	1/4	25
plates	12,000	1/4	25
dishes	8,000	1/6	16.6
total	48,000	1	100

The number of degrees in a circle is 360; therefore, to represent how much of the circle each item of production should represent, the calculation is as follows:

cups	1/3 of 360 degrees =	120 degrees
saucers	1/4 of 360 degrees =	90 degrees
plates	1/4 of 360 degrees =	90 degrees
dishes	1/6 of 360 degrees =	60 degrees

The circle is divided accordingly:

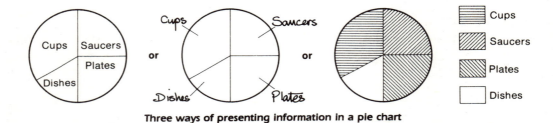

Three ways of presenting information in a pie chart

A cup, saucer and plate could be drawn in the relevant segment, providing the segments are large enough. The pie chart gives an immediate impression of proportions.

As a pie chart gives only a broad general impression, it is not suitable for showing figures in accurate detail. Among the techniques used for these are graphs, bar charts, histograms and line charts.

Line Graphs

One example of a line graph is the temperature chart of a patient in hospital where the fluctuating temperature of the patient is plotted on the vertical line (the y axis) against the horizontal line (the x axis) representing time. The manager of the cup production department could use this type of graph if he wants to be able to see at a glance how the department is doing. The daily production figures are therefore drawn on a graph. Assume the figures are as follows:

Day	Quantity	Day	Quantity	Day	Quantity
1	540	7	500	13	530
2	520	8	480	14	560
3	530	9	510	15	580
4	560	10	470	16	320
5	550	11	470	17	440
6	530	12	450	18	570

The graph below tells you immediately much more than the tabulation does. It shows fluctuation of output and possible reasons for it. Also, contrary to standard practice, the vertical (quantity) line does not start at zero. This is because it is known from past records that production of cups in this department does not normally fall below 300 or exceed 600 – therefore our scale only needs to cover those quantities.

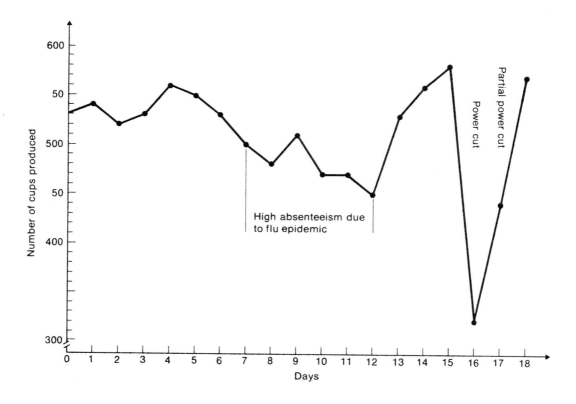

It is possible to construct a graph with more than one line on it. If the sales figures are required over a certain period in four different sales areas, the following graph could be used:

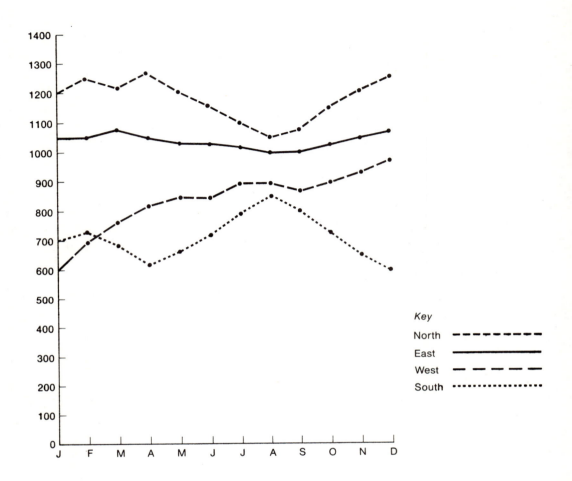

Key

North	- - - - - -
East	——————
West	– – – – –
South	··············

If this were a large chart kept only for sales office information, then different coloured lines could be used for each area, thus cutting out the need for different types of line. Referring to the graph above, we see:

- Northern area sales began to decline in May and throughout the summer were lower than the winter sales figures.
- Eastern area figures remained steady through the year. Maybe sales can be boosted?
- Western area – neglected area but with a new salesperson and other means, sales are climbing – the trend is upwards. When western area sales have settled down, maybe this man can be transferred to another region.

- Southern area – rather poor showing – not necessarily the salesperson's fault. The sales pattern is almost the direct opposite to the northern area pattern.

In the first graph, the quantity on the vertical scale started at 300, for the reasons given. In the second graph, the vertical scale starts at zero but since the lowest recorded quantity in the past 12 months was 600, next year's chart could start at, say, 400, and, because of a probable increase in regional sales, go up to 1600.

Line Charts

A line chart presents information by means of a straight line. Again the vertical line of the chart shows the variable (usually quantity) and the horizontal line is the fixed element (e.g. time). This does not always apply in the office situation. Sometimes it is more effective to reverse these roles. The third graph below shows a line chart in its conventional use.

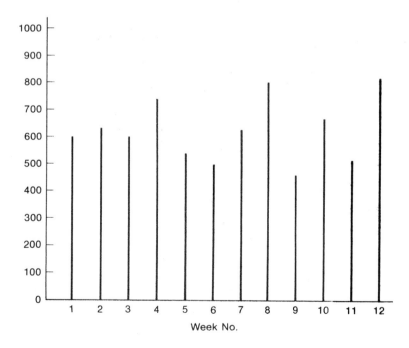

It will be seen that the vertical scale starts at zero, although the lowest quantity does not start at zero. The chart might lose some of its significance if it should start at 300, although it would not make any difference to the information it is conveying.

Bar Charts

A bar chart displays comparative information by means of bars or blocks. It can be used as an alternative to a graph, but is more effective when dealing with more than one item. Below is a block diagram of the north and west figures taken from the graph on p. 132.

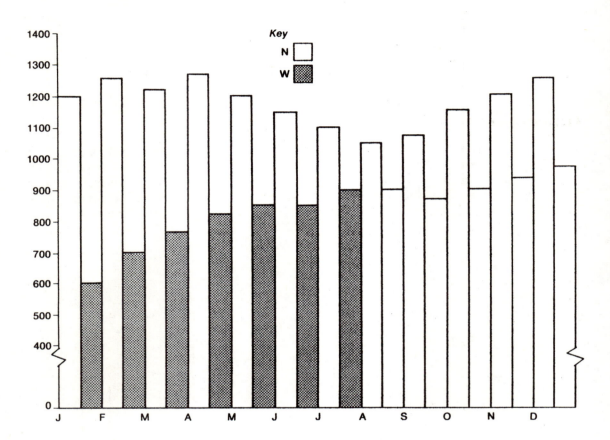

The zig-zag in the vertical scale denotes that the scale is broken. Some of west's results have been blocked out to accentuate the two areas, leaving some of west's blocks plain, to emphasise the need for this differentiation. In this application, the area of each block is not important – the width of each block is the same. The height of the block is dependent upon its value.

Histograms

A histogram looks like a bar chart but the surface area of the 'blocks' are proportionate to each other and to the total information which they represent.

134

Flow Charts

There are other applications of visual information used in commerce. One of these is an algorithm, or flow chart, which is a chart showing a step-by-step approach to a desired end (see below and overleaf).

Although it may be necessary in many work situations to change tabulations to charts by 'hand' it is now becoming more common for computers to do this work but only if they are capable of carrying out graphics and displays, and in any case, if a chart is to be used to display information in an office it needs to be quite large, using display boards which can be updated easily.

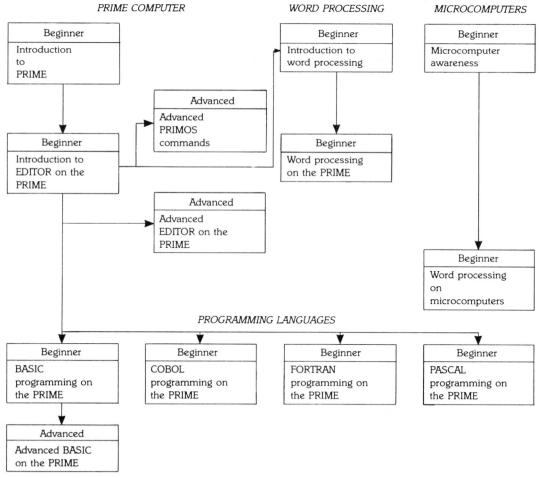

STAFF DEVELOPMENT COURSE PROGRAMME

Programmes are sometimes set out in the form of a flow chart

THE WEDDING MARCH

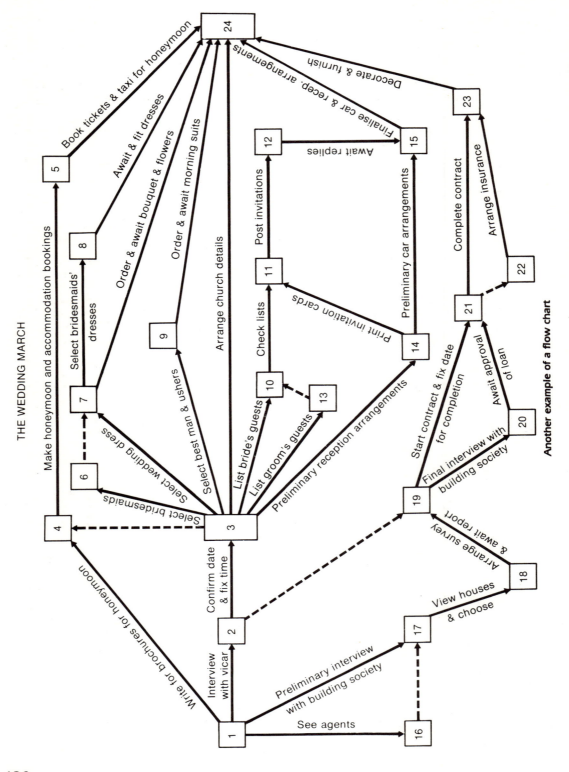

Another example of a flow chart

1 See agents
1 Preliminary interview with building society
1 Write for brochures for honeymoon
1 Interview with vicar

2 Confirm date & fix time

3 Arrange church details
3 List bride's guests
3 List groom's guests
3 Preliminary reception arrangements
3 Select best man & ushers
3 Select wedding dress
3 Select bridesmaids

4 Make honeymoon and accommodation bookings

5 Book tickets & taxi for honeymoon

6 Select bridesmaids' dresses

7 Order & await morning suits
7 Order & await bouquet & flowers

8 Await & fit dresses

10 List bride's guests
13 List groom's guests

11 Check lists
11 Post invitations

12 Await replies

14 Print invitation cards
14 Preliminary car arrangements

15 Finalise car & recep. arrangements

16 See agents

17 View houses & choose

18 Arrange survey & await report

19 Final interview with building society
19 Start contract & fix date for completion

20 Await approval of loan

21 Complete contract
21 Arrange insurance

23 Decorate & furnish

136

WALL PLANNERS

A very commonly used chart is a year planner. The illustration shows just a small part of a year planner used for staff holidays.

	HOLIDAY ROTA 199-												
	MAY		JUNE				JULY					AUGUST	
	21	28	4	11	18	25	2	9	16	23	30	6	13
J. Thomas			◯	◯							◯		
R. Smith					◯				◯	◯			
D. Watson	◯	◯	◯										
L. Evans						◯	◯					◯	
F. Smart							◯					◯	◯

The reservation indicators could be of different colours and/or shapes in sticky paper, or hatched lines

Other applications could be conference suite reservations (see Chapter 20) training courses, service engineers' commitments, speakers' engagements, sales figures, production output, etc.

Pictograms

Instead of using a line to show information on a graph, it is sometimes effective to use a symbol or series of symbols to connect the various points on the graph.

Similarly for bar charts, symbols may be used to show values instead of a rectangle.

Making these pictograms requires the ability to draw the symbols and to be consistent. They are often used in Government statistics mainly because they look more interesting and are easily recognisable.

The birth rate could be shown as a line of storks.

Beer production could be represented by barrels.

How the Government spends our money could be shown by a pile of coins divided up, so much for defence, education, social services, etc.

Numbers of cars registers over the years could be shown by a line of cars.

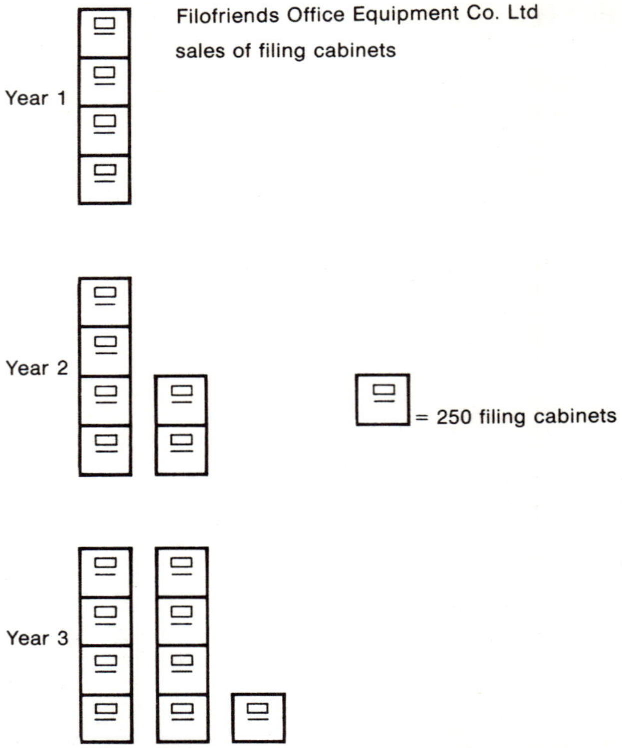

Filofriends Office Equipment Co. Ltd

sales of filing cabinets

Year 1

Year 2

= 250 filing cabinets

Year 3

A pictogram showing filing cabinet sales from a supplier expanding his business

QUICK REVISION

1 A pie chart presents information by means of slices of a circle. As it gives only a broad general impression, it is not suitable for ....

2 A graph shows ....

3 A line chart presents information by means of ....

4 A bar chart displays information by means of bars or blocks. It can be used as an alternative to a graph, but is more effective when ....

5 A histogram looks like a bar chart but ....

6 An algorithm is a chart showing a ....

7 Another name for an algorithm is a ....

8 Large visual display boards are used in offices for staff holidays, conference suite reservations, training courses, sales figures and ....

9 Instead of using a line to show information on a graph, or rectangles on a bar chart, it is sometimes effective to use symbols. These charts are known as ....

ASSIGNMENTS

1 Your sales representatives have planned visits to see potential customers in various places at varying times. Usually, these visits can be arranged a few weeks in advance. What sort of device would you recommend so that you can see at a glance (a) where they are at any given moment and (b) where they should be in a few weeks' time?

2 You are asked to check on the number of items of incoming and outgoing mail handled by the mail room over a period of 20 days, and to present the findings to a small group interested in possible improvements.

    (a)   What device would you use and how would you distinguish between incoming and outgoing mail?

    (b)   How would you show the numbers of letters and parcels dealt with each day for both incoming and outgoing mail?

3 (a)   Draw a pie chart showing the proportions of expenditure of the following. The sums are in billions of £s spent by the Government:

Health	23
Defence	20
Education	19
Social Security	51
Debt interest	17
Scotland, Northern Ireland and Wales	18
Other	49

    (b)   What general conclusions can you draw from this chart?

    (c)   What perceptible difference would it make to the pie chart slices if Social Security were reduced by £1bn and 'Other' increased by £1.6bn, and why.

4 During the week (Monday to Friday inclusive) your junior is expected to send out 125 invoices per day and 100 statements per day. Show by means of a suitable chart her week's target and her achievement by Wednesday evening if she has completed 400 invoices and 280 statements.

5 During a certain week a particular share index recorded the following close of trading prices:

Monday	1860
Tuesday	1845
Wednesday	1835
Thursday	1815
Friday	1840

    (a)   Show the above as a graph

    (b)   Given the benefit of hindsight, when would have been the best time to sell shares and to buy shares, and why?

CHAPTER 8

Mail Handling

INCOMING AND OUTGOING MAIL

Most firms large enough to be divided into departments have a mail room where letters and parcels are delivered and where all outgoing mail is stamped, or franked, before being taken to the post office or post box for collection.

A well-organised mail room will contain scales (two types) for weighing both letters and parcels, a franking machine, possibly other equipment for dealing with large quantities of outgoing mail, as well as mail room accessories and reference books for the staff to use to deal with any queries. Shelves and tables should be arranged to make it easy for the staff to carry out the sorting of incoming mail, and to place outgoing mail into the various categories ready for posting.

The illustration below shows one way in which a mail room could be arranged, and this is similar to a layout recommended by the Post Office for efficient handling of mail.

A well-organised mail room

Incoming Mail

Mail arriving at a firm may include many different documents besides letters. There may be invoices, quotations, estimates, orders, applications for jobs and advertising material. It is very important to distribute the mail to the different departments without delay, so that the office staff and managers are able to make a start on their day's work. In a large firm, mail room staff may take it in turns to come in before other office workers in order to make sure that all the mail has been taken round to the departments by the time the office workers are ready to start.

Letters may be opened in the mail room or may be distributed unopened. In a small office, the manager may open and deal with the letters himself.

One type of letter would never be opened except by the person to whom it is addressed. This is a letter marked 'Personal', 'Private' or 'Confidential', which would be handed to the addressee unopened as soon as possible.

Styles of addressing a confidential letter

In order to be certain that mail is in an office early in the morning, some firms arrange with the Post Office to rent one of the Post Office Private Boxes at a delivery office. Letters and packets may be collected at any time from a private box, except on Sundays, or days when the Post Office does not deliver. Firms using this service are given a number by the Post Office to use as part of their address. The Post Office makes a yearly charge for private boxes. A similar arrangement is possible for a private bag, into which a firm's mail is sorted at the delivery office, and which can be collected by the firm using it on normal Post Office delivery days. A charge is made by the Post Office for private bags. too.

If a firm has no private box or bag at the Post Office's delivery office, mail will be delivered in the normal way by a postman to the reception desk of the firm, and mail room clerks will collect it from there using trolleys if there is a large quantity of letters and packets.

Opening Mail

As it is so important to open and distribute the mail quickly, following a daily routine ensures that it is done efficiently:

- Face envelopes (i.e. turn envelopes so that address is the right side up and the right way round). While doing this, take out any envelopes marked 'Private' and place them on one side, unopened, for delivery with the opened mail.

'Faced' mail

- In some firms, it is usual to divide incoming mail into first and second-class, opening the first-class mail first, as it is (generally) more important. Second-class mail is a slower and cheaper service, normally taking two days to deliver. First- and second-class postal services are known as the 'two-tier' system.
- Open envelopes by slitting *both* long edges. This can be done with a paper knife, or, more quickly, with an electrically operated letter opener.

A paper knife

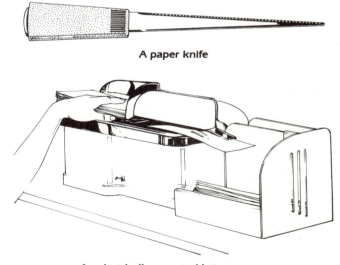

An electrically operated letter opener

- The electric letter opener removes a very narrow strip or 'sliver' of paper from the edge of an envelope, so narrow that it is unlikely to damage the contents, but in order to make sure that this does not happen, the envelope must be tapped on the desk so that the contents drop to the bottom of the envelopes. Slitting both long edges makes it easy to check very quickly that nothing has been left accidentally in the envelope. Some mail rooms keep opened envelopes for a few days in case of queries. The address or postmark on the envelope may be useful.

Nothing left inside the envelope!

- Unfold letters, or other documents, smoothing them out flat, and apply a date-stamp, taking care not to stamp over any of the typing or writing on the paper. Some firms use a stamp which automatically prints the time on the document as well as the date. Dating incoming mail is an important check on when it was actually received. An envelope marked 'Private' would be date stamped on the (unopened) envelope.

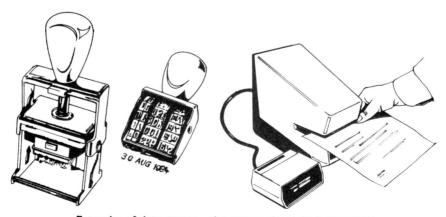

Examples of date-stamps – the one on the right is automatic

143

- Some letters, or documents, may have enclosures attached to them, or folded with them. Enclosures may be: catalogues, price-lists, leaflets, samples, photographs, cheques, stamps or postal orders. If they have not been attached to the letter, they should be stapled to it at the top left-hand corner. Pins and paper clips are not suitable as they have a tendency to catch on to other papers by mistake. Photographs may be kept together with paper clips but it is advisable to protect a glossy surface from direct contact with a clip.

If there is more than one sheet of paper in an envelope (a continuation sheet to a letter, or enclosures) make sure they are kept together – once separated, it may be difficult to tell to which letter they belong.

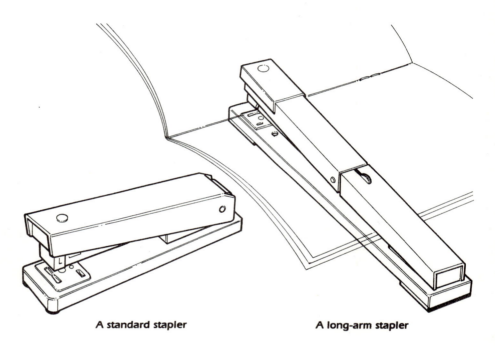

A standard stapler   A long-arm stapler

Letters containing money in any form should have the amount and the initials of the person opening the letter in pencil at the foot of the letter – this helps as a check in case of any later query. In some firms a remittances book is used into which all money received is entered before being taken to the cashier or the mail room supervisor. An entry in this book shows the date of receipt for each sum of money, the person or firm who sent it, and the amount. It also shows whether the money was received as a cheque, postal order or cash, and the signature of the person who recorded the information. The money goes with the opened letter and is eventually passed on to the cashier in the accounts department.

A register of incoming mail may be kept by a small firm; in most large firms this is no longer the practice.

DATE	SENDER	REMITTANCE	AMOUNT		SIGNATURE
199–			£	P	
June 1st	M. L. Mann and Co. Ltd.	cheque	20-00		P Fox
June 1st	Mrs. F. Hopkins	P. O.	2-00		P Fox
June 2nd.	Messrs. Page + Vines	Chq.	49-00		S. Smith.

A page from a remittances book

Missing envelopes should be noted in pencil and initialled at the foot of the letter by the person opening it. It is easy to tell, in most cases, whether a letter should have an enclosure, as there are several ways in which a typist or secretary may indicate that something is attached to a letter:

(a) 'Enc.' (which is the abbreviation for 'Enclosure' typed at the bottom left-hand side of a letter.

(b) A small label with 'Enc.' or 'Enclosure' printed on it, affixed to the letter. Enclosure labels may be numbered, for reference when replying to the letter.

(c) The symbol / typed in the left-hand margin alongside the sentence which refers to the enclosure.

(d) Three dots typed in the left-hand margin alongside the sentence which refers to the enclosure.

(e) The enclosures are listed at the bottom of the letter.

(c) and (d) are used less frequently than (a), (b) or (e).

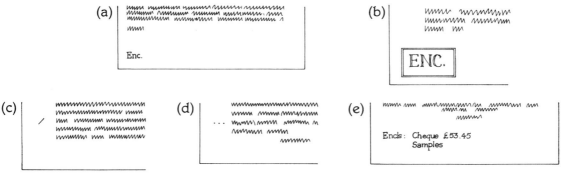

Different ways of indicating an enclosure

Distributing Mail

People distributing mail should look for the following to help them to decide where to send it:

- 'For the attention of (followed by name)'. This would be typed under the inside address on a letter immediately *over* 'Dear Sir'.
- The letter may have a subject heading typed underneath 'Dear Sir'.
- There may be a reference at the top of the letter. This is usually the initials of the sender of the letter followed by the initials of his typist or secretary.

If the letter does not contain any of the above information, it will be helpful to read it through quickly.

Not all letters come by post. Some are delivered by firms' messengers and are inter-departmental. This is known as internal mail and, if confidential, may be enclosed in large envelopes which are printed with lines for the name of each recipient so that after opening the name is crossed out and the next name written underneath. Letters between offices, departments and even branches of the same firm, are known as 'memos'.

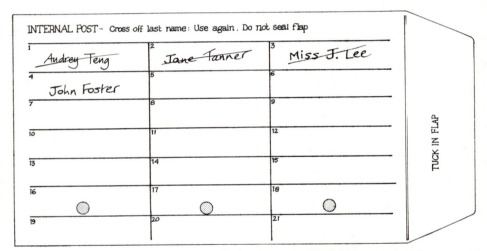

An envelope for internal mail (holes show whether it is empty or not!)

Parcels may arrive later in the day, as may mail which has to be signed for in the presence of the postman. Into this latter category will come registered letters and recorded delivery. There is more information about these Post Office services later in this chapter.

It may be the responsibility of the mail room supervisor to arrange for a letter to be seen by more than one person, if the letter mentions several topics. She could arrange for this to be done by:

- asking a typist to type a copy with several carbon copies
- photocopying it

- sending the letter to each person or department accompanied by a routing slip (see p. 245).

The choice of which method to adopt would depend on the urgency with which the letter had to be circulated. Photocopying is the quickest and most accurate, but it is also the most expensive. Carbon copies are the cheapest but the typist may make a mistake which could be serious. This method is slow, too. A routing slip also may take time as some people on the list could hold on to the letter thus delaying its progress round to the others on the list.

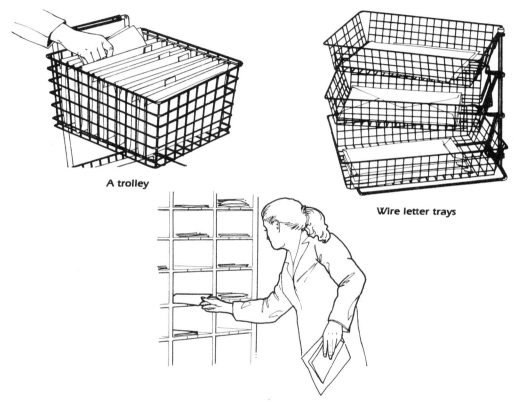

A trolley

Wire letter trays

Pigeon holes. Note that the letters are laid flat

Outgoing Mail

Mail for posting may arrive at any time during the day, but the afternoons are the busiest times in the mail room, and to avoid a sudden rush of mail, a system of regular collection from every department should be organised. Trays marked 'Outgoing Mail' placed where the messenger from the mail room can conveniently collect the mail at frequent intervals ensures that letters for posting are dealt with promptly. The mail room may also state a final collection time, after which no mail will be accepted for that day.

147

In some firms, letters are sent to the mail room already folded and inserted into envelopes, with a pencilled '1' or '2' in the top right-hand corner, to show whether the letter has to go by first- or second-class post. It will still be necessary to weigh a letter if it is bulky or seems heavier than the maximum weight allowed by the Post Office for minimum first-class or second-class postage. The addressee must pay any extra postage required, so accuracy is important.

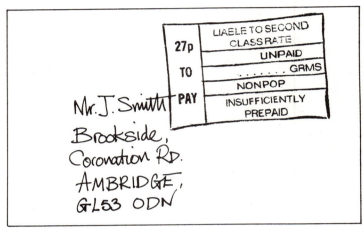

A letter with insufficient postage

Other letters which must be weighed are letters going abroad, whether by airmail or 'surface' mail. Airmail is expensive, and special thin paper and envelopes cut the cost down. There is also an airmail letter form (of A4 size) available at post offices which is the cheapest way to send letters by air. This is called an 'aerogramme'. 'Surface' mail is carried by train, ship or van, and is cheaper than airmail but slower.

In many firms, letters and other documents are sent to the mail room accompanied by correctly typed envelopes, and the mail room clerk's job is to fold and insert the letters into the envelopes. While she is doing this, she should:

- check by looking at the letter to see if there should be an enclosure. If the enclosure is missing, the letter should be placed on one side and later returned to the sender.
- if there is an enclosure, attach to it the letter by stapling or, if not suitable, using a paper-clip. Pins should never be used as the person opening the envelope may receive a sharp jab.
- check that letter has been signed.
- check that inside address is the same as that on the accompanying envelope. If not, again put letter and envelope on one side for querying

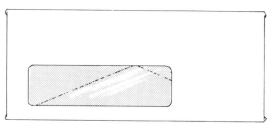

A window envelope. This envelope has a transparent panel. Aperture envelopes are similar but have no transparent panel, just a rectangular opening in the envelope

either with sender or mail room supervisor. 'Window' or 'aperture' envelopes are often used by firms to avoid the possibility of sending a letter to the wrong person or firm.

- fold the letter so that it fits the envelope with as few creases as possible. This is not as easy as it sounds, and most mail rooms have a special way of doing it. Some firms print their letterheading with small marks near the edges which indicate where the letter has to be folded.

The Postage Book

A postage book gives a detailed record of all letters, packets and parcels posted. An example is shown below.

STAMPS BOUGHT	NAME AND TOWN OF ADDRESSEE	STAMPS USED	DETAILS
£ P		£ P	
20 . 00	21 June 199–		
	F. Jones Ipswich	20	
	L. Naylor Cardiff	20	
	P. Knight Coventry	40	Rec. delivery
	S. Singh Calcutta, India	45	Airmail
	K. Wilson & Sons Ltd. Reading	1 . 38	Reg. letter
	J. Ross & Co Ltd Hove	20	
	A.B. Rowe & Co Rugby	3 . 10	Parcel
		5 . 93	
	Balance c/f	14 . 07	
20 . 00		20 . 00	
5 . 93	22 June 199–		
14 . 07	Balance b/f		

Stamps

Stamps need to be kept dry and free from damage in a special book. Below we shall learn about the franking machine, but it is always a good plan to keep a few stamps for an emergency, such as when the franking machine has broken down and you need to send out an urgent letter.

Using a stamp book

The Record of Stamps

A simple record of stamps is used in some firms as a check on the number of stamps used each day. Details of correspondents are omitted.

STAMPS BOUGHT	DATE	STAMPS USED	
£ P			£ P
15 . 00	21 June 199–	30 @ 15	4 . 50
		40 @ 20	8 . 00
		10 @ 4	40
		Balance c/f	12 . 90
			2 . 10
15 . 00			15 . 00
2 . 10	22 June 199–	Balance b/f	

MAIL ROOM EQUIPMENT

Franking Machines

A franking machine prints in red the value of a stamp on an envelope, postcard or label, as well as the date and time of posting, the place of posting, licence number of the machine, and an advertising slogan, if required. It

A franking machine

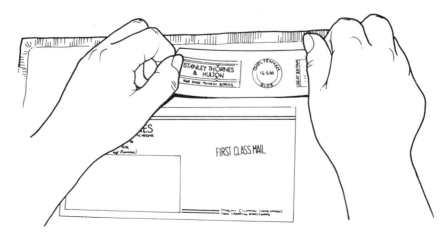

Affixing a franked label to an envelope too bulky to go through a franking machine

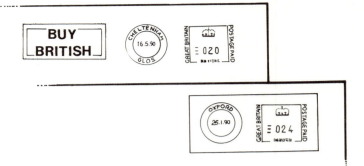

Franked envelopes, one with an advertising slogan and the other with a franked label.

RMRS Franking Machine Control Card

User	Meter no

Setting unit	Control Office

I certify that the following entries for the above machine for the week ended _____

are correct and that the correct date has been shown on each day's postings.

Initial column below to show date has been changed	Reading of Ascending Register	Reading of Descending Register	Total
Mon			
Tue			
Wed			
Thu			
Fri			
Sat			

Details of resetting during week

Please check date daily

Date	Amount

Note 1. This card should be posted on Saturday (or Friday if no postings are made on Saturday) whether or not the machine has been used in that week.

Note 2. The daily entry must be made on completion of each day's postings

Signed

Date

Post Office Examining Officer's initials

P3803

OP/00059 8/86

saves the time spent on keeping a record of stamps used, as well as the trouble of sticking stamps on envelopes, parcels and packages.

Franking machines may be purchased or hired from the manufacturers. A licence to use the machine must first be obtained from the Post Office. There is no charge for this.

A well-organised mail room will have a supply of postage stamps available in case the franking machine breaks down.

Franked mail, or 'metered mail' as it is also called, can by-pass Post Office facing and cancelling in the Post Office sorting office, often catching earlier trains and planes. Because such mail saves the Post Office time, it has to be posted in a special way – either handed in over the counter of a post office, tied in bundles and 'faced' or posted in a letter box in a special envelope.

If an envelope or label has the wrong value franked on it by mistake, it should be kept and returned to the Post Office (when the franking machine meter is taken for resetting would be a suitable time). A refund will be given less five per cent of the value franked.

Some firms still like to keep a record of outgoing mail, even though there is a franking machine in use, and this record will just consist of names and addresses of recipients of letters and parcels.

Larger franking machines incorporate equipment for sealing envelopes as well as stacking them after they have been franked.

The latest franking machines have a remote meter resetting system, which allows postage to be bought by phone. There is no need for visits to the Post Office – postage credit is reset in seconds. A control card (opposite) must be completed by the operator each week.

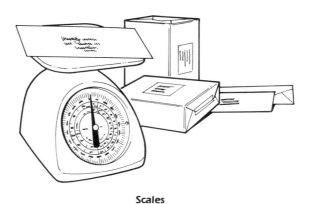

Scales

Scales

Traditional scales look like the one above, but many firms are now using electronic scales (see overleaf). Electronic scales can be used for letters and parcels and by pressing the right keys you can work out the weight and

Electronic parcel and letter balance

postage for mail to anywhere in the world. Every time postal rates change, though, you need a new 'microchip' from the Post Office – they will arrange an exchange for you.

Addressing Machines

An addressing machine may be linked to folding and inserting equipment, or used on its own.

Addressing machines are used by firms who send out a great deal of mail regularly to the same people – mail order firms, football pools, charitable organisations – and plates with the names and addresses on are typed (or duplicated) ready for use. Each name has a code, which is also printed on the envelope when the addressing machine plates are used (see below).

Addressing machines are now being replaced by word processors (see pp. 79–81) or computers (pp. 83–5) where lists of names and addresses can be stored in the memories.

Folding Machines

A *folding machine* will fold the letters and documents to be inserted into envelopes. A *folding and inserting* machine also inserts the letters into their envelopes.

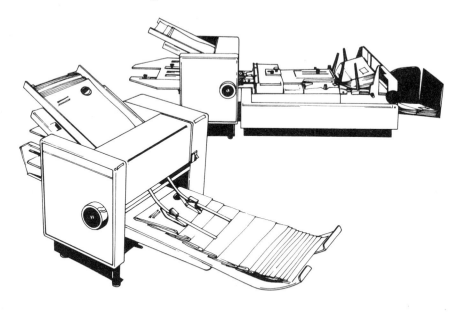

Folding letters and documents – by machine (top) and by hand (below)

Collators

Collators (like the ones below) are useful for sorting numbered papers into sets.

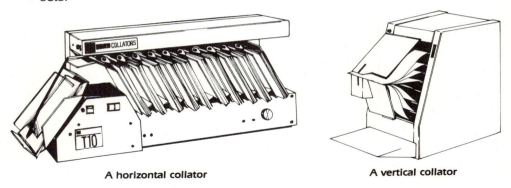

A horizontal collator

A vertical collator

MAIL ROOM SUNDRIES

Small items used in a mail room are known as mail room sundries. A list of these sundries is as follows:

- Brown paper – for wrapping parcels
- Clear adhesive tape – to use instead of string. (Fold the end of the tape *back* after cutting a piece off – this makes it easier to find the end next time you need the tape!)
- Corrugated paper – for packing breakables
- Envelopes – POP (Post Office preferred) sizes
- Adhesive packing tape – also to use instead of string
- Paper knife – if there is no electric letter opener
- Scissors
- Sponge moistener – for moistening stamps and envelopes
- Roller moistener – does the same job
- Sealing wax – sometimes used for sealing registered packets
- String

MAIL ROOM REFERENCE BOOKS

The *Post Office Guide* gives very clear and detailed instructions about parcelling everything, from musical instruments to umbrellas, and an up-to-date copy should be kept in every mail room for reference, not only in connection with parcels, but for information about postal rates and services to every country in the world. Separate leaflets (red for inland and blue for overseas) are issued by the Post Office after each change in postal rates. These give more detailed information than the *Post Office Guide*. The *Post Office Guide* may be bought from large post offices; the leaflets are free.

Other books useful in the mail room include:

- A large atlas
- A local *Classified Trade Directory (Yellow Pages)*
- *Thomson Local Directory*
- Telephone directories
- A–Z street maps
- Postal addresses and index to postcode directories
- Postcode Directories – (all these may be supplied on microfiche). *Thomson Local Directories* also include lists of postcodes in the area covered by each directory.

PARCELS

When you pack parcels, it is very important to make sure that you use strong, suitable, boxes. Every year the Post Office has to repack large numbers of parcels which become unfastened in the post and lose their contents. Parcels should be clearly addressed, with a stick-on label as well as a tie-on label, and should also have the name and address of the sender on the outside as well as the inside. Today, many firms send parcels by private carrier services.

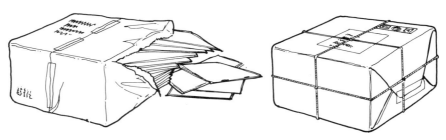

A parcel shedding its contents   A parcel correctly wrapped and labelled

A parcel label

Whenever possible, a strong box is preferable to wrapping paper especially if the article to be sent is heavy.

Plenty of packing materials – shredded paper is ideal (see p. 103) or crushed newspaper or any sort of crushed scrap paper – should be placed around the contents.

For small items padded bags give protection, especially for books, whose corners may be damaged in the post if unprotected.

When a box or padded bag is not available, use corrugated paper wrapped in strong brown paper.

Anything breakable should be marked clearly with the words FRAGILE – WITH CARE, and the Post Office will try to take extra care when handling the package.

Self-adhesive tape should be used along all sides of a parcel and, in addition, string should be firmly tied in at least two directions, knotting tightly where the string crosses.

Packing for Special Parcels

Large maps, plans, unframed pictures should be rolled and packed in a cardboard tube, securely sealed at both ends.

Small quantities of leaflets, brochures, examination papers should be packed in a padded bag or special bag (see illustration) as ordinary manilla envelopes are not strong enough for heavy contents.

Photographic prints must be placed between sheets of cardboard in an envelope marked DO NOT BEND.

Umbrellas and fishing rods (anything long and thin) should be packed between two strips of wood, wider and longer than the article and wrapped in corrugated paper and brown paper and marked DO NOT BEND.

Special packing

Liquids in tins or bottles should be surrounded by polystyrene chips or sawdust (this will absorb the liquid if there should be a breakage) and packed in a strong box.

Pictures in frames should be sandwiched between stout pieces of hardboard and wrapped in corrugated paper and strong brown paper.

Flowers must be packed in a strong box in layers separated by damp moss to keep the flowers fresh. If no moss is available, damp tissue paper or even damp newspaper will provide some humidity for the flowers.

Anything sharp (scissors or knives, for example) are only accepted by the Post Office if the edges or points are properly protected so that they cannot cause damage when being handled. Heavy cardboard should be used inside a cardboard box.

Bulk Posting of Parcels

There is a reduction in price for sending large numbers of parcels by post regularly – a lower rate for more than 30 parcels a week, and special terms for more than 200 a week, on a regular basis.

Compensation Fee

This is the Post Office service which is for parcels over a certain weight containing valuables, for inland post only. The maximum amount of compensation paid is scaled according to the amount of fee paid.

Details of Registered Post, Recorded Delivery and Compensation Fee (CF Parcels) are in the Postal Rates (Inland) leaflets obtainable at all post offices free. These are updated after each change of postal rates.

Cash on Delivery (COD)

Under this service the cost of the article delivered can be collected by the postman from the recipient. All parcels must be registered.

Other Services for Parcels Delivery

Delivering parcels is not a 'monopoly' of the Post Office as is the delivery of letters. As well as the Post Office, parcels may be delivered by:

- British Rail – station-to-station service and Red Star. With both these services the parcel must be collected by the addressee from a station. Red Star is the faster service of the two.
- Private carrier services – there are many of these listed in *Yellow Pages*.

Private firms delivering parcels may be cheaper than the Post Office service, may be quicker, too, and will usually accept larger and heavier parcels than the Post Office limits permit.

Trakback

Trakback is a new Royal Mail service for parcels for contract holders only. A signature is required by the person receiving the parcel. The label (illustrated below) has a barcode which is entered into a computer. Delivery can be confirmed by a free phone call to Trakback Response Centre.

MAIL HANDLING BY THE SECRETARY

Incoming Mail

In a large firm, letters may be delivered to a secretary for her to open and place on her employer's desk. The procedure detailed on pp. 142–5 should be followed, leaving envelopes marked 'Private' or 'Confidential' unopened.

The secretary should read all the letters through as she opens them as it is possible that she can deal with some of the queries without the need to pass them on to her employer. The ones needing urgent attention should be put on top of the pile.

Advertising material can be put on one side for examination and/or disposal later, when time permits.

In a small firm, all the mail is dealt with by the secretary, as one of her first duties in the morning.

Suspicious-looking packages should be dealt with as in Chapter 14 (they are not likely to arrive in most offices, but large firms take no chances and have an electronic screening device which is simple to use and helps to ensure the safety of staff).

Outgoing Mail

In a small office, the secretary is responsible for ensuring that the letters have been signed, go into the right envelopes, and are correctly stamped (see p. 148) and ready in time to catch the last post. She may also be responsible for posting them. Some firms have a system whereby an extra copy of each letter sent is placed in a letter book.

In a large firm, where there is a mail room, she must make sure her letters are signed, sealed and ready for collection by mail room staff to catch the last post.

For dealing with large quantities of mail, the equipment described on pp. 150–6 helps you cope efficiently and speedily. It is worth remembering that for the occasional 'mail shot' (sending large quantities of advertising material, circular letters, etc.) equipment can be hired for a short period, which is obviously cheaper than buying it and having it standing idle for weeks at a time.

INLAND AND OVERSEAS MAIL AND POST OFFICE SERVICES

Information from the Post Office

It is most important for any office employee who has the responsibility of dealing with the despatch of mail to have a thorough knowledge of the Post Office mail service, and the regulations covering the despatch of mail.

The *Post Office Guide* and up-to-date Post Office leaflets giving the cost of stamps and the postage rates in the UK and overseas are obtainable at most large post offices (see p. 157).

Inland Mail

'Inland mail' refers to letters, packets and parcels posted to destinations in the British Isles.

For letters and parcels there is a two-tier system, meaning that the sender may choose to send them first or second class. First-class post is dearer but arrives at its destination (usually) within 24 hours. Second-class post is cheaper, but slower, and it may take up to 4 days, depending upon when it is posted (e.g. a letter posted on Friday with a second-class stamp may not arrive at the address of the recipient until the following Tuesday).

Postcode Address File

The national Postcode Address File, containing details of every address and postcode in the country, is now on compact disc. This means that companies with this Address File can carry out checks in seconds on compatible computers by means of associated software.

The postcode system can be used for determining distribution depots, route scheduling and in the organisation of efficient after-sales service. It can be helpful in compiling and analysing statistics on a geographical basis, and orders, enquiries and even complaints can be allocated for action by use of the customer's postcode.

Certificate of Posting

This is a way of making sure that an important letter has actually been posted (and is not still in someone's pocket!). The service is free and the letter has to be handed in at a post office for the counter clerk to complete and stamp a receipt (it must *not* be posted in a letterbox).

This receipt, when taken back to the office, is proof that the letter has been posted, and when. Delivery of the letter is made by the postman in the ordinary way (through a letterbox) and no receipt form has to be signed by the recipient.

The Post Office

Certificate of Posting
for inland ordinary letters and parcels
and overseas ordinary letters

Received	items as listed	Accepting Officer's initials	Date stamp

Enter below in ink the name and full address as written on each item, and present them in the order listed.
(For Cash on Delivery parcels, enter also the reference number of the Despatch/Inpayment Document.)
No compensation will be paid in respect of money or jewellery sent in the ordinary post.

Name	Address	Postcode
1		
2		
3		
4		
5		
6		
7		
8		

P326 Dec 83   (continue overleaf if necessary)

Recorded Delivery

With this method, the Post Office issues a receipt on a yellow slip to the person posting the letter and also authorises the postman to collect a signature from the recipient, so that proof of posting and delivery is provided. Recorded Delivery is suitable only for letters and packets containing important papers – not valuables, because compensation is very limited. Papers suitable for sending by Recorded Delivery could be: passport, birth certificate, examination papers, legal documents – anything which could cause a great deal of inconvenience if lost.

Nothing intended for Recorded Delivery should be dropped into a letterbox.

E 701606	Recorded Delivery

Certificate of Posting
for Recorded Delivery
How to post

1 Enter below in ink the name and full address as written on the letter or packet.
2 Affix the numbered adhesive label in the top left-hand corner of the letter (or close to the address on a packet).
3 Affix postage stamps to the letter for the correct postage and Recorded Delivery Fee.
4 Hand this certificate, together with the letter, to an officer of The Post Office.
5 This certificate will be date-stamped and initialled as a receipt. Please keep it safely, and produce it in the event of a claim.

Name

Address

Postcode

Recorded Delivery should not be used for sending money or valuable items.

For Post Office use   Date stamp

Accepting Officer's Initials

Recorded Delivery no

E 701606

P2297

Registered Post

When anything valuable (up to a certain size and weight) has to be sent by post, it should be sent by Registered Post. Compensation is paid according to the amount of fee paid. Letters and packets sent by Registered Post are handled with special security measures by the Post Office and separately from ordinary mail. The counter clerk at the post office gives a receipt and the postman obtains one from the addressee. Registered Post is for inland post only – valuables being sent abroad by post are sent by another Post Office service.

Signing for receipt of recorded delivery or registered post

A letter or packet to be sent by Registered Post should be in a strong envelope, obtainable at post offices. These envelopes, already stamped with first-class postage are available in three sizes.

Nothing intended for registration should be dropped into a letterbox.

A correctly addressed registered envelope

Advice of Delivery

By completing an Advice of Delivery form (obtainable from any post office) advice of delivery will be sent to you for either Recorded Delivery or Registered Post.

The Post Office

1 Postal service

AR

Section 1
Return address

_____

_____

_____

Postcode

Advice of Delivery
of an inland Registered or Recorded Delivery letter

The Post Office does not undertake to deliver a letter or parcel to the addressee in person.

How to use this form

1 Write in Section 1 the name and address to which this form should be returned on completion.
2 Complete Section 2 overleaf in block letters.
3 Do not complete any other Section.
4 Affix postage stamps in the space below for the Advice of Delivery fee. For the current rate, please ask at the counter.
5 Hand in this form, unsealed, at the counter.

Stamps for Advice of Delivery Fee (to be cancelled by accepting officer)

P87 May 86   133316 9/86 GBR Ltd.

Consequential Loss Insurance

A registered letter or packet may be insured against loss, damage or delay by taking out Consequential Loss Insurance cover. An example of loss to the user of a postal service could be a winning competition entry failing to arrive before closure date, a passport lost in the post, samples delayed causing loss of sales. When posting a registered letter (or packet) for which this extra insurance is required, ask at the Post Office for a Consequential Loss

Insurance cover note. Fill this in with exactly the same name and address as on the packet and buy stamps to affix to the amount of cover required. The maximum is £10,000.

The cover note will be initialled and date-stamped by the counter clerk in the Post Office and should be kept in case a claim is made later on.

Consequential Loss Insurance is also available for COD service (see p. 160) and Special Delivery service (see p. 173).

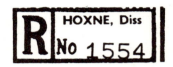

Label for consequential loss insurance

Redirection Service

The Post Office will redirect mail from an address which you have left to your new address.

A week before leaving, a Royal Mail redirection form has to be completed and handed in at the post office nearest to the *old address*.

You may select periods for redirection of one, three or twelve months.

The normal period for redirecting mail from a Poste Restante address (see below) is one month only.

Redirection service is for letters only. Normally, parcels will be returned to sender, unless the Post Office is notified separately (on the form) that parcels are to be redirected also.

Special Post Office Services

Poste Restante

This is a Post Office service which enables people on holiday or businessmen travelling around to collect their letters even when they are not sure where they will be staying. Letters must be addressed as follows:

Mr K Matthews
Poste Restante
Post Office
TUNBRIDGE WELLS
Kent
TW9 1AJ

or

Mrs E Holder
(to be called for)
Post Office
TUNBRIDGE WELLS
Kent
TW9 1AJ

Business Reply Service

This service, which requires a licence, is used by firms who wish to obtain replies from customers without putting them to the expense of paying postage. Business Reply forms may be in the form of a postcard, envelope, folder or gummed label. They may be first or second class (they are marked with a large 1 or 2). The envelope, etc. is posted in the normal way but without a stamp.

BUSINESS REPLY SERVICE
London No RG984

2

MISCO COMPUTER SUPPLIES LTD
4 The Western Centre
Western Road
Bracknell
Berkshire
RG12 1BR.

Business reply envelope, second class

Freepost

A firm that wishes to obtain a reply from a customer without putting him to the expense of paying postage may include in his address the word 'FREEPOST'. The reply bearing this word can then be posted in the ordinary way but *without a stamp*. The firm sending the letters pays the postage to the Post Office. A licence from the Post Office is needed to use the 'Freepost' service available from main post offices. An annual licence fee is payable. As with the Business Reply service, redirection is not permitted (unless extra stamps are added).

HALL & GRIFFITH LIMITED
FREEPOST
Elmstock, Oakshire.
EL78 4ZO

A freepost envelope

An international business reply service is available to 12 European countries and will be extended in the near future. Firms are able to pre-pay replies from clients overseas. Completed International Business Reply cards and envelopes will be returned as European All-up mail.

Overseas Mail

Parcels

Parcels should be labelled clearly and should always have the sender's name on the outside as well as the inside. The country to which the parcel is being sent should be clearly shown. An airmail label is necessary where airmail is being used. There is a choice between air and surface mail.

Generally, the maximum size for a parcel being sent overseas is 1.05 m in length and 2 m in length and girth combined but to many countries the limits are now 1.5 m length and 3 m length and girth combined. The maximum weight is 20 kg to most countries but some will only accept up to 10 kg. On the other hand, some countries will accept up to 22.5 kg. The weights and sizes to each country are given in the *Postal Rates Overseas Compendium*.

The Post Office has a scheme of insurance for parcels going overseas which will provide compensation in the event of loss. There are also other supplementary services such as Express Delivery, Cash on Delivery and Franc de Droits (payment of overseas customs charges by sender). If goods weigh less than 2 kg, they can be sent via the letter service. If the goods need to be sent very quickly then there is International Datapost, which is available to a growing number of countries for items up to 15 kg (see p. 172). If Datapost is not available then there is Swiftair for items less than 2 kg (see p. 170).

Customs

All packets and parcels posted to an overseas destination require a declaration label describing the contents. This applies to both airmail and surface mail. The reason for this declaration is to inform the customs officers in the country to which the parcel is sent what it contains – on some articles a tax has to be paid by the recipient and this tax is known as 'duty'. Duty is imposed on some goods to discourage people from sending them, the idea being that if the goods are manufactured in that country, the inhabitants want to sell their own and prevent foreign goods of similar type competing with them. Gifts may be allowed in duty free in certain countries if described on the label as 'gifts'. The *Post Office Guide* gives full details of regulations to all the countries of the world.

For letter packets there is a green label if the contents are less than £270 in value and a white form for goods in excess of that value. For parcels, the white form is used in most cases along with a despatch note. In other cases a combined declaration/despatch note is used. Other forms may be required depending on destination. The documentation for Swiftair is the same as letters and Datapost the same as parcels.

Post Office of Great Britain
Administration des postes de la Grande Bretagne

CUSTOMS DECLARATION
DECLARATION EN DOUANE

C2/CP3
(NON-ADHESIVE)

PP70

1. Name and address of sender *Nom et adresse de l'expéditeur*	2. Sender's reference, if any *Eventuellement numero de référence de l'expéditeur*

3. Name and address of addressee *Nom et adresse du destinataire*	4. Insert 'X' if the contents are a gift ☐ a sample of merchandise ☐ *Faire ici une croix (X) s'il s'agit d'un cadeau d'un échantillon*
	5. The undersigned certifies that the particulars given in this declaration are correct. *Le soussigné certife l'exactitude des reseignements donnés dans la presente déclaration.* 6. Signature
7. Observations	8. Place and date of posting *Lieu et date de dépôt*
	9. Country of origin of the goods. *Pays d'origine des marchandises* / 10. Country of destination. *Pays de destination*
	11. Total gross weight. *Poids brut total*

12. Number of items *Nombre d'envois*	13. Detailed description of contents *Designation detailée du contenu*	14. Tariff No. *No. tarifaire*	15. Net Weight *Poids net*	16. Value *Valeur*

Note: All unused space in columns 12-16 should be ruled through before presentation to post Office clerk.

OP/00209 9/86

CUSTOMS/DOUANE CI
(May be opened officially) *(Peut être ouvert d'office)*

Detach this part if the packet is accompanied by a Customs declaration. **Otherwise it must be completed.**
See instructions on the back
Detailed Description of Contents
(Désignation détaillée du contenu)

. . . .
. . . .
. . . .
. . . .
. . . .
. . . .

insert 'x' if the contents are:
(Faire 'x' s'il s'agit:)
a gift (d'un cadeau) . . . . ☐
a sample of merchandise
(d'un échantillon de marchandises) . . . . . . ☐

Value (Valeur) *(Specify the currency)*	Net Weight *(Poids-net)*

Customs declaration labels: white label (above) for goods valued at more than £270, green label (left) for packets containing goods valued at less than £270

169

Letters

To countries outside Europe, the cheapest way to send a letter is by using an aerogramme, obtainable at all post offices. The only disadvantage to these is that no enclosures are possible.

Other letters for countries outside Europe should normally be sent by airmail. They should be typed on thin (airmail) paper and placed in a special airmail envelope (with a blue airmail label). Cost is calculated by weight – the rates are given in the *Postal Rates Overseas Leaflet* or *Compendium*. If there is no urgency, letters can be sent by surface mail.

For letters to Europe there is only one class of mail known as 'All-up'. Airmail envelopes and labels should not be used. The *Postal Rates Overseas Leaflet* and *Compendium* both contain a list of those countries classed as Europe.

There is an EEC concessionary rate which means that letters can be sent to other EEC countries at the standard first-class rate.

Printed Matter and Christmas Cards

Firms with many overseas customers may send them Christmas cards and by using the printed paper rates, are able to save postage. The printed paper rates are available for both airmail and surface mail outside Europe and there is a surface mail printed paper service for Europe. For surface mail the full rate must be paid. The cards must not contain more than five words of greeting, besides the printed message and a signature, and they must be in unsealed envelopes.

Details of the rates are given in the *Postal Rates Overseas Leaflet* or *Compendium*.

The printed paper services can also be used for catalogues, price lists, direct mail and other publicity material or books and magazines.

Swiftair

Swiftair is an international express service for letters and printed papers and is available to all countries.

Mail by Swiftair receives priority treatment in the UK, and in many countries overseas the letters are delivered by special messenger. The list of countries where special messenger delivery is given is contained in the Swiftair leaflet on display at post offices.

A Swiftair label

Letters for Swiftair must be handed over a post office counter or included in the firm's collection (but kept separate from other letters). They must bear a red Swiftair label at the top left-hand corner on the address side of the envelope – below the blue airmail label, in the case of countries outside Europe. An extra fee is payable in addition to normal postage. A Certificate of Posting will be supplied free of charge on request at the time of posting.

Accelerated Surface Post (ASP)

ASP is cheaper than airmail and quicker than ordinary surface mail. It is a service for printed papers and combines air and surface (train, ship, road) transport.

The table below gives a comparison of times taken by various services.

	Airmail	Surface mail	ASP
Australia	4–5 days	6–8 weeks	12–18 days
East Africa	3–4 days	8–12 weeks	11–15 days
Japan	3–4 days	6–7 weeks	8–12 days
USA	3–4 days	4–6 weeks	10–18 days
India	4–5 days	6–12 weeks	11–15 days

ASP is available to Europe and 80 countries outside Europe.

Items to be posted by ASP should be put in separate bags, labelled ASP and the Post Office will collect them.

Bulk Airmail

Bulk Airmail is another airmail service for printed papers sent overseas and the cost is based on the weight 'pence per kilo'. Bulk Airmail also has to be kept in separate bags labelled ready for collection by the Post Office.

International Reply Coupons

These are sold at the larger post offices in Great Britain and Northern Ireland, and are exchangeable in all countries of the world, except South Africa and

An international reply coupon

Taiwan, for a stamp or stamps. The person to whom an International Reply Coupon is sent takes it to his nearest post office and exchanges it for a stamp issued by his own country – British stamps are not accepted in any foreign country. An International Reply Coupon is a convenient means of 'prepaying' the cost of a reply from abroad.

Services for Sending Mail Quickly

Datapost

Datapost is a Post Office service which is for urgent letters, packets and parcels (up to 27.5 kg). It guarantees overnight delivery within the United Kingdom and very speedy delivery to many countries overseas. Datapost is now available on demand at post offices from Monday to Friday (previously it had to be arranged on a contractual basis only). Datapost mail travels separately from ordinary mail and is accompanied throughout by Post Office staff (except when in transit on flights overseas). Items sent by Datapost overseas get fast Customs clearance, which is another advantage of the service.

Datapost is especially suitable for sending items where a guaranteed delivery is important – laboratory specimens from hospitals or samples to prospective customers.

A receipt is given for all Datapost items, so that firms using the service have proof of delivery.

Datapost is also available for the COD service (see p. 160). The Datapost Sameday service guarantees collection and delivery on the same day.

Datapost

EMS Datapost

A Royal Mail Service

57507342   1. Finance copy

Order number

Date sent

Contract number

To

Press Hard You are making six copies
Please type or press firmly with a ballpoint pen

57507342

D P 5 7 5 0 7 3 4 2 G B

Total items in consignment

This item

No.   of

Enter YES if Saturday delivery required

EMS Datapost

Payment method (Tick as applicable)   Cash   Account

Customer account number

Service register

Country code for Post Office use only

Is this item a Post Office prepaid Datapost pack?

Total weight of item
Kilos   gms

As applicable this posting is made under The Post Office Act 1969 or in accordance with the terms of the Datapost contract number shown

Signature of Sender

For Post Office use only

Date stamp of Accepting Officer   Office number

Charge/excess charge
£

Initials of Accepting Officer

Time

Date

Badge No.

CARRS input by

Serial No. of · _ CA116
Charge Slip ·

P 4061 May 89

1. Finance copy — period of retention 2 years

From

A Datapost label

Royal Mail Special Delivery

Royal Mail Special Delivery ensures that a first-class packet or letter will be delivered by first post the following morning (except Sunday) after posting *without fail*. If the letter arrives at the sorting office too late for the normal delivery service, a postman will go out specially to deliver it.

To send a letter (or packet – anything acceptable by normal first-class letter service) write your name and address *on the back* and ask for the service as you hand it in at the Post Office counter. You will be given a Certificate of Posting (see p. 162). You pay the Royal Mail Special Delivery fee in addition to first-class postage. If, for any reason, the letter is *not* delivered by first post on the next working day, the special delivery fee is returned.

Royal Mail Special Delivery can be used in conjunction with Recorded Delivery and Registered Post (see pp. 163–4).

The words 'Special Delivery' must be marked above the address on the left-hand side of the letter or parcel. A broad blue or black perpendicular line must also be drawn from top to bottom on both the front and the back of a letter and completely round a parcel.

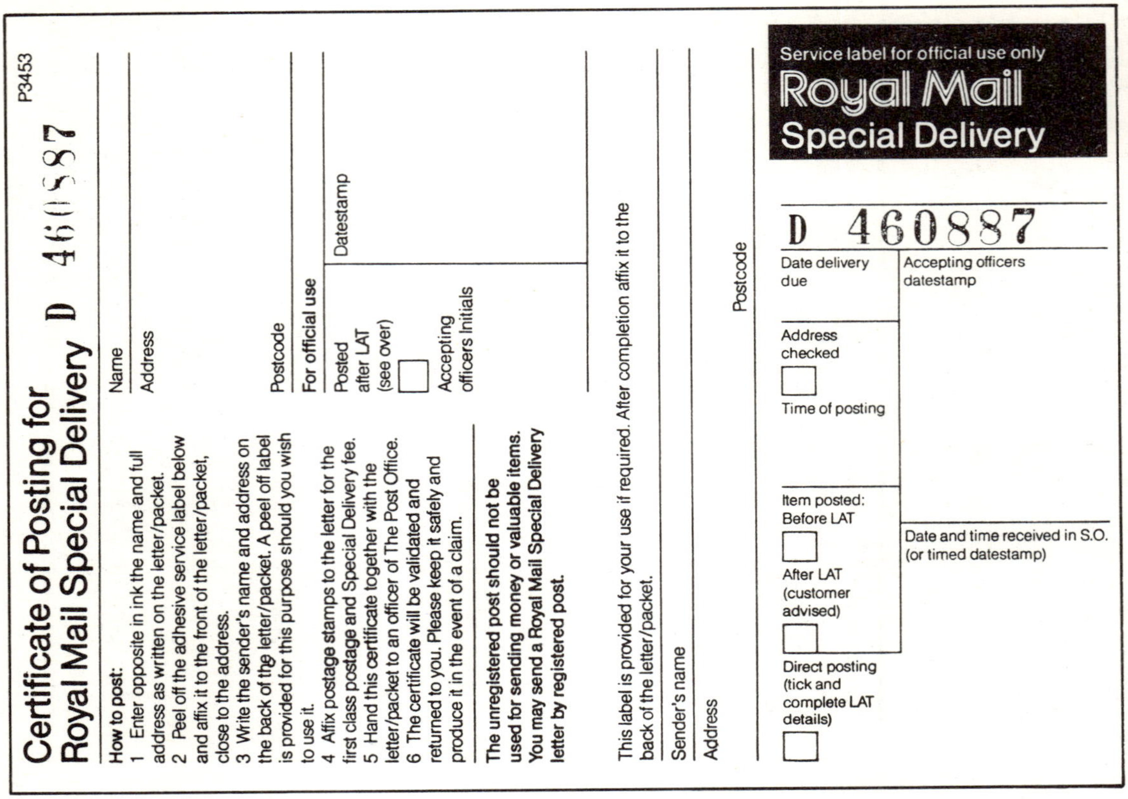
Certificate of Posting for
Royal Mail Special Delivery D 460887
P3453

How to post:
1 Enter opposite in ink the name and full address as written on the letter/packet.
2 Peel off the adhesive service label below and affix it to the front of the letter/packet, close to the address.
3 Write the sender's name and address on the back of the letter/packet. A peel off label is provided for this purpose should you wish to use it.
4 Affix postage stamps to the letter for the first class postage and Special Delivery fee.
5 Hand this certificate together with the letter/packet to an officer of The Post Office.
6 The certificate will be validated and returned to you. Please keep it safely and produce it in the event of a claim.

The unregistered post should not be used for sending money or valuable items. You may send a Royal Mail Special Delivery letter by registered post.

Name

Address

Postcode

For official use

Posted after LAT (see over)

Accepting officers Initials

Datestamp

This label is provided for your use if required. After completion affix it to the back of the letter/packet.

Sender's name

Address

Postcode

Service label for official use only
Royal Mail
Special Delivery

D 460887

Date delivery due

Accepting officers datestamp

Address checked

Time of posting

Item posted:
Before LAT

After LAT (customer advised)

Direct posting (tick and complete LAT details)

Date and time received in S.O. (or timed datestamp)

A Special Delivery Label

ELECTRONIC MAIL

Electronic Post

The Post Office offers a service called Electronic Post whereby the customer sends a computer tape to the appropriate Electronic Post Centre. The Post Office then prints the text and sends it to the address using first-class post. This service is particularly useful for bulk mailing, e.g. advertising leaflets.

Electronic Mail

Telex, Bureaufax and Intelpost are all forms of electronic mail - where messages are sent over the telephone as electrical signals which can be converted back into paper form at the other end. Privately owned facsimile transmission (Fax) machines, are also a form of electronic mail.

The latest developments in electronic mail are computer-based systems, which allow people to send and receive messages and other information through their own 'electronic mail-box'.

The 'mail-box' is a form of computer terminal linked to the telephone network, with a memory for storing messages and a means of putting messages into the system. A printer or typewriter is attached to allow messages to be printed as 'hard copy' when required.

An electronic mail service is particularly useful in a large company, where each office or department can have a mail-box and senior executives can have their own.

Telex and Teletex provide an external electronic mail system that gives written messages with the security of 'answerback' codes (see p. 56) which identify both sender and receiver.

International Electronic Post (INTELPOST)

Intelpost is the Post Office facsimile service (not to be confused with Bureaufax; see p. 54) for black and white copies of documents up to A4 size (297 mm × 210 mm). Colour originals may be used, but the copies will be black and white.

Copies will be sent by any Post Office which has the Intelpost sign, or a document for copying will be collected by messenger, on payment of an additional fee.

There are 114 Intelpost centres in the UK linked with 2000 major business centres in 30 countries abroad – in Western Europe, North America, the Far East and Australasia.

In addition to the Post Office over-the-counter service, Intelpost is available for firms which are too small for expensive electronic installations. The service can be desk-top, using equipment common to many offices, transmitting directly, without leaving the firm's premises, to others with a private facsimile (Fax) machine (p. 54).

Intelpost is particularly useful because access to it can be made, using a modem, for sending information from a computer down a telephone line, and from a telex machine. It is a public electronic mail system which is protected by law as it is a Royal Mail service and therefore confidential and secure.

When handing the document over to be copied the counter clerk will want to know:

- Name, address, postcode and telephone number.
- Number of sides to be transmitted.
- Method of delivery (special messenger, personal collection or ordinary first-class post).

There is no service on Saturdays, Sundays, or public holidays either in the UK or in other countries which operate the service.

After transmission, the Post Office at the other end will either:

- Deliver by special messenger.
- Deliver by first post the following day.

Alternatively, the copy can be collected from the Post Office.

For immediate delivery by special messenger, there is an additional charge. It is slightly dearer than Bureaufax, but as many words as you like can be written on the sheet as long as they are readable.

When documents are handed in for transmission by Intelpost, they should have a margin of at least 10 mm all round. They should not be folded, as the crease affects the facsimile quality.

Special short message forms (cheaper than the A4 size) are available for messages, especially birthday or congratulatory messages. Greetings cards are available at a small extra charge.

SECRETARIAL TIPS

1 If there are existing files in connection with an incoming letter, put them behind the letter when the pile of correspondence is placed on your employer's desk.

2 Letters dealing with more than one topic are avoided by good secretaries – who follow the 'one topic, one letter' maxim.

3 Make a firm stand about letters being dictated late in the afternoon which 'must go today' unless circumstances are exceptional. Dictation should be timed so that letters can be typed without pressure and finished well before the 'deadline' for the last post (see point 7 below).

4 Make a note of the deadline for mail and display it prominently near the collection baskets for letters.

5 Make sure that post office leaflets giving postal rates are *always* up to date. They are easily obtainable at most post offices. Equally vital, destroy the out-of-date leaflets immediately they have been superseded.

6 If you work for a firm with its own mail room, make sure you have some stamps and postal balances of your own, in case you have important letters to type after the mail room has closed.

7 Remember that franked mail cannot be posted in a letter box – it has to be taken to a post office (along with registered post and recorded delivery). It is important to reach the post office before it closes with this type of mail.

QUICK REVISION

1 Open first-class mail first, removing unopened   ....

2 Date-stamping mail is important as a   ....

3 Enclosures and continuation sheets should be   ....

176

4 Missing enclosures are indicated by ....

5 Money enclosed with letters should be ....

6 Departments to which mail has to be sent is indicated by ....

7 A letter to be seen by more than one person may be circulated by .... or .... or ....

8 If there are existing files in connection with an incoming letter they should be ....

9 Three important checks to be made before placing a letter in an envelope ....

10 A franking machine is an important item of mail room equipment which ....

11 Other mail room equipment for dealing with large quantities of mail ....

12 If large numbers of parcels are to be sent, two Post Office services should be considered: ....

13 Compensation fee is a Post Office service for inland post only, which ....

14 Reference books useful in the mail room are a large atlas, a local classified directory, Thomson local directory, A–Z street maps, phone books (telephone directories), postcode directories and ....

15 Near mail collection baskets should be a prominent notice stating ....

16 If you are a secretary in a firm with its own mail room you should keep a supply of stamps and have your own letter balances in case ....

17 A free service to obtain proof that a letter has actually been posted is ....

18 A service which gives proof of posting and delivery but only limited compensation is ....

19 A service which gives proof of posting and delivery and compensation according to amount of fee paid is ....

20 A service which enables business people moving around to collect their mail wherever they may be is ....

21 Freepost and business reply services are ways of ....

22 For letter packets to be sent overseas, a green label is required if the contents are worth less than ....

23 Letters can be sent to other EEC countries at a concessionary rate. This rate is ....

24 The international express service is ....

25 ASP is ....

26 Exchangeable for stamps in post offices in all countries except South Africa and Taiwan are ....

27 The only service which guarantees delivery on the day of posting is ....

28 Trakbak is a new post office service for ....

29 The post office facsimile service is ....

30 A computer terminal linked to the telephone network with a memory for storing messages and a means of putting messages into the system is known as ....

ASSIGNMENTS

1 *Working out postage*
Referring to p. 149 rule up a page from a postage book. Date it for a week ago. The value of stamps bought is £50. With up-to-date Post Office leaflets *Letter Rates* and *International Letter Rates,* find the correct postage and enter the following:

Grumble and Groan, Moanchester	letter second class
Brickfield Building Society Newcastle-upon-Tyne	letter first-class recorded delivery
British Instruments Ltd Camborne	letter 90 g first-class
Londonderry Travel Co Londonderry	parcel 750 g second-class
Sikh & Singh, Bombay	letter airmail 50 g
Jacques Rousseau et Fils, Lyons	letter 20 g
Heinze Wolff, Copenhagen	letter 15 g
Walker & Walton Ltd Bradford	letter Royal Mail Special Delivery
Thatch & Tile Barchester	registered letter value insured £750

Total, and bring down balance to the next day.

2 Rule up a sheet for a record of stamps as on p. 150 and enter the details in Assignment 1 in this simplified form. Total, and bring down the balance for the next day.

3 Your employer is going on a business trip involving staying in Geneva, Lucerne, Athens, Milan, Belgrade, Lisbon and Barcelona, and Washington USA.
Using the post office leaflet *Writing Home From Abroad* list the postal rates for letters and postcards sent from these countries to the UK. He would also like to know which will need airmail stickers.

4 You are employed as a secretary by a small firm. The number of letters sent out each day averages 20. There is a franking machine which is in need of repair – it was installed about 15 years ago. The local post office has recently closed down, and the nearest one is now two miles away. Your employer has asked for your opinion about buying an up-to-date franking machine to replace the existing one, or going back to using stamps. Write a report to him (invent the necessary details) setting out the advantages and disadvantages of both methods.

5 Why, in your opinion, is there a system in some firms of a 'letter book'?

CHAPTER 9

Stationery Supplies

Stationery forms only a small part of the stock held in a firm, but it is becoming more and more expensive, so that issues of stationery should be carefully controlled.

Stationery covers such obvious items as:

- typing paper – bond and bank, A4 and A5. Bank is white and coloured.
- letterheading – A4 and A5 (portrait or landscape, see p. 180)
- memoranda – A4 and A5
- envelopes, all sizes and types
- printout paper for computers
- carbon paper

Other items which may be issued from the stationery store could be:

- ballpoint pens
- pencils
- staplers and staples
- perforators
- adhesive tape
- paper clips and pins
- rubber bands
- treasury tags
- bulldog clips
- folders – all sizes (see pp. 104–5)
- labels
- scissors
- rubber thimbles
- string and brown paper
- rubber stamps and pads
- typewriter ribbons and cassettes

- correcting ribbons
- correcting fluid
- typewriter erasers
- typewriter eraser shields
- printheads for computers
- daisywheels for typewriters
- daisywheel albums
- disk storage boxes

PAPER SIZES

A5 paper is half the size of A4.

A5 paper may be used either with the short edge inserted into the typewriter (this is called *portrait*) or with the long edge inserted into the typewriter (this is called *landscape*).

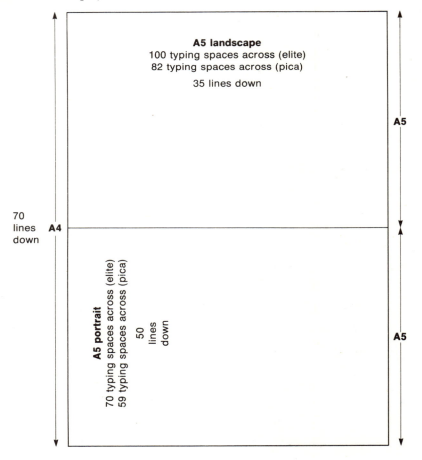

ENVELOPE SIZES

The Post Office sets out sizes for envelopes in the *Post Office Guide* (see p. 157) which they prefer (POP, or 'Post Office preferred' envelopes).

There are three different *shapes* of envelopes which would be kept in a stock of stationery, in varying sizes:

- Pocket, which opens on the short side (see below).
- Banker, which opens on the long side (see below).
- Window (or aperture) envelopes, which save typing the address on the envelope (see p. 149).

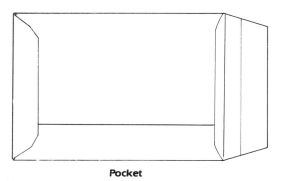

Pocket

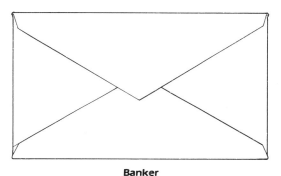

Banker

STOCK CONTROL OF STATIONERY

In a small office, the secretary (or her assistant) may be responsible for issuing stationery. It is important that no unnecessary 'stockpiling' of stationery occurs for two reasons – stock costs money and storage space in an office is always valuable. A method of avoiding stockpiling is to keep a careful record of everything in the stationery store on a stationery stock card as illustrated overleaf.

The stationery stock card shows the minimum amount below which the stock should not fall, and the maximum amount likely to be required. This should not be exceeded, otherwise money is tied up and storage space is being used unnecessarily. Maximum/minimum levels enable the secretary or clerk in charge of stationery stock to see at a glance from the stock card whether issues of certain items are increasing and to whom. Stock cards also enable the reordering to be done well before stock falls too low. In the card illustrated the person in charge should never allow the number of boxes of treasury tags to fall below 10, but she should never stock up to give a total of more than 40. The right-hand column keeps a record of the number in stock and when these fell to 11, she decided to reorder.

Stationery Stock Card

Item _Treasury Tags_
(boxes of 50) mixed colours

Maximum Stock: 40 boxes
Minimum Stock: 10 boxes

Date 199–	Receipts			Issues			Balance in Stock
	Quantity Received	Invoice No.	Supplier	Quantity Issued	Requisition No.	Department	
Jan 1							30 boxes
" 8				1 box	153	Reception	29 "
" 11				10 boxes	401	Filing dept.	19 "
March 1				8 boxes	477	Personnel dept.	11 "
" 3	25 boxes	450	Office Equipment Supplies Ltd.				36 "

A completed stationery stock card

A spreadsheet on a computer (see p. 85) could be used for stationery stock control.

REORDERING STATIONERY

Reordering of stationery stock is often done by the purchasing department and an order from the stationery supervisor is sent to this department at regular intervals – perhaps once a month – or when shortage causes an emergency. A stock requisition form may be used:

Stock Requisition		No. _____
Dept.		
Quantity	Description	Stock Ref. No.
Received by	Signed	Authorised
	Date	Date

SECRETARIAL TIPS

1 Keep empty boxes in which typing paper is delivered for placing 'orders' in readiness for collection.

2 Place one copy of each requisition on top of relevant order so that it is clear to whom it belongs.

3 File the other copy of each requisition in numerical order to be used when stock-taking.

4 Do not make exceptions to the rule stating when stationery is issued – or very soon *everyone* will expect to be treated as a special case.

5 Bank and bond paper are delivered in boxes containing one ream; there are 500 sheets in a ream. When staff requisitions stipulate less than a ream, it saves time counting out sheets to measure them – every 50 milli-metres (two inches) equals approximately 400 sheets of bond paper. Cut a notch measuring 50 mm in a piece of cardboard.

6 Send a copy of the checklist of stationery available to all members of staff, together with a copy of the notice showing days and times when issued.

7 Make sure that two people have a key to the stationery cupboard, in case one of them is absent at any time. Keep key safely out of sight.

8 File stock cards in alphabetical order of item, and mark them with coloured tabs when re-ordering is becoming imminent.

QUICK REVISION

1 Stocks of stationery in a firm should be carefully controlled for two reasons: ....

2 Maximum/minimum levels of stock enable the person in charge of stationery to see ....

3 A computer program for recording stationery stock control is a ....

4 A stock requisition form is used by staff for ....

5 A checklist of all the items in the stationery store should be on the outside of the door and also ....

6 Together with the checklist on the door should be a ....

7 A quick way to save time-wasting counting of sheets of paper is to measure them. Two inches (50 mm) equals ....

8 So that it is clear to whom stationery orders belong place a ....

1 (a) Complete the first stock card below.
  (b) What was the total number of reams issued in January? February?
  (c) Which department used the most during these two months?

2 Give 4 *brief main* guidelines for your junior assistant as reminders about important priorities when issuing stationery, for her reference while you are on a fortnight's holiday.

3 Suggest suitable days and/or times when stock-taking could be carried out with the minimum disruption to your own job and to the other members of staff, remembering that stock-taking is a time-consuming job because it has to be done carefully and accurately.

4 The purchasing officer is querying the increase in the numbers of ballpoint pens ordered in July and August last year. He wants a list of departments with the total numbers ordered during these months (use the stock cards opposite).

STOCK CARD

Item __Bond Paper__   **Maximum stock** _400 reams_

__A4__   **Minimum stock** _100 reams_

| Date 199– | Receipts | | | Issues | | | Balance in stock |
	Quantity received	Invoice No.	Supplier	Quantity Issues	Requisition No.	Department	
Jan 8							110
" 11	250	9981	Office Equipment Supplies Ltd				
" 18				20	301	Reprographic	
" 25				5	324	Purchasing	
Feb 1				1	361	Reception	
" 8				5	374	Personnel	
" 15				15	381	Reprographic	
" 22				5	390	Sales	

STOCK CARD

Item _Ballpoint pens_ Maximum stock _600_
Black Minimum stock _250_

Date 199–	Receipts			Issues			Balance in stock
	Quantity received	Invoice No.	Supplier	Quantity Issues	Requisition No.	Department	
July 1							500
" 8				10	472	Accounts	490
" 9				20	524	Mail Room	470
" 14				50	545	Wages	420
" 20				15	556	Production	405
" 22				25	561	Mail Room	380
" 27				12	570	Reception	368
" 30				25	576	Personnel	343

STOCK CARD

Item _Ballpoint pens_ Maximum stock _600_
Black Minimum stock _250_

Date 199–	Receipts			Issues			Balance in stock
	Quantity received	Invoice No.	Supplier	Quantity Issues	Requisition No.	Department	
Aug. 3							343
" 3				30	574	Wages	313
" 10				20	589	Sales	293
" 10				10	594	Buying	283
" 17				20	609	Mail Room	263
" 17	250	0398	Shaw & Short Ltd.				513
" 24				10	617	Accounts	503
" 24				5	624	Filing	498

185

CHAPTER 10

Money at Banks and Post Offices

BANK ACCOUNTS

There are two types of bank account – current and deposit (or savings). In order to encourage customers to leave their money in a deposit account, interest is paid.

Most banks allow customers to withdraw money from a deposit account on demand (after completing a withdrawal slip). Giving seven days notice of withdrawal avoids loss of interest.

A current account is quite different. It is the most widely used, although many bank customers have both a current and a deposit account. A current account enables the customer to write cheques to pay bills and to take out any cash needed for day-to-day expenses. Traditionally, no interest is payable on a current account, but some banks now offer a new type of account, which pays interest when the account is in credit. These new current accounts charge a fixed yearly rate (payable monthly) known in advance by the bank's customer.

A typical enquiry desk at a bank

In a traditional account, a credit balance is set by the bank against any charges due (and they vary from bank to bank). The charges are based on the number of transactions (cheques, direct debits, standing orders, see p. 199).

How to Open a Current Account or a Deposit Account

Go into the nearest branch of the big four, or Co-operative Bank, or Trustee Savings Bank and find the enquiry counter.

Tell the clerk you wish to open an account (either current or deposit). You will then be asked for:

- a description of your occupation,
- some money (it need only be a few pounds),
- a specimen signature (so that no one else can sign your cheques or withdraw money from your deposit account),
- a reference (your employer would be suitable, or a friend with a bank account).

You will be given (in about a week) a cheque book (for your current account) printed with your name on each cheque (see below).

Cheques

What a Cheque Is

A cheque is an order in writing addressed to the bank to pay, when required, a sum of money to the person named on the cheque. It is quite legal for a plain piece of paper to be used, or even a tablecloth or fish (this has actually happened) but it is now the practice for the banks to issue special cheque forms, in books.

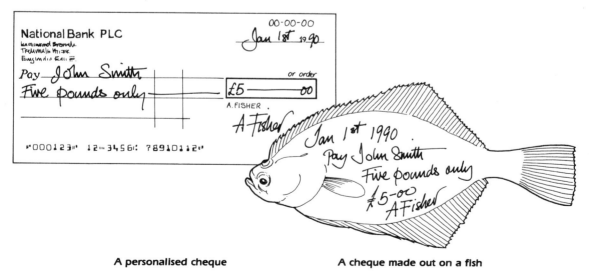

A personalised cheque   A cheque made out on a fish

A cheque is not legal tender – as a bank note is – and anyone is entitled to refuse a cheque in payment of a debt, but a cheque is an official document recognised in law.

Reasons for Cheques

A cheque enables money to be transferred from one person to another without notes and coins leaving the bank. A large sum of money can be paid more conveniently and quickly by cheque, with no counting of notes or coins or the security risks involved when cash is handled.

Banknotes and coins...   ...attract thieves

Writing Cheques

Cheques must be written in ink or ball-point pen and *not* in pencil. Most cheques are attached to the cheque book by a 'counterfoil', or cheque 'stub'. The counterfoil is left in the cheque book after the cheque has been made out and removed, as a record for the customer, so it is sensible to fill it in as a copy of each cheque.

Sept. 10 19 9—

SPECIMEN ONLY Issued by Bank Education Service.

September 10 19 9— 00-00-00

BANK OF EDUCATION
HOMETOWN

Pay _____ *or Order*

£ _____

£ _____ B HOPEFUL

000651

"000651" 00" 0000: 10475375" 11

Counterfoil

The person receiving the money represented by a cheque is the 'payee'. The name of the 'payee' is written clearly on the cheque against the word 'Pay' and should also be written on the counterfoil, with the date and the amount.

A cheque must be dated with the date on which it is written. Banks will not accept post-dated (dated in advance) cheques for immediate withdrawal of cash.

Name of 'payee'
on counterfoil

Sept 10 19 9—

Miss Joanne
Phillips

SPECIMEN ONLY Issued by Bank Education Service.

September 10 19 9— 00-00-00

BANK OF EDUCATION
HOMETOWN

Pay Miss Joanne Phillips _____ *or Order*

£ _____

£ _____ B HOPEFUL

000651

"000651" 00" 0000: 10475375" 11

Name of person who will
receive cheque – 'payee' .

189

On the line beneath the payee's name the amount to be paid is written *in words*. It is written again in figures in the 'box' provided. The two amounts must be the same – if not, the bank will not pay out the money. Any space left should be ruled up so that no one can dishonestly add any figures. 'Noughts' are best avoided as they can look like sixes if written badly. Dots must not be used either – write long dashes instead. The word 'only' may be added after the amount in words as an extra safeguard (see below).

	SPECIMEN ONLY Issued by Bank Education Service.
Sept 10 19 9-	*10 September 199-* **00-00-00**
	BANK OF EDUCATION
Miss Joanne	**HOMETOWN**
Phillips	*Pay Miss Joanne Phillips* ____ *or Order*
	Ten pounds only —— £10 ——
	B HOPEFUL
£ 10 —	
000658	"000651" 00"0000': 10475375" 11

Signature

The customer signs his (or her) name always in the same way, and it should agree with the specimen signature he gave to the bank when he opened his account. The signature is at the foot of the cheque. This signature is the name of the 'drawer' of the cheque.

	SPECIMEN ONLY Issued by Bank Education Service.
Sept 10 19 9-	*10 September 199-* **00-00-00**
	BANK OF EDUCATION
Miss Joanne	**HOMETOWN**
Phillips	*Pay Miss Joanne Phillips* ____ *or Order*
	Ten pounds only — £10 ——
	B HOPEFUL
£ 10 —	*B. Hopeful*
000651	"000651" 00"0000': 10475375" 11

The counterfoil does not have to be signed

Signature of drawer

190

'Stale' Cheques

A cheque is 'valid' (that is, it will be cashed by a bank) up to six months after it has been made out. After six months, it is out of date, and is 'invalid' and will be returned to drawer marked R/D (refer to drawer).

Cheques which 'Bounce'

Cheques which 'bounce' have not been *cleared* and so are dishonoured, for any one of the following reasons:

- if the drawer of the cheque has no money in his current account
- if the amount in words does not agree with the amount in figures
- if drawer's signature looks different from his specimen signature
- if an alteration has not been initialled
- if cheque is post dated (dated in advance)
- if cheque has been 'stopped' by the drawer
- if cheque is 'stale'.

Completing the Counterfoil

It is useful to the 'drawer' if he has a record of what he wrote a cheque out for as well as to whom and also he may like to deduct the amount of the cheque from his current account balance and make a note on the counterfoil.

What the cheque
was made out for

10 Sept/19 9— Miss Joanne Phillips for: driving lesson £ 10 —— Bal. in account £65 000651	**SPECIMEN ONLY** Issued by Bank Education Service. 10 September 19 9— 00-00-00 ## BANK OF EDUCATION **HOMETOWN** *Pay* Miss Joanne Phillips ——— *or Order* Ten pounds only —— £ 10 ———— B HOPEFUL B. Hopeful ⑈000651⑈ 00⑈0000⑊ 10475375⑈ 11

Balance in account on
10 September 199-

The completed cheque and counterfoil

Correcting Mistakes on Cheques

Providing it is a simple one, a mistake on a cheque may be crossed through (once only, not scribbled over) and the correction signed by the drawer of the cheque. If the error is a large one (the wrong payee's name for example), it is better to tear up the cheque, cancel the counterfoil and start again.

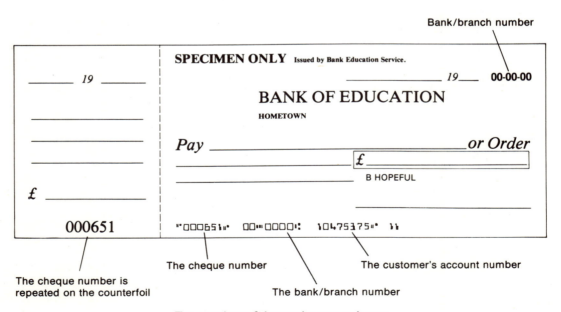

The counterfoil does not require initialling; it stays in the cheque book

A correction crossed through and initialled

'Stopping' a Cheque

The bank should be informed at once if a customer has lost his cheque book, or a cheque which he has posted has not been received. The bank should be telephoned if possible giving date, number and amount. Then, later, it will be necessary to complete a 'stop instruction' form which the bank will provide.

Bank/branch number

The cheque number is repeated on the counterfoil

The cheque number

The bank/branch number

The customer's account number

The meanings of the numbers on a cheque

For example, after Mrs Mary Jenkinson had posted her cheque in payment of an account, she was very surprised when, later, the bill was sent to her again. Upon enquiry she found out that her cheque had never been received and must have gone astray.

She immediately went to her bank and found out that the cheque had not been presented for payment. Mrs Jenkinson at once completed a form instructing the bank to stop payment of the missing cheque should anyone present it at the bank. She then made out a second cheque in payment of the still unpaid bill. The staff of the bank keep a careful watch for the lost cheque among those which are presented for payment, and a record of the 'stop' is placed on Mrs Jenkinson's computer records. The computer automatically rejects the cheque if it is eventually presented for payment.

Withdrawing Cash from a Current Account

Cash can be withdrawn by writing out a cheque or by using a cash dispensing machine (see p. 199).

Most banks have a quick service counter for customers who only want to cash a cheque. This avoids standing in a queue for a long time behind people with other business to transact.

When cash is withdrawn by cheque, the cheque has to be made out by the customer to 'Self' or 'Cash'.

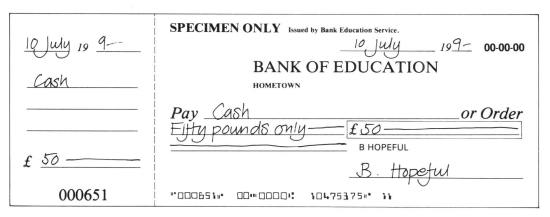

10 July 19 9—

Cash

£ 50

000651

SPECIMEN ONLY Issued by Bank Education Service.

10 July   199—   00-00-00

BANK OF EDUCATION

HOMETOWN

Pay Cash   or Order

Fifty pounds only——— £50———

B HOPEFUL

B. Hopeful

"000651" 00"0000: 10475375" 11

An open cheque made out to 'Cash' (for withdrawing money in cash from a current account)

An 'open' cheque has no crossing. It will be cashed by a bank, and is therefore not as safe as a crossed cheque, which has to be paid into a bank account. Banks mainly issue books of crossed cheques for this reason.

If a crossed cheque which has been lost or stolen is later paid into a bank account illegally, it is always possible to trace the person who stole or found the cheque.

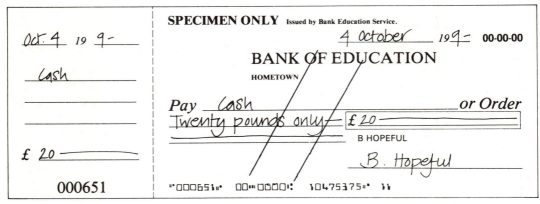

A crossed cheque made out to 'Cash'

An 'open' cheque can be crossed simply by ruling two parallel lines from top to bottom across the middle (see above). All cheques sent by post should be crossed, as a safeguard against theft.

Cheque books are provided free to holders of current accounts.

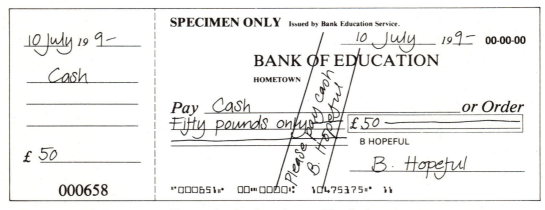

The crossing has been 'opened' by signing

It is extremely foolish to sign a cheque and leave the amount blank. The cheque could be filled in for any sum of money and the bank would accept it, even though the writing would be different from the signature. Because the latter is genuine, the cheque would not be queried.

1 Nov 19 9–	1 November 199– .00-00-00
Mr T Keene	**BANK OF EDUCATION**
	HOMETOWN
_____	*Pay* Mr T Keene _____ *or Order*
_____	£ _____
£ _____	B HOPEFUL
	B. Hopeful
000658	"000651" 00"0000: 10475375" 11

A 'blank' cheque (amount is not specified). Anyone could fill in any amount in words and figures

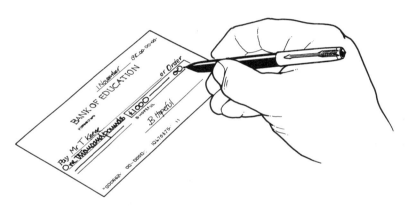

Even though the amount is written in different handwriting . . .

. . . the cheque is not queried

Paying in a Cheque Made Out to Another Person

A bank will accept this if it is endorsed (signed) on the back by the payee. Such a cheque has to be paid into an account; it cannot be cashed.

Special Cheque Crossings

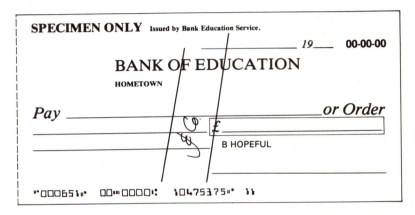

An ordinary cheque crossing (printed on by the banks) consists of two parallel lines which usually has '& Co' printed between the lines, but this is not essential. This is known as 'general crossing'

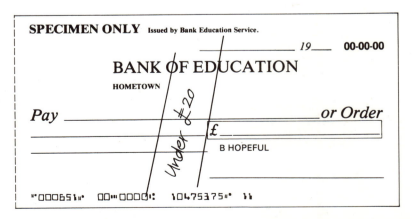

This cheque must be for an amount under £20. It is a safeguard against anyone altering the amount by adding an extra nought

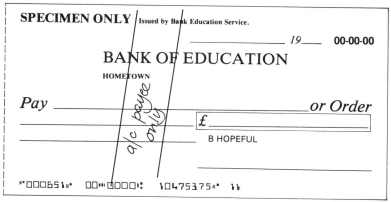

This is an extra safeguard – the cheque must be paid into the payee's account and no other

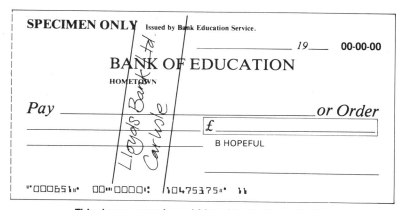

This cheque must be paid into Lloyd's Bank, Carlisle

Cheque Cards

Current account holders may have a cheque card, if they wish (after they have had a current account for about six months and proved that they can handle it responsibly). A cheque card enables them to cash a cheque for up to £50 at any branch of any bank, or write a cheque for goods bought up to the value of £50 in the UK and in the major cities of Europe. A cheque card is an undertaking by the bank issuing it to honour the cheque written in association with it. New limit for cheque cards (ranging from £100 to £250) is soon to be raised by *some* banks. Building societies already offer a £100 limit cheque card.

Cash Dispensing Machines

Cash dispensing machines have been set up in more than 10,000 branches of banks to allow customers to withdraw cash quickly (without waiting in a queue at the counter) or after the bank is closed. Most have reciprocal arrangements with other banks. The customer is supplied with a special plastic card which is inserted into the cash dispensing machine and the customer taps out his or her secret number on the keys. The secret number is known only to the computer and the customer. If the card and the number agree, the cash dispenser releases the amount of money that the customer has 'keyed' in.

A cash dispenser

Some machines release only a fixed amount (say £10 or £20). Others release amounts up to a limit agreed with the customer. They are all programmed with information about the amount of money in an account and will release any amount up to the maximum – provided there is enough money in the account!

Service Points

These have special buttons to request the print-out of a customer's current balance and to request that a full statement or a new cheque book be sent by post. Again, this saves joining a queue at the counter.

Credit Cards

Credit cards are not run by the banks but by separate credit card companies linked to the banks. For example, Barclaycard is linked to Barclays Bank and Access to a number of banks including Lloyds, Midland and National Westminster.

With a credit card a customer may buy goods or services (e.g. tickets, meals) at any place linked with his credit card in the UK and many other countries. Such places display the sign. Instead of paying cash at once, the customer signs a special slip which gives the value of the purchase, like a bill. The credit card is made of plastic, embossed with the customer's name and credit number, and carries his specimen signature.

 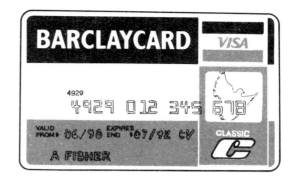

Credit cards

Credit cards and cheque cards are now issued with 'holograms' produced by laser beam in varying designs to make them harder to forge. A hologram makes a pattern in two or three dimensions when it reflects the light.

If the total is settled before the date shown on the statement, no credit charge is made; but if payment is delayed or if the customer only pays a part of the sum owing, interest is charged on the balance owing by the credit card company.

Standing Orders

A standing order is an instruction in writing to a bank by a customer (usually on a printed form – see overleaf) to pay on the customer's behalf, from his or her current account balance, amounts which are paid regularly (insurance premiums, mortgage payments, TV rental, hire purchase payments, savings into a building society or SAYE savings scheme, and subscriptions to clubs). This avoids the possibility of forgetting to pay these amounts at the right time.

Direct Debit

This is similar to a standing order except that the amount may be varied by the payee without reference to the current account holder. It is a great help to building societies and organisations such as the AA, because a direct debit avoids having to ask for the customer's permission to change (usually increase) the amount payable. Notification that a direct debit is to be changed is sent to a customer by the bank.

It is worth remembering that in some cases (not all) direct debits are deducted from a current account *before* the date specified by the account holder, which may result in him or her being overdrawn without realising it.

199

```
TO COLLEGIATE BANK                    Standing order
                                      Specimen Only

Branch    Hometown

                   Date  25th February 199-

Please make payments and debit my/our  current   account No. 57367401
in accordance with the following details, to:

Bank  Bank of Education

Branch  Newtown

Sorting code number  00 - 00 - 04

For account of  XYZ Insurance Co.

Account number, if any  10475375

Reference, if any  _____

Amount   £ 15

Payments to be made _____ weekly/monthly/quarterly/half yearly/annually*

Date of first payment  14th March 199-

Date of final payment  14th March 19--

This order cancels the existing one* for £ __

                              B. Hopeful

*Delete as appropriate
```

A standing order form

Paying Money into a Current Account

Payment is made into a current account at a bank by completing a paying-in slip or a bank giro credit slip (p. 202). These paying-in slips have a counterfoil. The bank clerk date stamps both, one for the bank records and the counterfoil for the depositor to keep. The paying-in slip (or credit slip) on p. 203 gives:

A the date

B the amount

C the name of the person paying in
D the name of the person whose account is to be credited
E the account number

For the convenience of the bank clerks who have to balance or check their tills at the end of each day, the sum paid in is divided between cash (notes and coins), cheques and postal orders. The 'cash' figure is subdivided into notes and silver and bronze coins.

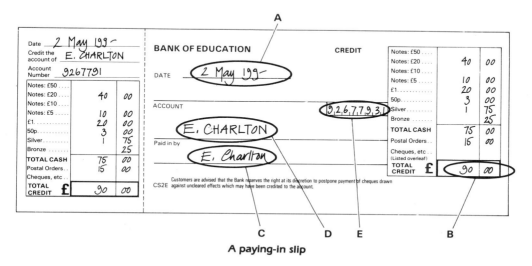

A paying-in slip

In the illustration above, note that two £20 notes have been paid in (i.e. £40), two £5 notes (i.e. £10), twenty £1 coins (i.e. £20), six 50p pieces (i.e. £3), silver coins to the value of £1.75 and bronze to the value of 25p.

Details of cheques and postal orders, are written on the back of the paying-in slip (and on the back of the counterfoil). This is useful where there are a number of cheques and/or postal orders. The total is brought forward to the front of the paying-in slip.

The paying-in slip is used when you go to a branch to pay money into your account held at that branch.

Paying-in slips vary slightly from bank to bank.

Bank Giro Credit

Any payment into another account can be made through any bank by bank giro credit, so long as the bank and branch where the account is held are known. Most electricity, gas and water boards encourage customers to pay their bills in this way by printing bank giro credit forms on the bottom of their bills. The bank, branch and account number of the organisation is already printed on the form, so all the customer has to do is to fill in the amount to be paid in, sign the form and hand in the form with the amount.

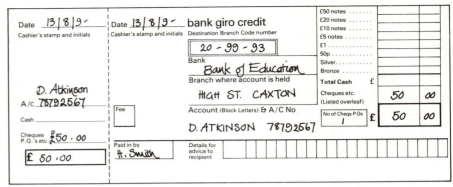

Bank giro credit form

One cheque may be made out for several bills being paid in this way. Bank giro credit slips are available in banks.

A bank giro credit schedule is a list for paying salaries into employee's bank accounts.

Bank Giro Credit Schedule

This is a list for paying salaries into employees' bank accounts each month. A cheque for the total sum to be transferred is made out by the firm in favour of the bank itself. This method of payment is safer and more convenient than giving cash, or writing cheques.

BANK GIRO CREDITS   24·2·91 DATE

Lloyds Bank   HIGH STREET, SUTTON   BRANCH

Please distribute the credit slips attached, as arranged with the recipients

Our cheque £ 9732.54 is enclosed.

LIST NO 8   *J. Williams* SIGNATURE
                                                    DIRECTOR

CODE No.	BANK AND BRANCH		ACCOUNT	NET AMOUNT
	BARCLAYS	LINCOLN	A.J. SMITH	1458.24
	LLOYDS	BRISTOL	K. BLAKE	1253.06
	MIDLAND	SUTTON	P. WEST	1658.16
	NATIONAL WESTMINSTER	CHEAM	T.H. GREEN	1261.14
	LLOYDS	WESTMINSTER	D.M. MORGAN	1021.14
	BARCLAYS	CROYDON	F. ROGERS	953.00
	MIDLAND	STRAND	K. JONES	1164.28
	COUTTS	BRISTOL	B. WATTS	963.52
			TOTAL (or Forward Total) £	9732.54

Bank giro credit schedule

Bank Statements

These are sent to a holder of a current account at regular intervals, or on request. It shows all money paid into the current account, all cheques written and all credit transfers, standing orders and direct debits – as well as any dividends paid into the account. The last figure in the right-hand column is the amount in the account when the statement is made up.

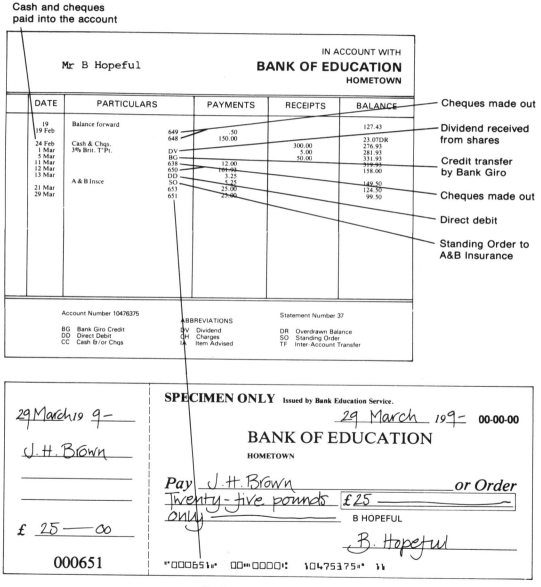

Cash and cheques paid into the account

DATE	PARTICULARS		PAYMENTS	RECEIPTS	BALANCE
19 19 Feb	Balance forward	649 648	.50 150.00		127.43
24 Feb	Cash & Chqs.			300.00	23.07DR 276.93
1 Mar	3% Brit. T'Pt.	DV		5.00	281.93
5 Mar		BG		50.00	331.93
11 Mar		638	12.00		319.93
12 Mar		650	161.93		158.00
13 Mar	A & B Insce	DD SO	3.25 5.25		149.50
21 Mar		653	25.00		124.50
29 Mar		651	25.00		99.50

— Cheques made out
— Dividend received from shares
— Credit transfer by Bank Giro
— Cheques made out
— Direct debit
— Standing Order to A&B Insurance

Account Number 10476375

ABBREVIATIONS

Statement Number 37

BG	Bank Giro Credit	DV	Dividend	DR	Overdrawn Balance
DD	Direct Debit	CH	Charges	SO	Standing Order
CC	Cash &/or Chqs	IA	Item Advised	TF	Inter-Account Transfer

29 March 19 9—

J. H. Brown

£ 25 — 00

000651

29 March 199— 00-00-00

BANK OF EDUCATION

HOMETOWN

Pay J. H. Brown _____ or Order

Twenty-five pounds £25 _____

only

B HOPEFUL

B. Hopeful

"000651" 00"0000: 10475375" 11

Bank statement of account

203

When a customer has overdrawn his account, the letters DR or OD are printed at the right-hand side under 'Balance'. DR and OD mean 'overdrawn balance', i.e. being 'in the red'.

Electronic Funds Transfer (EFT)

The 'cashless society', where there will be no need to carry notes and coins, has come nearer with the increased use of credit cards and cheque cards. Electronic funds transfer (EFT) takes the cashless society one step further, as it allows for the automatic transfer of money between companies and people by means of computers. Through EFT, customers can transfer funds without writing cheques or bank giro slips, call up their bank statements on a television screen for checking, and see details of standing orders or direct debits. It will be possible virtually to eliminate time-consuming visits to banks. Also, companies will receive cash due to them much more quickly, as it will not be necessary for cheques to leave the receiving branch. Details regarding the cheques will be fed into a computer, thus cutting down the 'clearing' time (three days by traditional methods) and automatically crediting money to the accounts so that it is available at once. Companies will be able to keep an up-to-date record of their cash position – a very important advantage of EFT.

What is required is a normal television set (either black and white or colour), a Prestel keypad and a telephone jack socket. The keypad is connected to the telephone socket and the television set, and the service is ready. As an alternative to a Prestel keypad, EFT can be run through a home or business computer using a modem.

Customers of some banks can now benefit from electronic funds transfer at the point of sale (EFTPOS). The cheque card (called a Switch or Connect card) is simply handed to the cashier at the checkout point of the store when payment is requested. Payment from the relevant bank account takes place automatically, eliminating the need to write a cheque.

OTHER BANK SERVICES

For Travellers

Traveller's cheques are a worldwide form of international currency. Anyone (not just bank customers) can buy traveller's cheques from a bank, in denominations of £2, £5, £10, £20 and £50. The bank makes a small charge.

When bought each cheque must be signed. When being cashed, each traveller's cheque has to be signed again (endorsed) by the same person who signed when they were collected from the bank. This endorsement has to be made in the presence of the cashier at the bank. Therefore it is

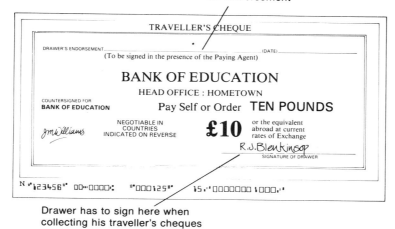

Drawer has to sign here when presenting his traveller's cheque for cashing; an 'endorsement'

Drawer has to sign here when collecting his traveller's cheques

A traveller's cheque

necessary to make sure that when traveller's cheques are collected in this country from the bank, they are signed for by the person most likely to cash them when abroad.

Traveller's cheques are a safe way to carry money abroad (or in this country) as if lost, they will be replaced. Many hotels, shops and restaurants will accept traveller's cheques in payment.

Eurocheques

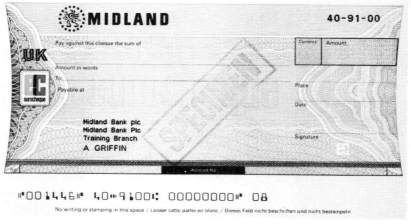

A eurocheque

Eurocheques are offered by banks and allow holders to pay by cheque in Europe and in Mediterranean countries exactly the same as they would in Britain. Eurocheques can be written in 39 different foreign currencies and cut out the bother of arranging for traveller's cheques before a trip or holiday abroad, and also having to cash them while in a foreign country. The added advantage with eurocheques is that there is no need to pay out a large sum of money beforehand to obtain traveller's cheques.

Cash may be withdrawn by eurocheque from any European bank displaying the eurocheque sign.

The eurocheque service is no cheaper than traveller's cheques, but a great deal more convenient.

Foreign Currency

Banks will provide foreign currency in exchange for cash (or debit a current account for the value of the foreign currency). It is always useful to carry some foreign money for a journey abroad, so that some money is available for small items on arrival (drinks, bus fares, telephone calls).

Safe Custody of Valuables

All the large banks offer safe custody. This covers services including:
- storing a sealed envelope with contents unknown to the bank,
- storing sealed or locked packages, boxes or cash boxes, the contents of which need not be declared, and may consist of jewellery, valuable stamp collections, paintings or silver.

Items in safe custody are held in a strong room to which access can only be made by two members of the bank staff with separate keys, so in order to avoid a long wait when collecting articles from safe custody, it is wise to telephone first.

Although all banks now charge for safe custody (charges vary from bank to bank), it is sensible to take valuables to a bank for safekeeping while away, rather than leave them for burglars to find. Valuables deposited for safe custody must be insured.

Night Safes

A night safe is built into the outside wall of a bank. The customer has a small box or wallet into which he places his money with a paying-in slip (see p. 201) completed in the usual way. He then locks his bag or seals it with a special punch and takes it to the bank. He unlocks the hatch in the bank's outer wall and drops the box or wallet down a chute. The box can be collected unopened when the bank is open.

A night safe

Other Services

Insurance

Banks will advise on the best type of insurance to take out for children, wives, husbands, and businesses.

Wills

A will is an instruction to carry out wishes regarding the distribution of someone's property after his death. A bank will act as an executor or trustee (a trustee is someone who looks after property or money left in a will to someone who may only be a child, until they are grown up). The bank makes a charge for acting as an executor. An executor carries out the instructions in a will.

Investments

Banks employ specialists who will give advice to customers about the best ways of investing their money. The bank cannot force customers to take their advice, and if someone wishes to buy shares in a diamond mine on a remote island that cannot even be found on a map, the bank cannot stop him! Banks charge for advising about investments, too, in some cases.

Bank Drafts

A bank draft is a means of transferring money from the account of one bank customer to another, and is preferred by creditors to a cheque where a large sum of money is involved. A bank draft is considered to be as good as cash, as the customer pays for it in advance.

A bank draft is guaranteed by the bank and is useful when two strangers are involved in a business transaction (e.g. selling a car).

207

BANK OF EDUCATION

TO
BANK OF EDUCATION

NEWTOWN Branch
18 February 19 9~

On demand
pay to the order of A. Solicitor

Five hundred pounds only

£ 500 —

For and on behalf of BANK OF EDUCATION

Head Office
Hometown

J.C. Scott MANAGER

A bank draft

The buyer may wish to drive the car away immediately and not wait for the seller to wait for the cheque he has received in payment to be 'cleared' as it may 'bounce' (see p. 191).

Bill of Exchange

A bill of exchange is the method of payment used by many firms when dealing with overseas customers. It is drawn up by the exporter (the payee) stating the amount owed and the date it is due. The importer signs (thus accepting the bill). The bill of exchange is then a legally binding promise to pay.

The advantage to the importer of a bill of exchange is that of paying for the goods after they have been received, and, possibly, resold. The exporter has the advantage of not having to give credit to a (possibly) unknown foreigner, and can sell the bill before the date of repayment, if the money is needed.

Getting Cash Out of a Branch of Another Bank

A cheque must be written 'Pay cash' or 'Pay self' in the usual way, and when handed in to the cashier, a cheque card has to be used for identification. At present, there is a cash limit of £50 per day but by special arrangement in advance, through the customer's own branch, cheques can be cashed up to an agreed amount (i.e. £20 daily) at another specified branch, without

208

producing a cheque card. This is especially useful to bank customers on holiday. New limits for cheque cards (ranging from £100 to £250 is soon to be raised by *some* banks. Building societies already offer a £100 limit cheque card.

References

A bank will provide a reference for a department store, if requested, to the effect that a bank customer is able to manage his financial affairs sensibly and should therefore be allowed to buy goods on credit from the store.

Most firms sell to other companies on credit and may have to wait up to three months for their money (though one month is more usual). When a firm receives an order from a new customer, he will ask his bank to make enquiries (from other banks) and let him know if his new customer pays his bills regularly.

Firms engaged in foreign trade find this service especially useful when they are doing business with a new overseas buyer. Banks have links with other banks all over the world.

Confidentiality

All transactions with a bank are confidential. No information will be given to *anyone* about a customer's account without the customer's written permission. Until recently the only exceptions to this were the executors of a will and the Inland Revenue for income tax purposes. Now the banks help those investigating drug trafficking by notifying them of large cash deposits.

Lending Money

This is one of the three chief reasons for banking, and it is the way banks make their profits – by lending customers' money at interest to other customers in need of it. So that the money is absolutely safe, they will not lend without security (collateral) which means that if a customer wishes to borrow a large sum of money he has to deposit at the bank something of great value, such as the deeds to a house, an insurance policy on which he has paid the premiums for a number of years, or share certificates. If, for any reason the loan cannot be repaid, the bank then has the right to take possession of the collateral. Thus customers' money is safeguarded.

An overdraft is the cheapest way to borrow money. It means that a current account is overdrawn to a maximum amount and for a maximum period, both agreed with the bank manager.

A personal loan, which is borrowed for a certain purpose (buying a car, for instance, or some hi-fi equipment), has to be repaid within a certain period, agreed with the bank manager. A personal loan is normally repaid in monthly instalments from a current account.

Interest is charged on overdrafts, personal loans and budget accounts – the actual amount of interest varying from bank to bank. Bank interest on loans is often much lower than that of other moneylenders.

POSTAL ORDERS

The postal order is the most commonly used Post Office remittance service. It is especially useful for transferring small amounts of money to someone who has no bank account, as it is encashable over the counter of any Post Office. It could, for example, be used to send money as a birthday present. Postal orders may be sent overseas – the *Post Office Guide* gives full details.

A crossed postal order with counterfoil

A counterfoil is provided with each postal order for the use of the sender. It should be filled in and kept as a record. It should not be sent with the postal order.

The sender should fill in the details and the person cashing the postal order must sign it. If crossed, it must be banked. Postal orders are valid for six months. They should always be crossed when they are sent away as payment for goods ordered by mail order, or to a football pools firm – uncrossed postal orders are a great temptation to a thief as they are so easily cashed.

GIROBANK

Girobank is a computerised bank administered through post offices. It offers many similar services to the clearing banks. Directories are kept at post offices of all Girobank account numbers, and an in-payment form may be bought to pay bills over the post office counter to any organisation having a Girobank account.

All public utilities (water, electricity and gas boards) print at the foot of their bills a Girobank transfer number, with their account numbers already printed on it. Payment can then be made at any post office.

Girocheques are forms for transferring payment out of the Girobank and may be used exactly as an ordinary bank cheque. Girocheques may also be used to withdraw money from a Girobank account, at any post office.

In addition to the above, Girobank offers the following services to account holders:

- deposit accounts earning interest,
- personal loans (customer must be over 18),
- bridging loans (customer must be over 18),
- standing orders,
- direct debits,
- free bank statements,
- cheque card (holder must be over 18),
- credit card (holder must be over 18). Girobank Visa can be used with Girobank LINK cash machines or Barclays Bank cash dispensers in the UK and abroad wherever a machine displays the Visa symbol.
- traveller's cheques and foreign currency,
- international money transmission,
- provision of change (sorted coin).

There are no bank charges as long as a customer's account remains in credit. When the customer is overdrawn (in debit or 'in the red') a charge is made which includes an amount for each payment from the cheque account.

A Girobank Transcash form (front)

SECRETARIAL TIPS

1 A cheque-signing machine saves time for busy managers – the signatures are printed on the cheques by a metal plate. Security is provided by a key-locking system and special ink.

2 Payment of cheques guaranteed by a cheque card cannot be stopped.

3 When large numbers of bank notes have to be paid regularly into a bank, a bank note counting machine will save time. A bank note counting machine is able to count both new and unused banknotes at the rate of approximately 100 in 7 seconds.

4 The counterfoil of a bank paying-in slip (or bank giro credit slip) is the only receipt from the bank for cash and cheques paid in. It is vital to keep this safely as it is not unknown for money to be credited to a wrong account. As an additional safeguard, photocopy the paying-in slip before taking it to the bank and keep the photocopy as your record.

5 Money may be sent abroad by Post Office Girobank (see pp. 210–11) and it is worth remembering this and referring to the *Post Office Guide* for details. The service is known as 'Transcash'.

6 Try to avoid visiting the bank on Monday mornings and Friday afternoons when banks are at their busiest.

7 Some branches of major banks now open on Saturday mornings.

QUICK REVISION

1 The length of time for which a cheque is valid is   ....

2 A cheque is 'dishonoured' for several reasons, the main ones being:
   account overdrawn cheque has been 'stopped'
   alteration has not been initialled
   cheque is 'stale'
   cheque is postdated or   .... or   ....

3 'Endorsing' a cheque is   ....

4 A written instruction to a bank (usually on a printed form) to pay a fixed amount regularly on behalf of a customer is a   ....

5 A written instruction similar to the above, but which can be varied by the payee without the account holder's permission is a   ....

6 To pay money into a current account it is necessary to complete a bank giro credit slip or a   ....

7 Payment into another account may be made through any bank by means of a   ....

8 The document sent out regularly by banks to customers showing all money paid in and withdrawn is a   ....

9 Electronic funds transfer (EFT) allows ....

10 Traveller's cheques are a safe way to carry money when travelling (especially abroad) because ....

11 A more convenient way to have access to cash (in Europe) is by ....

12 The routine for placing cash into a night safe is: ....

13 A bank draft is used when ....

14 A bill of exchange is used when ....

15 A reference from a bank is useful to firms when ....

16 Postal orders are a useful way of sending small amounts of money to someone without a bank account. They are also a convenient way to transfer money ....

17 Postal orders must never be sent ....

ASSIGNMENTS

1 (a) As a result of trips to Europe, goods will be imported from and products exported to various European countries. List the different ways of transferring money to and receiving money from foreign firms, giving the advantages and disadvantages (if any) of each.

(b) During one of your employer's business trips, your junior assistant is away ill and unable to collect her salary. You know she has no bank account (she is paid in cash) – what is the best way of sending the money to her? The petty cash balance allows you sufficient cash to pay what is due to her.

(c) During the absence of your boss, you will have to deal with day-to-day money matters, which will include receiving money from customers both by cheque and cash. There is an office safe, but it is obviously sensible not to keep too much money in it. How can you deposit money in the bank while avoiding visits during banking hours? Explain any procedures necessary.

CHAPTER 11

Petty Cash and VAT

WHAT IS PETTY CASH?

The word 'petty' means 'small'. Petty cash means, therefore, small amounts of money paid out, or received.

Every firm finds it necessary to have cash available for payment of small items, for which the services of a bank would not be convenient. Examples of payments by petty cash are: tea, coffee, milk, sugar for the office staff, bus or taxi fares, parking meter fees, postage stamps, cleaner's wages, small items of office stationery.

Looking after Petty Cash

Money used for petty cash must be kept in a lockable cash box with a removable tray, so that bank notes can be stored safely under the tray. The box must be locked in a cupboard, out of sight, when not being used.

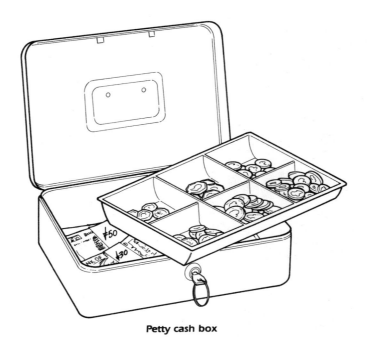

Petty cash box

The person in charge of petty cash is sometimes a secretary, sometimes a senior clerk. He or she saves the chief cashier's time by paying out (disbursing) money for small items.

The petty cash book is usually kept on a system called the imprest system. The word 'imprest' means 'advance' or 'loan'. Under the imprest system a sum of money to equal the amount which has been spent is disbursed by the chief cashier to the petty cashier at the end of a regular period – usually a week or a month.

Thus, if the clerk in charge of petty cash has started the week with £100, and spent £18.30 by Friday, she will ask the chief cashier for £18.30. This amount (the imprest) will bring the total in her cash box back to the original £100. The amount left in her cash box before going to the chief cashier for an 'imprest' is £81.70. This £81.70 is known as the 'balance' – that is, the amount *not* spent or paid out to other people to spend, out of the £100 imprest.

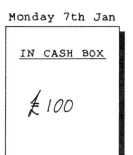
Monday 7th Jan
IN CASH BOX
£100

Friday 11th Jan
IN CASH BOX
£81.70

Monday 14th Jan
IN CASH BOX
£81.70 and vouchers totalling £18.30

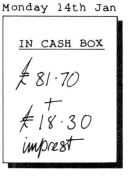
Monday 14th Jan
IN CASH BOX
£81.70 + £18.30 imprest

| Petty Cash Voucher | Folio _____ No. _____ |
| | Date _____ 19 |

For what required	AMOUNT	
	£	p

Signature _____

Passed by _____

Petty cash vouchers authorise the payments made from petty cash

Petty cash vouchers must be signed by the person *receiving* the money, and also by the person authorising the payment – e.g. a manager, supervisor or senior secretary. The clerk in charge of the petty cash must not pay out any money, however small the sum, without a petty cash voucher. In addition, a receipt should be produced for anything bought out of petty cash, when it is possible to obtain one. Bus and train tickets should be kept and handed to the petty cash clerk.

The postage book (p. 149) is kept as a record of stamps bought and used, and acts as a receipt – the Post Office does not normally give a receipt for stamps sold by them, although they will do so if it is required specially. A voucher would have to be signed for stamps bought for an office, of course.

Filling in a Petty Cash Form

In the petty cash account sheet on p. 219 each item has been entered twice – once under 'Total Paid' and once under its own special heading – one of the analysis columns.

- 'Stamps' under 'Postage'
- 'Tea, coffee, sugar' under 'Office expenses'
- 'Cleaner's wages' under 'Cleaning'.

Analysis columns enable the office manager, petty cash clerk and chief cashier to see at a glance whether too much is being spent on a certain item. Analysis column headings vary from office to office, which is why they are left blank for the petty cash clerk to fill in. It is useful to head one column 'Miscellaneous'. This can be used to enter any item which does not normally have to be paid for out of petty cash, i.e. does not fit under other headings.

A column headed 'Stationery' would be used for all items normally bought at a stationers – string, ball-point pens, shorthand notebooks, pencils, rubber bands, staples, adhesive tape, envelopes, A4 and A5 bond and bank, blotting paper, postcards, typewriter ribbons, typewriter erasers, liquid typewriter corrective, carbon paper, paper clips, rubber stamps and pads, glue, scissors, ink, bulldog clips, treasury tags, rules, folders, index cards, and so on. Only occasional items should be bought with petty cash – most stationery is bought by the buying office and issued under stationery stock control in a large firm (see Chapter 9).

A column headed 'Travel' would be used for bus fares, train fares and taxi fares. Larger amounts would have to be authorised by the department dealing with travel and would not come out of petty cash (air fares, for example).

'Office Expenses' can be used for small items – tea, coffee, sugar, milk, flowers.

PETTY CASH ACCOUNT

Dr.	CASH RECEIVED			CASH PAID			Total Paid	ANALYSIS			Cr.
	Date	Folio	Amount	Date	Details	VN		Postage	Office Expenses	Cleaning	
	199 –		£ P				£ P	£ P	£ P	£ P	
	Jan 7	CB3	20 . 00	Jan 7	Stamps	101	4 . 40	4 . 40			
				" 9	Tea, coffee, sugar	102	3 . 90		3 . 90		
				" 11	Cleaner's wages	103	10 . 00			10 . 00	
							18 . 30	4 . 40	3 . 90	10 . 00	
					Balance		1 . 70				
							£ 20.00				
	Jan 14		1 . 70		Balance b/d						
			18 . 30		Cash received						

Date cash received.

'Folio' refers to the page in the cash book to which the petty cash total is transferred.

Totals of all analysis columns should be the same as total of 'Total Paid' column. It acts as a check.

A petty cash account form

217

Any item which occurs fairly regularly would need its own analysis column heading – i.e. meter fees for parking or flowers for reception.

'Cleaning' would include soap, polish, dusters, window cleaning as well as the cleaner's wages.

'Postage' would include any surcharge paid on letters arriving understamped (see p. 148) and purchase of international reply coupons, registered envelopes and stamped envelopes, as well as stamps.

Each analysis column is totalled separately, and the combined totals should agree with the 'total paid'. If they do not agree, a mistake has been made. This 'cross-checking' ensures that any mistakes can be spotted and corrected.

The difference between the 'total paid' and the amount of cash received is the 'balance' – i.e. the amount remaining in the petty cash box.

The 'balance' is brought down first on the petty cash sheet, and the amount of imprest (i.e. cash to restore the balance to its original amount) is written underneath. The petty cash sheet is then ready for the next entries.

The folio number of the petty cash sheet refers to the page number in the cash book in which petty cash is entered – e.g. 'CB3' means 'cash book, page 3'.

Where VAT has been paid, this is entered in a separate column, either the last of the analysis columns or the first. Do not forget that VAT is part of the amount in the total column, not added to it. In small firms, where petty cash only amounts to a very small sum each month, VAT is not shown separately. Receipts must be produced to reclaim VAT.

VALUE ADDED TAX (VAT)

Value added tax (VAT) is a tax on most business transactions which take place in the United Kingdom and the Isle of Man. Imports are also taxed. Examples of 'business transactions' are:

- sales of goods, new and second-hand,
- rental and hiring of goods,
- some gifts,
- services provided for payment (dentist's, hairdresser's, for example),
- admission to premises (cinemas, theatres, stately homes),
- facilities provided by clubs.

The present standard rate of VAT is 15 per cent.

Some goods and transactions are not liable to VAT. The main ones are:

- exports,
- food (*not* catering, i.e. meals in restaurants and cafes),

- books and newspapers,
- prescriptions and aids for the handicapped,
- children's clothing and footwear.

Articles and transactions not liable to VAT are zero rated.

Notice No. 701 from local VAT offices explains rates in detail.

How VAT Works

As soon as the taxable turnover (not profit) of a business exceeds £25,400 the business becomes liable for VAT. 'Turnover' is the value of all taxable supplies made in the UK (and Isle of Man). If registration for VAT is necessary, VAT is added to prices charged to customers. This is *output* tax. Similarly, suppliers to the firm will add VAT to all goods and services, e.g. trading stock, telephone, stationery. This is *input* tax. On the return form received from Customs and Excise, input tax is subtracted from output tax and the balance paid to them. If input tax is more than the output tax, Customs and Excise will refund the difference.

Who has to be Registered for VAT

It is the *person* not the *business* who is registered for VAT. Each registration covers all the business activities of the registered person.

What Records have to be Kept

- Copies of all invoices and credit notes issued and received (see pp. 226–8).
- Copies of customs entries for imported goods.
- Copies of documents in connection with exports.
- Record of output and input tax.
- Petty cash receipts for taxable goods bought (see p. 216).

SECRETARIAL TIPS

1 Enter totals in petty cash sheet in pencil, until they have been checked and balanced. This avoids messy alterations.

2 Allocate petty cash vouchers a number when receiving them, and file them in numerical order.

3 Do not use the 'Miscellaneous' column for too many items – if the amount under this heading becomes larger than under most of the others, re-analyse what is being entered under 'miscellaneous' and, if necessary, make another column heading. This also applies to entries under 'Office Expenses',

which can be another rather vague description which defeats the purpose of having analysis columns.

4 Some firms have a 'ceiling' on the limit for any one petty cash item – this is to ensure that petty cash is not being used to buy items which should be purchased through the purchasing department in the normal way (see p. 9). Anyone presenting a voucher which exceeds the 'ceiling' should not be reimbursed without reference to the Chief Cashier.

5 A quick check of the petty cash can be made at any time by adding the money on the vouchers to the cash in the box. The total should equal the amount started with.

ASSIGNMENTS

1 Make out a petty cash sheet (see p. 217) for the following, deciding on the amount of imprest you require by totalling the items FIRST before you enter them. Bring down the balance at the end of five days and restore it to the original amount. Work out VAT for the items marked with an asterisk. Date for 14 days ago.

*Pot plant fertiliser	£1.23
*Oasis	47
Taxi fare from station for Mr G Field	£3.00
Charity collecting box	£2.00
Milk	£2.70
Tea	99
Coffee	£1.95
Saccharine tablets	45
Bus fare for Mary Gill	£1.90
*First Aid Box	£7.00
Surcharge on under-stamped letters	33
International Reply Coupons	£3.00
Stamps	£10.00
*Photocopying	50
*Clear adhesive tape	£2.60

2 Find the mistakes (there are 4) in the petty cash account on p. 221, and rewrite it correctly.

3 You work in an office with three other typists, who have to make frequent short trips by bus (or occasionally taxi, if urgent). You are responsible for buying fresh flowers for the reception area, and also for keeping stocks of tea, coffee, sugar and biscuits. The milk bill is paid for out of petty cash, too. Postage amounts to about £35 a week, payable out of petty cash, as also is the cleaning and disinfecting of the telephone – £7. Make out vouchers and a petty cash sheet, with a suitable imprest, to cover one week's petty cash.

VAT is not payable (or is paid and not reclaimable) on food, postage, bus and taxi fares.

220

PETTY CASH ACCOUNT

DR — Cash Received / Cash Paid — Analysis — **CR**

Date	Folio	Amount £ P	Date	Details	Voucher No.	Total paid £ P	VAT £ P	Postage £ P	Office Expenses £ P	Travel £ P	Miscellaneous £ P
199-											
Dec 8		11.88		Balance b/d							
		38.12		Cash received							
			Dec 8	"Get Well" Card - Sally Hayes	82	0.65	0.10				0.55
			" 8	Flowers for " "	82	5.00	0.75				4.25
			" 9	Aerogrammes	83	0.71		0.71			
			" 9	Stamps	83	15.00		15.00			
			" 9	Registered letter envelopes (large)	83	1.85		1.85			
			" 10	3 cups & saucers	84	7.50	0.88		6.62		
			" 11	Tea, sugar & coffee	85	4.50			4.50		
			" 12	Milk	86	3.20			3.20		
			" 12	Taxi fare - Bill Barnes	87	9.40				9.40	
						45.81	1.73	17.56	15.32	9.40	4.80
						4.19					
					£	50.00					
Dec 15		45.81		Balance b/d							
		4.19		Cash received							

221

CHAPTER 12

Business Documents

All firms, large and small, make their profit by selling goods or providing services for which people are prepared to pay.

BUYING

Buying goods starts with an enquiry. This may be in the form of a letter or on a specially printed form (see below).

SHAW & SHORT LTD
Wholesaler

Whitaker Street
MANCHESTER
Tel: 432 888   **M96 8TB**   Telex: 990 111

ENQUIRY FORM

To: . . . .   Date: . . . .
. . . .
. . . .
. . . .

Dear Sir

I am interested in buying . . . .

Could you please send me details - prices, delivery dates, leaflets and/or catalogues as soon as possible?

Yours faithfully
SHAW & SHORT LTD

Peter Mason
Purchasing Officer

An enquiry form

The reply could be in the form of a quotation, giving details of the item required.

QUOTATION
OFFICE EQUIPMENT SUPPLY CO LTD
Knightley Road
Bromswood
Lancs
T45 7BC

Tel 859 333   Telex: 674231

To: Shaw & Short Ltd

Whitaker Street

Manchester

M96 8TB

Date: 1 Dec. 199-

No: BAM 16

For the attention Mr Peter Mason, Purchasing Officer
Dear Sirs

In reply to your enquiry dated ...... 15 Nov ...... we have pleasure in quoting you as follows:

Quantity	Description	Catalogue No	Price	VAT	Total
1	Addressing machine	HG 732-89	£190	£27.79	£217.79

Delivery: ex stock   Terms: $2\frac{1}{2}\%$ 30 days

P Benson
Sales Manager

A quotation

Alternatively, the reply could be in the form of a price list, giving details of the item required and other products supplied by the firm.

PRICE LIST

OFFICE EQUIPMENT SUPPLY CO LTD
Knightley Road
Bromswood
Lancs
T45 7BC

Tel: (0567) 859 333   Telex: 674231

COMPUTER ACCESSORIES

Catalogue No.	Description	Price
AC 4978	Print wheel album	£5.96
TL 9214	Print-out binders 265 × 305 mm per ten	£33.15
TL 9220	Print-out binders 325 × 280 mm per ten	£37.26
TL 9231	Print-out binders 450 × 280 mm per ten	£46.12
TL 9330	Diskette tray holds 40 8″ diskettes	£23.50
TL 9321	Diskette tray holds 90 8″ diskettes	£29.50
AC 4981	Diskette mailer 8″ per ten	£15.00
SL 7538	VDU screen filter 280 × 220 mm	£25.95
SL 7539	VDU screen filter 340 × 260 mm	£27.95

AUDIO-TYPING EQUIPMENT

Catalogue No.	Description	Price
SN 6153	Mini cassette dictating/ transcribing machine	£285.00
SN 6154	Mini cassette transcribing machine	£255.00
SN 6152	Mini cassette recorder	£95.00
SN 6175	Mini cassette recording discs per ten	£25.00
SN 6167	Foot control	£26.00
SN 6170	Headset	£10.60
SN 6171	De luxe headset	£13.00
SN 6169	Hand microphone	£38.00
SN 6172	Tie-clip microphone	£15.00

VAT Reg. No. 633 2887 19   DELIVERY   ex stock

TRADE DISCOUNT 10% (on orders over £250)   TERMS $2\frac{1}{2}$% 30 days

5 August 199__   (This cancels all previous price lists)

A price list

It is usual to write to several firms, the final choice being based on price, delivery, suitability, and terms of payment.

When the final decision is made as to the most suitable supplier, an order is sent. This has to be signed by the purchasing officer or one of his assistants. Orders are numbered and dated with copies for Accounts Department, the head of the department who will use the equipment and for purchasing department files.

		SHAW & SHORT LTD
		Whitaker Street
		MANCHESTER
		Tel: 859 333 Telex: 674231

Date __12 December 199-__

To __Office Equipment Supply Co Ltd__

__Knightley Road__

__BROMSWOOD Lancs__

__T45 7BC__   No _____526_____

Please supply & deliver

Cat	Qty	Description	£	p
HG 732-89	1	Addressing machine + VAT	190 27.79	
			Total	£217.79

Terms __2½% 30 days__

Delivery __Ex stock__   Signed _____
                                         Purchasing Officer

An order form

SELLING

Upon receipt of an order, the firm supplying a product sends the goods with an advice note to the customer, advising them of the contents of the package. If the goods are delivered by road transport, the carrier will have a delivery note, which has to be signed by an employee of the firm receiving the goods, as a receipt. An invoice is also sent by the supplier. This is numbered, dated, quotes the customer's order number and sets out the full price, plus VAT and terms of payment.

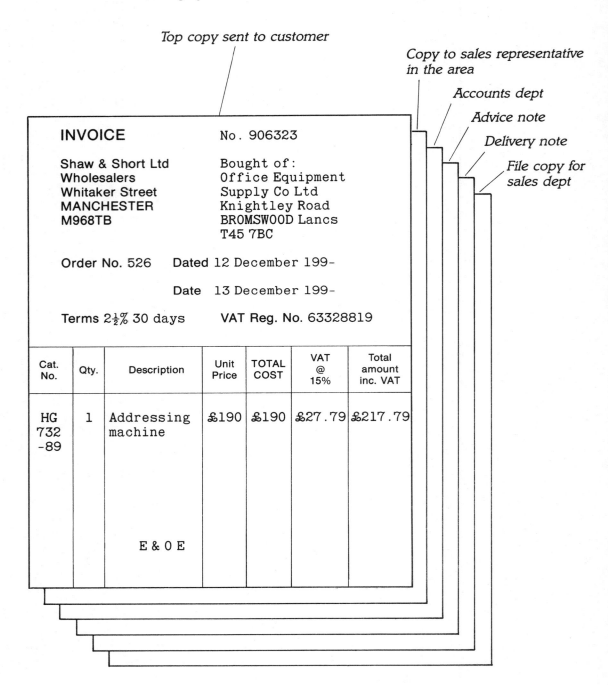

Top copy sent to customer

Copy to sales representative in the area

Accounts dept

Advice note

Delivery note

File copy for sales dept

INVOICE   No. 906323

Shaw & Short Ltd   Bought of:
Wholesalers   Office Equipment
Whitaker Street   Supply Co Ltd
MANCHESTER   Knightley Road
M968TB   BROMSWOOD Lancs
                 T45 7BC

Order No. 526   Dated 12 December 199-

                   Date   13 December 199-

Terms 2½% 30 days   VAT Reg. No. 63328819

Cat. No.	Qty.	Description	Unit Price	TOTAL COST	VAT @ 15%	Total amount inc. VAT
HG 732 -89	1	Addressing machine	£190	£190	£27.79	£217.79
		E & O E				

In the invoice on p. 226, note that VAT is worked out on £190 less 2½ per cent cash discount (i.e. £185.25).

The copies are different colours for easy identification. They would be NCR or one-time carbon and possibly continuous stationery to save time (see p. 74).

E & O E stands for 'errors and omissions excepted'. This means that if the typist makes a mistake when typing the price, it does not bind the seller (in this case, the typist could have typed £19.00 which would have made a great deal of difference).

Usually, a statement is sent to a customer by the supplier of goods at the end of each month, showing how much is still owing.

STATEMENT

Shaw & Short Ltd
Wholesalers
Whitaker Street
MANCHESTER
M96 8TB

Office Equipment Supply Co Ltd
Knightley Road
BROMSWOOD   Lancs
T45 7BC

Date	Invoice No.	Purchases	Payments and Returns	Balance
199-		£		£
13 December	906323	217.79	————	217.79
19 December	906341	12.00	————	229.79
21 December	906353	————	7.00	222.79

The last balance in this column is the amount owing

A credit note is sent if there has been an overcharge due to a mistake on the invoice, or for goods or packing cases returned. A debit note is sent if goods have been undercharged. Credit and debit notes are shown on a statement.

DEBIT NOTE

Shaw & Short Ltd
Wholesalers
Whitaker Street
MANCHESTER
M96 8TB

No 387
12 December 199-

Dr to:

Office Equipment Supply Co Ltd
Knightley Road
BROMSWOOD
Lancs
T45 7BC

Order No: 433   VAT Reg No 63328819

Date	Description	Amount
199-		
19 December	Undercharge on Invoice	£12.00

CREDIT NOTE

Shaw & Short Ltd
Wholesalers
Whitaker Street
MANCHESTER
M96 8TB

No 423
21 December 199-

Dr to:

Office Equipment Supply Co Ltd
Knightley Road
BROMSWOOD
Lancs
T45 7BC

Order No: 487   VAT Reg No 63328819

Date	Description	Amount
199-		
21 December	Packing cases returned against Invoice No. 906353	£7.00

SECRETARIAL TIPS

1 An easy way to work out VAT (currently 15 per cent)

   By moving the decimal point one place to the *left* and ignoring the last figure you have 10 per cent. Halve this amount (which gives you 5 per cent). Add these two amounts together and you have 15 per cent.

   Example: 15 per cent on £257.50

   Step 1: 10% – £25.75

   Step 2: 5% – £12.88 rounded up because of the odd halfpence

   Total: 15% – £38.63

2 Working out 2½ per cent is done in the same way as above, except that 5 per cent is divided by 2 (in the example above this would be £6.44) which is 2½ per cent of £257.50.

3 Remember that VAT (see pp. 218–19) is worked out *after* any discount has been deducted.

4 Printing separate up-dated pricelists is cheaper (and more efficient) than including prices in an expensively produced catalogue. Prices may change several times a year, and customers will be annoyed if the price quoted in the catalogue is not correct.

5 When buying new equipment for an office is under consideration, and after demonstrations have been seen (from more than one manufacturer), the equipment which meets with approval should be available in the office for members of staff to try it out under realistic working conditions, before a final decision is made to buy it.

QUICK REVISION

1 The first step in a business transaction is an enquiry, sent by a potential ....

2 The supplier then sends a .... Alternatively, the supplier could send a ....

3 If the purchase goes ahead, the next document is an ....

4 The supplier sends his bill in the form of an ....

5 Overcharges by the supplier are corrected by ....

6 Undercharges by the supplier are corrected by ....

7 The final document in a business transaction is a statement which shows ....

8 A cash discount is offered to a buyer to induce him to pay promptly. A trade discount is given to ....

9 'E & O E' is the abbreviation for 'errors and omissions excepted' which means ....

ASSIGNMENT

1 (a) You work in the Sales Department of Office Equipment Supply Co. Ltd, Knightley Road, Bromswood, Lancs, T45 7BC. On a copy of the invoice form on p. 226, make out an invoice for the following, taking the prices from the pricelist on p. 224. The name of the customer is Shaw & Short Ltd, Wholesaler, Whitaker Street, Manchester, M96 8TB. Invoice No. 7766532 (date for today). Order No. 87109 (dated 3 days ago).

50	print wheel albums
100	print-out binders 450 mm × 280 mm
10	VDU screen filters 280 × 220 mm
5	VDU screen filters 340 × 260 mm
10	Mini cassette dictating/transcribing machines
100	Mini cassette recording discs
10	Headsets
10	Hand microphones

(b) Make out a statement to be sent to Shaw & Short Ltd on a copy of the form on p. 227 showing the total on the above invoice, and include a payment of £500 made a week after the date of the order. Date the statement for four weeks after the date of the invoice.

SECTION 2

CHAPTER 13

Written Communications

ADDRESSING ENVELOPES

A correct postal address consists of:

- name of person to whom letter is being sent,
- number of house (or name if it has no number),
- name of street, road, avenue, crescent, lane, etc.,
- district (where it applies), or name of village, in the country,
- post town,
- county,
- postcode.

Of the above, the post town is very important. This is where the mail is sorted out for a particular district and is the basic unit of the postal system. It must *always* be included in the address and shown in BLOCK CAPITALS on the envelope.

The name of the county in which the post town is situated is necessary as this helps with sorting. Exceptions to this are county towns and certain very large cities such as London, Manchester and Birmingham. Some county names may be abbreviated and there is a list of correct abbreviations in *Postal Addresses and Index to Postcode Directories,* which is published by the Post Office.

The postcode is used in the automatic sorting of mail and must always be the last part of an address. Every address in the United Kingdom has a postcode.

Figures should be used in typing postcodes for 'zero' and 'one'.

The illustration overleaf shows the postal code areas in the United Kingdom, reproduced courtesy of The Post Office.

Particular care should be taken with people's names. If the signature on a letter is illegible, check in the files, or even telephone the secretary of the sender, rather than misspell a name. The reason for typing a signatory's name on a letter, below the complimentary close, is very obvious!

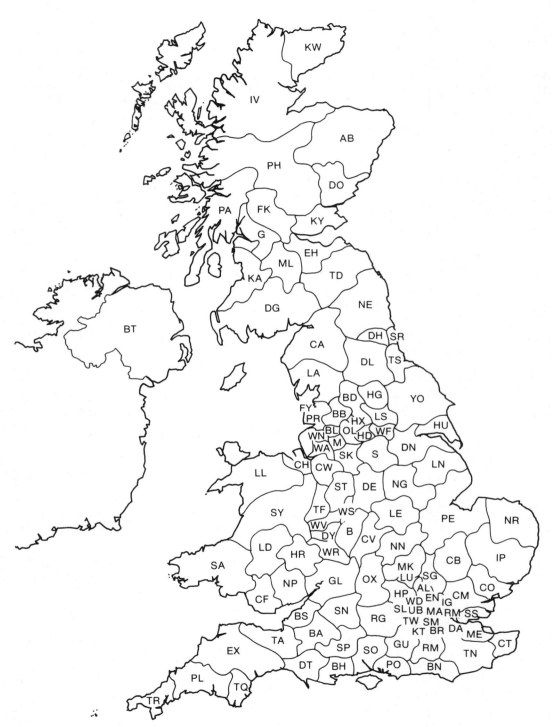

Postal code areas

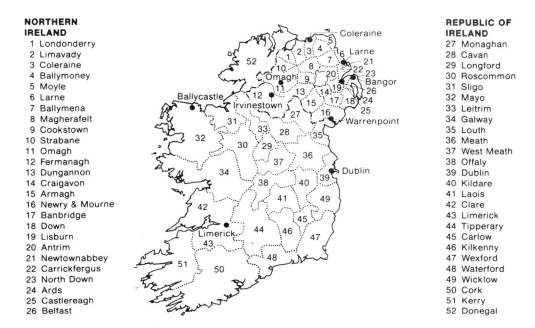

NORTHERN IRELAND

1 Londonderry
2 Limavady
3 Coleraine
4 Ballymoney
5 Moyle
6 Larne
7 Ballymena
8 Magherafelt
9 Cookstown
10 Strabane
11 Omagh
12 Fermanagh
13 Dungannon
14 Craigavon
15 Armagh
16 Newry & Mourne
17 Banbridge
18 Down
19 Lisburn
20 Antrim
21 Newtownabbey
22 Carrickfergus
23 North Down
24 Ards
25 Castlereagh
26 Belfast

REPUBLIC OF IRELAND

27 Monaghan
28 Cavan
29 Longford
30 Roscommon
31 Sligo
32 Mayo
33 Leitrim
34 Galway
35 Louth
36 Meath
37 West Meath
38 Offaly
39 Dublin
40 Kildare
41 Laois
42 Clare
43 Limerick
44 Tipperary
45 Carlow
46 Kilkenny
47 Wexford
48 Waterford
49 Wicklow
50 Cork
51 Kerry
52 Donegal

Districts of Northern Ireland and Counties of the Republic of Ireland

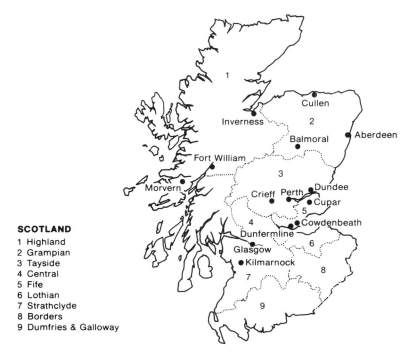

SCOTLAND

1 Highland
2 Grampian
3 Tayside
4 Central
5 Fife
6 Lothian
7 Strathclyde
8 Borders
9 Dumfries & Galloway

Regions of Scotland

235

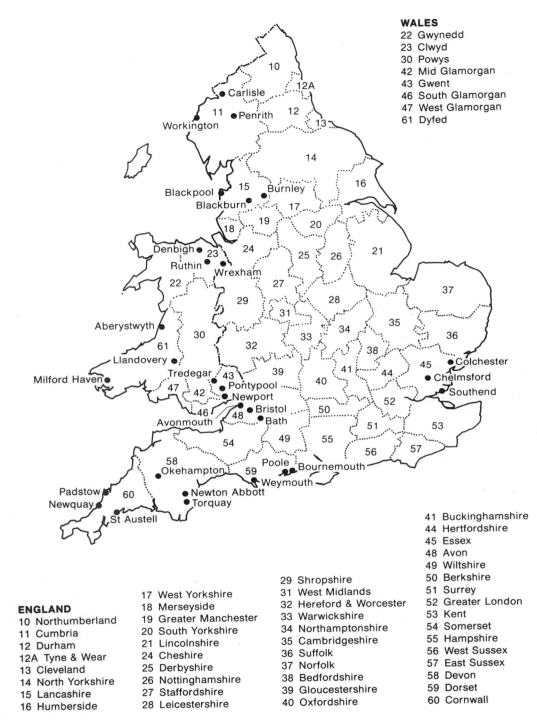

WALES
22 Gwynedd
23 Clwyd
30 Powys
42 Mid Glamorgan
43 Gwent
46 South Glamorgan
47 West Glamorgan
61 Dyfed

ENGLAND
10 Northumberland
11 Cumbria
12 Durham
12A Tyne & Wear
13 Cleveland
14 North Yorkshire
15 Lancashire
16 Humberside

17 West Yorkshire
18 Merseyside
19 Greater Manchester
20 South Yorkshire
21 Lincolnshire
24 Cheshire
25 Derbyshire
26 Nottinghamshire
27 Staffordshire
28 Leicestershire

29 Shropshire
31 West Midlands
32 Hereford & Worcester
33 Warwickshire
34 Northamptonshire
35 Cambridgeshire
36 Suffolk
37 Norfolk
38 Bedfordshire
39 Gloucestershire
40 Oxfordshire

41 Buckinghamshire
44 Hertfordshire
45 Essex
48 Avon
49 Wiltshire
50 Berkshire
51 Surrey
52 Greater London
53 Kent
54 Somerset
55 Hampshire
56 West Sussex
57 East Sussex
58 Devon
59 Dorset
60 Cornwall

Counties of England and Wales

236

County Abbreviations

Abbreviations for county names which the Post Office will accept (other abbreviations cause confusion and should not be used):

Beds	Bedfordshire	Northd	Northumberland
Berks	Berkshire	Notts	Nottinghamshire
Bucks	Buckinghamshire	Oxon	Oxfordshire
Cambs	Cambridgeshire	Salop	Shropshire
Co Durham	County Durham	S Glam	South Glamorgan
E Sussex	East Sussex	S Humberside	South Humberside
Glos	Gloucestershire	S Yorkshire	South Yorkshire
Hants	Hampshire	Staffs	Staffordshire
Herts	Hertfordshire	Tyne & Wear	Tyne and Wear
Lancs	Lancashire	Warks	Warwickshire
Leics	Leicestershire	W Glam	West Glamorgan
Lincs	Lincolnshire	W Midlands	West Midlands
M Glam	Mid Glamorgan	W Sussex	West Sussex
Middx	Middlesex	W Yorkshire	West Yorkshire
N Humberside	North Humberside	Wilts	Wiltshire
N Yorkshire	North Yorkshire	Worcs	Worcestershire
Northants	Northamptonshire		

Position of inside address for window envelopes: Window envelopes have a transparent panel or an aperture through which the inside address can be read.

Window or aperture envelopes save typing separate envelopes and prevent letters being sent to the wrong addresses.

When window envelopes are used, the position for typing the inside address is indicated by four small right-angles, or a rectangle.

Careful folding is necessary to make sure that the full address can be read.

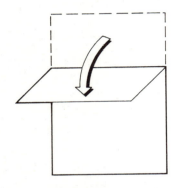

**With the sheet down,
fold top third towards you**

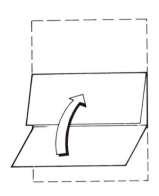

**Fold lower third up
so that address shows**

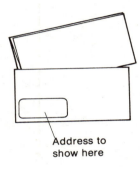

Address to
show here

**Place letter in envelope
with last crease at foot**

FORMS OF ADDRESS

When writing to *individuals* it is polite to give them a title: Mr, Mrs, Ms, Miss. Titles such as The Revd (for the Reverend), Dr (Doctor), Captain, Professor, are used in place of Mr, Mrs, etc. Esq, (Esquire) is still used but is a rather out-of-date title for a man. It is typed after the surname and takes the place of 'Mr'.

Until recently, formal styles of address were always used. The modern approach is more free, but does not make life easy for a secretary who has to decide on an appropriate form of address. The following are formal guidelines:

● People under eighteen are addressed by name only:
   Elaine Carter, Peter Jones

● Unmarried adult sisters should be styled:
   The Misses D. and E. Evans

The correct way to address a letter to a married woman (legally and traditionally) is to use her husband's initials, not hers. However, it has now

obviously become a necessity to use a woman's own forenames by commercial organisations such as banks, building societies and public limited companies.

A widow should be addressed by her own initials, but she may prefer to retain her husband's. Courtesy indicates that she should be addressed in the way she prefers.

When it is necessary to distinguish between father and son with the same first name, use 'senior' or 'junior' abbreviated:

    Mr James Johnson snr (father)
    Mr James Johnson jnr (son)

A minister of religion may be addressed as:

    The Revd T. Smith

Salutation would be: Reverend Sir. Complimentary close would be: I am, Reverend Sir
Yours faithfully

Less formally – salutation: Dear Vicar, or Dear Mr Smith. Complimentary close: Yours sincerely.

A mayor or mayoress may be addressed as:

    The Right Worshipful the Mayor (Mayoress) of ...

Salutation would be: Sir (Madam). Complimentary close would be: I am, Sir (Madam)
Yours faithfully

Black's Titles and Forms of Address gives comprehensive guidance on addressing titled people.

Firms should be addressed as 'Messrs' only when their names do *not* include 'Limited', the abbreviation 'Ltd' or 'PLC' (Public Limited Company, see pp. 3–4).

Firms whose names start with the word 'The' or when a title is included in the name, e.g. Sir William Watkins & Co. should not be addressed as 'Messrs'. *Always* address a letter to an individual in a firm, e.g. Marketing Director, Assistant Buyer, including name and initials, if possible.

Decorations, Honours and Qualifications

These are typed after the name, in order of importance. The order is:
Decorations and honours, e.g. VC (Victoria Cross)
CBE (Commander of the British Empire)

Educational qualifications, e.g. PhD (Doctor of Philosophy)
MA (Master of Arts), BA (Bachelor of Arts)
BSc (Bachelor of Science)

Professional titles, e.g. FRS (Fellow of the Royal Society)
FRSA (Fellow of the Royal Society of Arts)
ARCM (Associate of the Royal College of Music)
MP (Member of Parliament) – typed last because it is a professional title which may last for five years only.

Note: groups of letters denoting qualifications, etc., are typed as follows:

- *Open punctuation:* No spaces between letters in each group. Two spaces after last letter in group: BSc MA FRSA MP.

- *Full punctuation;* Fullstop after each letter; no space between letters; one space after final fullstop in group. B.Sc. M.A. F.R.S.A. M.P.

Circular Letters

A circular letter is one of which many copies (sometimes hundreds of thousands) are sent out. Usually, circular letters are sent for advertising purposes to inform possible customers about 'special offers' or new products to be introduced or new branches of a firm to be opened. The appearance of a circular letter must be of a high standard – it is possible by the use of a word processor (see pp. 79–81) to make each letter appear as if it had been individually typed. The other way of producing circular letters is by a duplicating process – preferably offset-litho which produces good quality copies. A circular letter does not contain an inside address and may have 'Date as postmark' printed where the date would normally be typed. This ensures that whenever the copies of a circular letter are prepared, they can still be used months later.

240

FORM LETTERS, COMPLIMENT SLIPS AND MEMORANDA

Form Letters

Form letters are business letters sent from one firm to another, or to members of the public (e.g. to someone who has applied for a vacancy, giving the time of an interview). Form letters are pre-printed (either by a duplicating process or a word processor – see Chapter 4) on letter headings and are used in offices where a large number of similar letters are sent out and the only information which varies is the name, address and date.

241

```
STAR INSURANCE CO LTD
170 Cheapside
LONDON
EC2V 8DU
Tel (01) 314867


[                        ]



[                        ]


Our ref LAD/H/J4/DAW
Your ref


Dear Sir/Madam

With reference to policy no        on life assured
may I remind you that I still require

to enable me to proceed.


Yours faithfully
STAR INSURANCE CO LTD



Manager
Life Administration
```

A form letter to be used with a window envelope

The variable information is added by the typist or clerk (it can be added in writing). Form letters save time and can be prepared beforehand during a slack period in an office. The appearance of form letters should be of a high standard as they are to be sent out of the firm. Departments in a firm sending form letters may be:

- Sales Department acknowledging orders (today this is done less frequently than it used to be, because of the cost of postage).
- Personnel Department arranging interviews and advising applicants about the outcome of interviews.

```
HALL & GRIFFITH LIMITED

32 Lime Avenue
ELMSTOCK
Oakshire
Telephone Elmstock 36277


Our ref MS/

Date as postmark


Dear Sir/Madam

Thank you for your letter dated
asking for an appointment to see Mr/Mrs/Miss
                      of                  Department.
Unfortunately Mr/Mrs/Miss
is away at present and is making no appointments for
several weeks.
Please write again next month if you wish to make an
appointment later.

Yours faithfully
HALL & GRIFFITH LIMITED


M Steele
Personnel Manager
```

Another example of a form letter

Compliment Slips

These contain the number and address of the firm, together with telephone numbers, and telex number (if applicable). 'With compliments' is printed on, leaving just sufficient space for a brief message, or the sender's own name and title to be added. The size of compliment slips varies, but is usually about 10 centimetres (4 inches) square. Compliment slips can be used for enclosing with catalogue price lists – in fact, anything which is being sent by post where a letter is not necessary but where the recipient must know the name and address of the sender. They save typing letters and are used by many firms whose outgoing mail includes items for which the recipient is not expected to pay – the word 'complimentary' means 'given free'.

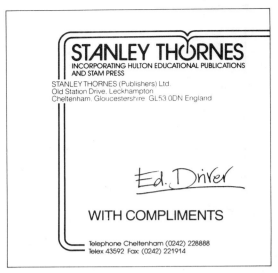

A compliment slip

Memoranda

It is usual to send written communications between offices on memoranda forms called 'memos'. One single 'memo' is a 'memorandum'. All that memos contain (besides the message) is the name of the sender, the name of the recipient, the date and, sometimes, a subject heading. There is no salutation ('Dear Sir'), no complimentary close ('Yours faithfully') and no

---

MEMORANDUM

To: Typing Pool Supervisor   25 November 199-

From: Peter Mason, Purchasing Officer

Subject: Demonstration of Facsimile Transmission Machine

The Sales Manager of Office Equipment Supply Co Ltd will be visiting the firm on the 1 December to demonstrate a facsimile transmission machine. I am sure you will be interested in this demonstration, and if you telephone my secretary sometime before the 1 December, she will let you know a convenient time to see the machine. A later demonstration can be arranged for members of your staff to see it.

                                  P.M.

---

inside address. It is usual for memos to be initialled, not signed in full, by the employees sending them.

Circulation Slip or Distribution Slip

A 'circulation slip', or 'distribution slip' (sometimes also called a 'routing slip') is attached to a document that has to be read by a number of employees in turn. It consists of a list of names, and as each person passes on the document to the next on the list he ticks his own name. The document may be a letter which has been received in the incoming mail and has to be seen by more than one person (see pp. 146–7).

Magazine on Telecommunications
Please read and pass on in order shown below:

Name	Dept	Initial/date
G H Lamb	Purchasing	G.H.L. 10/10
Mrs K Potts	Sales	K.P. 11/10
D S Ames	Accounts	

Please return to: R Harris

by: 13/10

A circulation slip

When extra copies of memos for distribution to other members of staff are needed, a list of the names is typed at the bottom left hand of the memo, preceded by the letters 'cc' (copy circulated'):

cc   Mr B Adams
     Mrs C Carter
     Ms F Jones
     Miss L Noon

Six copies in total – top copy, 4 for distribution, one for filing.

Memos dealing with a confidential matter should be marked 'Confidential' and placed in a sealed envelope, similarly marked.

Composing Letters and Memoranda

Experienced senior secretaries often compose replies to letters from brief notes pencilled on them, or are able to reply without instructions. It is important to keep business letters brief, but at the same time retain a courteous tone.

Note that after the salutation 'Dear Sir', 'Dear Sirs' or 'Dear Madam', it is correct to type 'Yours faithfully' (Not 'Yours sincerely'). After a salutation which includes a name ('Dear Mr Brown'), it is correct to type 'Yours sincerely' (not 'Yours faithfully'). The name of the firm printed on the letterheading is usually typed in capital letters after 'Yours faithfully'. It is incorrect to type it after 'Yours sincerely'.

Signing a letter on behalf of the writer can be done in two ways:

Yours faithfully
VINER'S WINE MERCHANTS LTD

for Sally Snape

K Robbins (Ms)
Area Manager

Yours faithfully
VINER'S WINE MERCHANTS LTD

Sally Snape

Dictated by Ms Robbins and
signed in her absence.

It is necessary occasionally to write a letter on behalf of an employer. The complimentary close would then be:

Yours faithfully
VINER'S WINE MERCHANTS LTD

Sally Snape

Sally Snape (Mrs)
Secretary to Ms K Robbins,
Area Manager

Yours sincerely

Sally Snape

Mrs Sally Snape
Secretary to Ms Kate Robbins,
Area Manager

Or (the reason for this is that the recipient is more interested in the name of K. Robbins than that of Sally Snape):

Yours faithfully
VINER'S WINE MERCHANTS LTD

for K. Robbins ss

K Robbins (Ms)
Area Manager

An alternative complimentary close: Instead of 'Yours sincerely', 'Yours truly' is sometimes used. It should not be followed by the name of the firm or organisation.

Memoranda, or memos, are used internally in firms (see p. 244) to confirm decisions made, to give instructions, or to ask for information. They are much less formal than a letter to be sent to another firm – first names are often used, but the 'house style' should be checked in this respect.

Care should be taken in the tone of a memo, as brevity should not mean brusqueness. Adding the words 'please' or 'thank you' does not take up much space (or time) and can alter the whole tone of the message.

```
MEMORANDUM
To:     Miss Kay Bartlett  Chairman's Personal Assistant
From:   John Vernon                            30 March 199-
SHAREHOLDERS' MEETING
The date for the next shareholders' meeting has to be
fixed this week. Could you please meet me in my office at
1100 tomorrow for a brief discussion? It should only take
a few minutes.


cc      Ms L Benson
        Mr D Franklin
```

BUSINESS LETTERS

Large firms or organisations issue booklets to their office staff, setting out the format for business letter layout and punctuation, known as the 'house style'.

In the absence of these guidelines, a secretary in a new job should follow the layout of the copies of outgoing letters in the files. When more experienced, she can than make alterations if she feels they would improve the appearance of her work. 'Open' punctuation (the omission of fullstops after abbreviations) is widely used today in typing, because it is quicker, but some employers may prefer the conventional 'full' punctuation, in which case their wishes should be followed.

The appearance of business letters is vitally important. They must always be immaculate, including spelling. Often, the first impression of a firm is given by a letter.

A draft of a long, complex letter, or one containing technical terms, enables the sender not only to check the facts, but re-arrange his ideas, if necessary. Word processing make this a relatively simple operation.

Extra copies for distribution should have all recipients' names typed on each copy and the relevant one marked with a highlighting pen in each case. If it is important that copies have to be sent *without* other recipients knowing, then a list of names is made on file copy *only*.

Finally, address on envelope and inside address on letter should agree in every detail (or window envelopes used, which save time and the possibility of errors).

Blind carbon copies

If the sender of a letter does not want the distribution list known to the recipient, the letter is taken out of the machine when it is finished and the carbon copies only re-inserted. The letters 'bcc' ('blind carbon copies, circulated to') are typed by the names:

    bcc   Mrs K Garside
           Mr F Hill
           Miss B Thompson

The distribution list above would appear on all carbons but not on the top copy.

When only the sender should know who will receive copies, an individual name is typed on each copy and a full list on the file copy only.

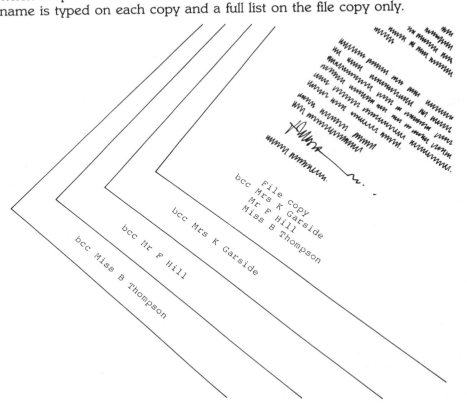

248

DICTATION

Taking Dictation

Used pages in a shorthand notebook should be fastened back with an elastic band, so that the notebook automatically opens at a fresh page.

For reminders or corrections during dictation, margins should be ruled down either left- or right-hand side of notebook. Tops and bottoms of pages should be dated and one corner folded back (the opposite corner to the writing hand) on several pages for quick 'flipping' over.

Mark anything which has to be given priority with a clear sign, such as an asterisk, or similar unmistakable sign.

If dictation is interrupted, this pause should be used to read quickly through notes, and to add punctuation or to improve any 'fuzzy' outlines. When dictation is resumed, a secretary will be asked to read back some of the last part of her notes.

Writing on a lap is both uncomfortable and leads to unreadable outlines. A flat surface should be insisted upon.

Any new technical word, or a name of which the spelling is unknown, should be marked with a wavy line during dictation (and in the margin as well, if time allows) and either queried later, or looked up in the files.

Most secretaries are expected to punctuate – fullstops should always be inserted while taking dictation, as they help transcription. Other punctuation can be added while transcribing. Some dictators indicate paragraphs, which should be clearly marked in the shorthand notes by an unmistakable sign – two short vertical lines close together is one useful way.

A line should be drawn from top to bottom of each page after it has been transcribed. If there is an interruption, (and there frequently is) a mark in the shorthand notes with a highlighting pen where transcribing stopped will save omitting a line when re-starting.

Audio-typing

Errors are often due to uncertainty over what is being said on the cassette – perhaps a technical or unusual word. When starting a new job, keep a notebook listing all new words and phrases in alphabetical order, checking the spellings carefully, and use it as a reference until the words are familiar.

Dictating

Even a skilled and experienced audio-typist finds it difficult to produce accurate work rapidly without the co-operation of the dictator. It is essential to have a system of indicating the length of each letter (usually an index slip), the number of carbon copies required, and the Post Office service to be used (if different from normal).

Dictation which contains changes of mind are irritating, confusing and frustrating for the audio-typist. A format of short sentences (not so easy to achieve as it sounds) should be the aim. One idea should be dealt with in one paragraph, dictated as though talking face to face and avoiding unnecessarily long words. Jotting a few thoughts down beforehand is a great help, even though a dictating machine is supposed to remove the need, but muddled thought is better clarified in writing than when spoken.

Hints for Dictators

Start dictation by specifying the number of copies, who is to receive them, and any other special instructions (enclosure, airmail, registered post, etc.).

Use the index slip to indicate length of letter.

Whether or not punctuation and paragraphs are dictated should be agreed between dictator and typist. It is helpful if new paragraphs are indicated: the dictator knows what is coming but the typist does not.

Proper names and technical words should be spelled out. If capital letters, brackets or quotation marks are to be used, this should be mentioned before the word and after if appropriate.

Tell your secretary the terms you are going to use ('upper case' or 'capitals', for example) and use them consistently.

Do not smoke while dictating.

The microphone on a dictating machine picks up surrounding noise. (Most offices are far from soundproof). Find a spot away from the window (traffic noise can be obtrusive) and switch off the machine when the telephone rings or visitors come in.

Speak clearly and naturally, with plenty of emphasis. A recorded voice sounds quite different from a natural voice: listen critically to your own dictation.

TYPING SPEECHES AND DRAFTS

Speeches should be typed in double line spacing. A convenient size for pocket or handbag is A5, but some speakers prefer A4. Sheets of paper (or perhaps cards, if the speech is not a long one) should be fastened by treasury tags through the top left-hand corner so that they turn over easily and lie flat. This prevents the embarrassing situation in which a speaker finds pages in the wrong place, or discovers that a page is missing.

A draft is a typed or written copy of a document (or letter) which is later to be amended. If it is a typed draft, it should be in double line spacing with wide margins, so that there is room for corrections.

The word DRAFT should be typed in spaced capitals at the top of the document; underlining in red makes this more prominent, so that there is no possibility of it being overlooked.

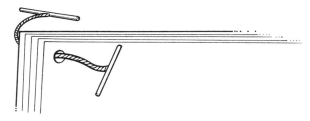

Treasury tag through top left-hand corner

Gauging Typing Space

Assessing the amount of space needed to type from shorthand notes is a matter for each individual shorthand writer. Shorthand outlines vary in size and the number of outlines written on each line of a notebook vary, too, so a shorthand-typist must learn to gauge for herself the number of typing lines she will need for a page of her own shorthand.

When gauging the amount of typing space needed for a handwritten passage, count the number of words in any one complete line – choose one which has about the same number of short and long words, so that you get an average line.

If the number of words is (say) 10, count the number of lines in the document and multiply by the number of words. Number of lines (say) 30 ($30 \times 10 = 300$).

The maximum number of words which can be typed on an A4 sheet of paper is approximately 406 made up from: 70 typing lines from top to bottom edge of paper, 12 lines for top and bottom margins, $58 \div 2$ (double line spacing) = 29. Average number of words in a typing line with 1″ margins left and right (elite pitch) is 14 ($29 \times 14 = 406$).

Therefore, the calculation of 300 (above) indicates that the typed document will fit on to one sheet of A4 paper with double-line spacing. If the line spacing is 1½, an additional 9 lines can be typed, which would give a total of 532 words. Single line spacing would give a total of $70 \times 14 = 980$ words.

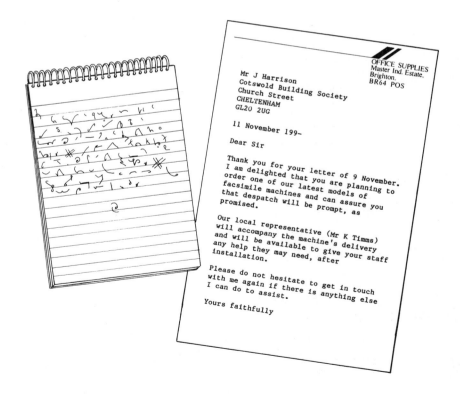

The above figures are only approximate, but help when it is necessary to decide whether a continuation sheet will be required for a passage to be typed on A4 paper and where a footnote is to be typed (if there is one).

When trying to decide whether a letter or A4 memo will need a continuation sheet, deduct 12 lines (i.e. 168 words) for the printed heading when making calculations.

SECRETARIAL TIPS

1 Dictating machines have another use apart from audio-typing – they can be used to leave occasional messages either from boss to secretary or vice versa.

2 When you have a great many envelopes to type, 'chain' feed them into your machine as follows:

- Open envelope flap and feed flap downwards into machine.

- Type address.

- As typed envelope is moved out, feed in next one to be typed.

- Type the address in the correct position.

- As you turn the cylinder knob to remove the typed envelope, feed in the next one to be typed, flap downwards, as before. This brings the blank envelope into position for typing, as the typed envelope is removed. It is known as 'chain' feeding.

- If you have hundreds of envelopes to type, it is a great time-saver! Postcards can be chain fed in the same way.

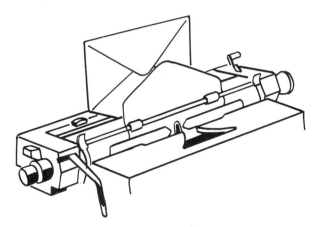

3 Keep spare, sharpened pencils handy (even if a pen is normally used) in order to save a crisis if a pencil point breaks or ink supply dries up during dictation.

4 Date the covers of shorthand notebooks when they are finished with, and keep them for at least 6 months. If a copy of a letter is

lost, the shorthand notes are available for reference.

5 The title 'Ms' is useful when it is not known whether a woman is married or single.

6 Postcards are a cheaper way of sending brief details (e.g. acknowledgement of an

order) than form letters, as they need no envelopes. They do, however, require the same postage as letters (i.e. first or second class).

7 When typing speeches use double or treble line spacing and wide margins both left and right – this keeps the lines short and easy to read. A convenient size for pocket or handbag is A5, but some speakers prefer A4.

8 A separate letter, however short, for each

topic, makes it easier for the recipient to deal with, rather than one long letter with several headings for various subjects.

9 Make sure that headings to memos indicate clearly the subject matter, so that initially all that is needed by the recipient is a quick glance, to find out what the content is.

10 If in doubt about whether to use the title of recipient or not on a memo, use a title.

QUICK REVISION

1 Firms should be addressed as 'Messrs' only when   ....

2 When writing to a woman and it is not known whether she is married or single, use the title   ....

3 When writing to a Member of Parliament who has other qualifications, 'MP' is typed   ....

4 The order for the other three main types of honours, degrees and qualifications is: ....

5 A useful enclosure which saves writing letters, sent with catalogues, price lists, etc. is   ....

6 A routing slip, distribution slip or circulation slip is used to   ....

7 A simpler way than form letters of sending brief details is by   ....

8 Confidential memos should be marked 'Confidential' and   ....

9 'House style' when referring to letters and memos means   ....

10 Copies of letters or memos which are to be sent without other recipients knowing are   ....

11 Use an interruption during dictation to read quickly through notes, add punctuation and   ....

12 If interrupted while transcribing shorthand notes   ....

13 Shorthand notebooks, when full, should be   ....

14 When a new job involves audio-typing keep a notebook listing all   ....

15 Speeches should be in double- or treble-line spacing with   ....

16 The complimentary close 'Yours sincerely' does not have   ....

17 When in doubt about whether to use the title of the recipient of a memo or not, use
....

18 When several subjects are to be dealt with, memos and letters should be ....

ASSIGNMENTS

1 You are secretary to the Area Sales Manager. His name is Mark Knowles. Compose memos from the following details. Date for today, and make other dates appropriate.

(a) Ask the Transport Manager to arrange for a car to take your boss to Gatwick at 1100 a week from today.

(b) Notify all Area Managers to attend a meeting on the second Monday next month to discuss latest sales figures. Time of meetings is 1000 and will last until 1600 (approx.). Lunch will be provided.
The names of the Area Managers are:
Mrs Mary Sanderson
Alan Webb
Peter Barnes
Ms Jane Shaw
John Carter

(c) Confirm to the Wages Department that Miss Sarah Willings, Mrs Diane Fuller, Mrs Barbara Downs and Ms Janine Bright are to have their salaries raised on the first of next month (insert suitable date) by £30 per month. These memos will have bcc (blind circulated copies).

(d) Type a letter (on suitably headed paper) confirming the booking made by phone for a single room with bath for the nights of Wednesday and Thursday at the Holiday Inn, Great North Road, Newcastle-upon-Tyne, in the first of next month (insert suitable dates) for your employer.
Mention that he will be arriving about 2100 and would like a meal. He wants an early morning call at 0700 with breakfast (Continental will be adequate) at 0730 on the Friday.
Sign the letter yourself, as secretary to the Sales Manager.

2 You are secretary to Miss Elizabeth Stevens, Personnel Officer. Type a letter to the Vicar (The Revd Michael Pitt MA OBE), The Old Rectory, St Augustine's Square, Chelmsford, Essex CM4 3RN, and head it 'Youth Club Visit'.
Confirm that the suggested visit on Wednesday 27th (insert suitable month here) will be convenient for the Training Officer, Mr Mark Dunn, to take a group from the Youth Club around the factory and offices. The tour will be in two parts each lasting about an hour, with a short break for coffee at 1100.

Suggest that the party arrives about 0945 and that the maximum number should be 15 plus the Vicar. Confirmation of these arrangements in due course will be appreciated.
cc to Mark Dunn.

CHAPTER 14

Safety and Security in the Office

THE SECRETARY'S RESPONSIBILITIES

A secretary's responsibilities in connection with security include the following:

1 *Confidential papers* – they should be locked away whenever she is out of the office. Fire-proof filing cabinets ensure papers are not destroyed in the event of fire. Important papers can be microfilmed (see pp. 117–18) so that additional copies are filed away from mail files. All unwanted papers should be shredded (see p. 103).

2 *Cash* (including petty cash – see p. 214) should always be locked away when the office is empty. If money is regularly taken to the bank, vary the day, time and route to prevent an attempted theft.

3 *Confidential telephone conversations* – should never be repeated and if your comments may be overheard by anyone not to be trusted, ask caller to ring back, or have call switched to a more private place.

4 *Any package which looks as if it may contain explosives* (look for oil or grease marks, a smell of almonds, wires sticking out or a small hole in the wrapping), should be put on a table in an empty room with the door locked until it can be inspected by the Crime Prevention Officer. *Do not attempt to open the letter.* Mail bomb detector equipment is available which will sense explosives through a thick packet, and it is possible to put through handfuls of letters in rapid succession or packages up to 18 inches wide. This detector equipment does not affect films or magnetic tapes. It is plugged into an ordinary 13 amp power point and is simple to use.

5 *Visitors* (see pp. 69–70) should never be allowed to wander around a firm unescorted. Provide ashtrays for the smokers.

6 *Tops of cupboards* should not be stacked with boxes and files, and gangways should not be blocked.

What's wrong with this office?

7 *Keep filing cabinet drawers closed.*

8 *Serial numbers on equipment* should be noted, so that in the event of theft, they may be traceable by the police.

9 *Torn or worn floor covering* should be reported and replaced.

10 *Overloaded electrical adaptors and trailing wires* should be eliminated by a competent electrician.

At the end of the day, a secretary should check:

- taps are turned off in the cloakroom,
- lights are switched off,
- electrical equipment is unplugged (apart from computers),
- safe and filing cabinets are locked,
- doors and windows are locked.

A duplicate set of keys left with a responsible member of staff is a help in case of loss or in an emergency.

SAFETY LEGISLATION

Accidents are usually caused by a moment's lack of thought and under the Health and Safety at Work Act (passed in 1974) employees as well as employers have duties as well as rights in regard to safety in offices.

The Industrial Injuries Act of 1946 provided a scheme of insurance against accidents at work for all employees, including office workers, and this was the beginning of regulations to protect them. In 1963 the Offices, Shops and Railway Premises Act was passed, which laid down regulations for lighting, heating, washing and toilet facilities, as well as minimum space (400 cubic feet) for each office worker, first aid and safety. Firms employing over 150 people had to arrange for one employee to be trained in first aid.

The most important development in office workers' conditions is the Health and Safety at Work Act (HASAWA) which includes all the regulations already in existence but is much more comprehensive and also applies to schools and colleges, which the previous legislation did not. Control of Substances Hazardous to Health (COSHH) regulations came into force in 1988, and in 1989 all employers (regardless of their line of business) were required to provide health and safety information in the form of leaflets and posters.

Between 1963 and 1974, the formation of trade unions for office workers influenced working conditions and helped to improve them, as did also the shortage of office workers after the Second World War - even a generous salary does not compensate for miserable working conditions.

REPORTING ACCIDENTS

Fire is most commonly caused by smokers' cigarette ends and many firms today are recruiting non-smokers, partly for this reason, and also for health reasons. Unscheduled fire drills should be held often and all staff must be able to use the fire extinguishers, which should be checked regularly. Other

Keep fire-fighting equipment, hoses and hydrants free from any obstruction

causes of fire are faulty wiring, and chemicals such as paint or aerosols. Scrap paper should be shredded and disposed of, not left in untidy piles. Fire exits must be clearly marked, kept unblocked, and fire doors left unlocked while staff are on the premises. The alarm should be raised *at once* if fire is discovered.

Bomb threats by telephone happen occasionally. Scotland Yard recommend:

- ask where bomb is, when it is to go off, what it looks like, who and where the caller is and why the bomb has been left.
- keep caller talking as long as possible, listening for any accent and background noises – the police will want to know as much as possible.
- inform firm's Safety Officer (if there is one) or the manager, who will decide whether to clear the building immediately. Call the police. Very often these telephoned bomb threats are hoaxes but no one can ever be sure.

First aid boxes should be prominently displayed and replenished regularly. Where there is a first aider in a firm, all staff should know him or her.

Know who your first aider is

An accident book should be kept to record details of any accident and the treatment that is given, both to employees and visitors to the firm, in case of any claim for compensation being made against the firm at a later date, because of serious developments from an accident.

DATE 199-	NAME	ADDRESS	ACCIDENT OR ILLNESS
28 February	Graham Timms	34 Lynwood Close Roker Sunderland	Nosebleed - sent to surgery.
2 March	Maureen Evans	5 Willow Way Washington Co. Durham	Foreign body in eye - removed in reception.

An accident report form

SECRETARIAL TIPS

1 Keep a book near all equipment used by staff in which faults can be entered, dated and initialled.

2 Arrange for a duplicate set of door keys to be left with a responsible member of staff in case of an emergency (such as other set of keys mislaid, and/or keyholder absent).

3 Have doctor's and nearest hospital's telephone numbers by the telephone and/or switchboard.

4 Get help with lifting heavy items, such as typewriters.

QUICK REVISION

1 Three ways of foiling potential thieves on the way to the bank are ....

2 Two ways of ensuring that confidential papers do not get into wrong hands are ....

3 Ensure that any stolen equipment can be traced by ....

4 The Act which includes all the health and safety regulations already in existence but is more comprehensive and also applies to schools and colleges is the ....

5 Two factors which have helped to improve the working conditions of office staff are ....

6 Common causes of fire are cigarette ends, chemicals and ....

7 Three important regulations about fire exits are ....

8 When a firm employs over 150 people, first aid is catered for by ....

9 An accident book is necessary because ....

10 First aid boxes should not only be displayed prominently but ....

ASSIGNMENTS

1 List as briefly and clearly as possible 5 main guidelines for a new office junior on accident prevention.

2 Draft a leaflet on health and safety to be distributed around your office.

3 Describe the action you would take after a visitor falls and goes into a coma in your office.

CHAPTER 15

Staff Recruitment

A senior secretary may be given the responsibility of recruiting a junior, assistant, or asked to advise on the appointment of her own replacement, if she is promoted, or leaves the firm. Sometimes, she 'sits in' on parts of an interview or supervises the tests given. Interviewing for other posts vacant in a firm is often carried out by members of the Personnel Department.

There are several ways of recruiting a new member of staff:

- internal advertising (in a large firm),
- applying to the Department of Employment Job Centres,
- applying to private employment agencies (especially useful for temporary secretarial staff),
- advertising in newspapers (usually local, for secretarial jobs),
- Prestel (see pp. 53–4).

An internal advertisement can be on the notice boards around a firm, or in the firm's house journals, or both.

ADVERTISING

An advertisement in a newspaper may ask applicants to send in a curriculum vitae (CV) with a covering letter, or write for an application form. Advertisements should be concise and brief without omitting essential details – if it is important that the applicant should be able to write shorthand, for example, then this should be stated. Ability to type can be taken for granted when advertising a vacancy for a secretary (whether junior or senior) but standards can be stated (e.g. RSA Stages II or III) as can English qualifications. Most recently trained secretaries will be familiar with word processing. If word processing is vital, the advertisement should state that training would be given, if the candidate is otherwise suitable.

It is important to make it quite clear in advertisements whether experienced staff only are required, or whether college leavers are being recruited, otherwise a great deal of time will be wasted by both applicants and the prospective employer.

The use of a box number in an advertisement, instead of the name of the firm, avoids telephone or personal calls, but may result in an employee applying to his or her own firm! Also, delay is caused by replies having to be collected from newspaper offices, or passed on by them.

After applications have been received, they have to be divided into the 'possible' and the 'hopeless', with the 'possibles' whittled down even more (if there are a great many of them) to a reasonable number of applicants to interview (a short list).

Careful forward planning is essential, particularly when a key position is being filled.

Allowance must be made for applicants who may find it inconvenient to attend on the day or at the time specified by sending out letters calling them for interview well in advance (or telephoning them). After an appointment has been made, the successful applicant has to give notice to her current employer so that it may be several weeks before she can take up her new position.

The letter calling an applicant for an interview should set out date, time and address, with brief directions together with name of nearest tube or number of bus passing by. The name should be given of the person to be asked for at the reception desk. The applicant should be requested to contact the firm at once if day or time of interview is unsuitable, and give an alternative.

A list of applicants, with times of appointments, will be needed by the receptionist.

There should be a 'job description' for a secretarial post in a large firm consisting of a description of the duties involved. This could be compiled partly by the present holder of the job, partly by the head of her department, and partly (in some cases) by the Personnel Department. A copy of a job description should be sent with an application form, or in reply to a letter of application.

References

These are usually taken up by the firm after an interview with an applicant considered suitable for the position.

INTERVIEWING

Have the job description, specification and assessment in front of you, together with the CV, completed application form and/or letter of application. Some firms send an application form which the candidate brings completed, in which case ask for it before the interview starts and have it in front of you. In addition, prepare a list of questions to ask each applicant and

APPLICATION FOR EMPLOYMENT

PLEASE USE BLOCK CAPITALS

CONFIDENTIAL

OFFICE STAFF:
PLEASE SEE PAGE 2

Position applied for

Personal information

Surname	Forename(s)
Address	Date of birth
	Place of birth
	Nationality
Telephone	Marital status

Education/training

	From	To	Examinations passed and grades
Secondary schools			
College/University (including evening, day-release and correspondence courses)	From	To	Certificates/degree obtained
Other professional qualifications, including membership of professional institutes and societies			

Employment Please enter your last or current employment first

Name and Address of Employer	From	To	Position Held	Reason for leaving

Additional information Include here your spare time interests

Office staff only:

Please indicate in order of preference which of the positions below you are interested in and for which you would be suitable.

- ☐ Audio-typist
- ☐ Filing clerk
- ☐ Secretary
- ☐ Book-keeper
- ☐ Word processor operator
- ☐ Shorthand-typist
- ☐ Copy-typist
- ☐ Switchboard Operator
- ☐ Receptionist

References Approaches to referees will only be made by agreement with the applicant, normally following an interview

1.

2.

I declare that the above information is correct.

Signature _____ Date _____

264

type them out with a space at the side of each for a tick, or short comment. This acts as a useful reminder during and after the interview, when a choice may have to be made between several otherwise suitable applicants.

Remember that applicants will be nervous and ill-at-ease, possibly also very shy. Start off with informal comments, such as 'How was your journey?', or 'Did you have any difficulty in finding us?' and use the candidate's name. There may be a subject of common interest on the application form or CV which could be mentioned – the area where the applicant lives, the school she went to, the sport she is interested in.

If a test of typing or shorthand is to be given (and this is the only way to ensure that there is a certain standard of competence), arrange this towards the end of the interview, and give applicants an opportunity to familiarise themselves with the typewriter beforehand. Speed tests are unrealistic, because the applicants are already nervous, and typing under pressure will make them more so. A dictated passage, to be typed back in the applicant's own time, or a handwritten passage to be copy-typed, is a far fairer test. Allowance must be made for nerves and unfamiliarity with the type-writer.

Most of the relevant information about the applicant should already be on the CV and application form, so that the purpose of an interview is mainly to find out something about the applicant's personality, attitude towards the job and, of course, appearance. 'What do you know about this firm?' is a useful question which may draw forth some interesting replies – it will at least tell the interviewer whether the applicant has gone to the trouble to find out anything at all about the place where she may work.

Other Questions to Ask Applicant

- What were your favourite subjects at school? (if relevant).
- What have you been doing since you left school or college? (if relevant).
- What do you hope to be doing in five/ten years time?
- What do you count as an achievement?
- What does 'being a success' mean to you?
- Why are you leaving your present job?
- What do you do in your present job?
- Are you prepared to undertake further training: (a) in your own time (b) in the firm's time?
- Give some reasons why we should offer you this job.
- Why have you applied for this job?
- Would you be interested in promotion within the firm?
- Would you be interested in taking on any responsibilities?
- What clubs or societies do you belong to and what positions of responsibility have you held in them?

It is important to remember that the object of an interview is to get the applicant to talk, not for the interviewer to hold forth at great length. A CV is illuminating in the information it *does not* give, e.g. reasons for leaving a job or whether further training is being undertaken or considered, and these are also questions which can be asked. Make sure that questions are so phrased that the applicant cannot answer them by just 'yes' or 'no'.

Allocate a reasonable amount of time for each applicant and allow time for questions from her.

List of Suitable Questions for Applicant to Ask

- Why has the vacancy occurred?
- What will be my duties besides typing?
- What sort of typewriter will I be using – electronic or manual?
- Will I be using a word processor or a computer?
- Who will I be working for?
- Where will I be working, and can I see that office?
- What are the possibilities of further training or day release?
- Are promotion and pay increases on merit or automatic?
- Are there welfare and medical services?
- Are there social activities and sports clubs?
- Is there a canteen?
- What are the hours of work?
- What is the holiday allowance?
- What is the salary? (if not mentioned by interviewer – this is one of the main reasons why you are going to work, after all)
- Is there a pension scheme?
- Are there any fringe benefits? (e.g. luncheon vouchers, opportunity to buy firm's products at reduced rates)
- Will I have to join a trade union?

If the applicant does not cover all of these, make sure the information is given. It is important to make it quite clear to college or school-leavers that the salary offered is 'gross' and that statutory deductions (see p. 270) reduce it quite considerably. Many first-time applicants do not understand the difference between 'gross' and 'net' salary.

It is the interviewer who should end the interview, and this can be done by standing and saying, for example, 'Thank you for coming and for your interest. You will be notified in a few days about a decision'. A decision should be made as promptly as possible.

The successful candidate should be notified by letter, possibly after an initial telephone call. Unsuccessful candidates should be notified once the letter accepting the post has been received. Wait until then, because the second choice may be needed if the first offer is turned down.

JOB DESCRIPTION AND SPECIFICATION

A Job Description

TITLE:	Personal Assistant
DEPARTMENT:	Production
HOURS:	Monday to Thursday: 0900 to 1730; lunch break: 1300 to 1400; Friday: 0900 to 1630
RESPONSIBLE TO:	Production Manager
AUTHORITY OVER:	Junior shorthand-typist; copy-typist
FUNCTION:	To provide secretarial support for the Production Manager and supervise the clerical work of the department.

DUTIES

1. Collect and open mail.

2. Correlate diaries with own diary; make and confirm appointments for Production Manager and his assistant.

3. Deal with telephone calls and take messages in absence of Production Manager and his assistant.

4. Take dictation; use audio-typing equipment; word processing; maintain absolute discretion regarding confidential material.

5. Type agenda for meetings; take minutes.

6. Make travel arrangements and arrange itineraries.

7. Compose memos and routine letters.

8. Supervise and check work of junior staff.

A Job Specification

Personal characteristics:
- ability to work under pressure and on own initiative
- reliability
- tact and discretion

- presence of mind
- good grooming
- punctuality
- loyalty to the firm
- ability to maintain good relationships with other members of staff, especially those who are juniors
- common sense

Qualifications
- high standard of English
- accurate shorthand, typing and word processing skills
- efficient and pleasant telephone manner
- thorough knowledge of primary clerical duties
- ability to receive and look after visitors in a welcoming manner
- ability to 'screen' telephone and personal calls with tact

It is important that a new employee is met and looked after on arrival. Someone from the office where she will work should go to Reception to meet her, make her welcome, and show her where the cloakroom, canteen and surgery are.

All new employees, whatever their age, find the process of learning names, and the way round the building, bewildering and frustrating. Induction courses are planned to help to overcome some of this.

INDUCTION COURSES

These will cover:
- the history of the firm,
- the layout (plans of the building may be given),
- diagrams showing the management and responsibilities of various heads of departments (see p. 4).
- a talk about the firm's progress and future plans,
- explanation about pensions, holidays, social activities, welfare, fire drills, safety,
- a tour of the firm, including the factory, if it is a manufacturing firm,
- introductions to various supervisory members of staff.

In some very large organisations, induction courses may last several days – in smaller ones, only a few hours. It is an opportunity for the new employee to ask questions, and to begin to get his or her bearings.

Some firms arrange a medical examination for new employees, which will take place during the first week.

Check-list for interviewing applicant for post of Personal Assistant

Name   . . . .

Appearance   makeup   . . . .

                         hair   . . . .

                         clothes   . . . .

                         shoes; tights   . . . .

Voice   . . . .

Manner   . . . .

Articulateness   . . . .

Interest in firm   . . . .

Interest in job applied for   . . . .

Qualifications: English   . . . .

                         typing   . . . .

                         shorthand   . . . .

                         word processing . . . .

                         audio-typing   . . . .

                         secretarial   . . . .

Interest in further training   . . . .

Interest in promotion   . . . .

Domestic/family circumstances . . . .

Possession of driving licence . . . .

Any specialised experience   . . . .

Foreign languages   . . . .

Unusual hobbies or interests . . . .

Suitability for job   . . . .

Not suitable for this vacancy, but could be

considered later   . . . .

Grades: A   exceptional   D   good
            B   excellent   E   fair
            C   very good   F   below standard

On the first day of work a new employee should bring:

- A National Insurance number (obtainable from the Department of Social Security for school or college leavers).
- Income tax form P45 which sets out how much tax has been deducted by the previous employer. If there has been no previous employment, an emergency income tax code will be allocated until the income tax form (Claim for Allowances) has been completed. Any tax overpaid while an emergency tax code is in operation will be refunded when a notice of the correct coding is received.

DEDUCTIONS FROM SALARIES

Income tax and National Insurance contributions are statutory (required to be made by law). Other deductions are agreed by the employee (i.e. they are voluntary) and can include savings fund, social fund, Trade Union dues, contribution to a pension scheme. When all deductions have been totalled and taken away from the gross pay, the remainder (known as the net pay) is paid to the employee.

Contributions to a Pensions Scheme

The pension may be run by the employer (a private one) in which case the employee contributing is known as 'contracted out', or may be the Government's scheme, in which case the employee is known as 'not contracted out'. Every worker over 18 has to contribute to a pension scheme – either a private one or the Government's, and has the statutory right to choose which one.

National Insurance contributions are scaled according to gross pay (currently over £43 per week). There are three rates:

- standard – paid by most employees,
- reduced – paid by certain married women, linked to earnings, and widows,
- nil – because a worker has reached pensionable age (*but* the employer still has to pay his contribution.

Unemployment benefit is based on National Insurance contributions.

Income Tax

Income for the purposes of income tax means:

- wages (or salaries),
- overtime,
- bonuses of Christmas gifts in money,
- interest from savings accounts,
- dividends from shares,
- pension,
- holiday pay,

270

- commission,
- rent from furnished lettings,
- profits from businesses and professions,
- social security benefits,
- tips received in connection with employment,
- perquisites.

1 Income from trade, profession or vocation 6 April 1989 to 5 April 1990

Business name and address	Type of trade, etc.	Amount for year £
	Enterprise allowance	
	Balancing charges	
	Deductions for Capital Allowances	

2 Income from employment etc.: 6 April 1989 to 5 April 1990

Income received for duties performed wholly in the UK including fees, bonus, commission, tips benefits, expenses, leaving payments and compensation.

Occupation and employers name(s) and address(es)	Amount for year £

Income received in respect of duties performed wholly or partly abroad

Employment concerned	Amount for year £

Dates absent from UK when working abroad. Enclose statement if necessary.

To claim dedn. enter an "X" here

3 Other Income: 6 April 1989 to 5 April 1990

Property in the UK

* delete as appropriate
*Unfurnished lettings
*Furnished lettings
*Furnished holiday lettings
*Ground rents or Feu duties
*Land

Address	Gross income including premiums	Expenses (enclose statement)	Amount for year £

The first page of Income Tax form P1

Certain allowances can be offset against income tax. These allowances are given for the following, but must be claimed on Form P1 – the Tax Inspector will not know the wage-earner is entitled to them unless he is informed:

- Interest on mortgage repayments to a building society.
- For a dependent man, allowances are given on earned income for his wife, and other dependent relatives, such as children, or his mother.
- For a wage-earning wife, an allowance is given against the income she earns.
- An unmarried man receives a single person's allowance.
- Any special protective clothing needed for a job – boots, overalls, spectacles, gloves.
- Any special tools required for a job.
- Books for teachers.
- Subscriptions to trade unions and other official professional organisations connected with a job or profession.
- Special income tax allowances for the blind.
- Interest on a bank loan which qualifies for tax relief (not all do).

Income which is completely tax-free:

- war widow's pension,
- child benefit allowance,
- maternity allowance,
- sick pay,
- industrial injury or disablement pensions,
- first £70 interest from National Savings Bank ordinary account.

There is no tax relief for National Insurance contributions.

Some tax may be paid direct on your behalf, e.g. Building Society interest.

Any of the above information which is relevant should be entered on Form P1 so that the correct code number can be allocated for an employer to know how much tax to deduct from the gross pay.

Income Tax Forms

Form P1   Return of income, completed by employee and sent to Inland Revenue office. An income tax code is based on the information contained on this form.

Form P2   Sent by Inland Revenue to employee, notifying code.

Form P6   Sent by Inland Revenue to employer, notifying code.

Form P7   Guide to PAYE for employer.

Form P8	Guide to completing P11.
Form P11	A record kept by employer showing pay and deductions for the tax year, 6 April to 5 April (see p. 276-7).
Form P14	Return sent at end of tax year to Inland Revenue (summary of P11).
Form P15	Completed by employee who has lost P45.
Form P35	Completed by employer showing pay, tax, National Insurance contributions and sick pay for all employees.
Form P45	In three parts. Part 1 is sent to tax office; parts 2 and 3 given to employee to take when leaving employment to hand to new employer.
Form P46	Sent to tax office with details of new employee who has no code number.
Form P60	Final statement of pay, tax deductions and National Insurance contributions for the year, given to employee by employer as soon as possible after end of tax year (5 April).

Using Tax Tables

There are two tax tables – A and B. Table A (on p. 274) shows the amount of money which can be earned free of tax with a cumulative total. Table B (on p. 275) shows the amount of pay on which tax is due. These amounts are worked out by the tax codes which each employee is given by the Inland Revenue, based on the tax return the employee has completed. Code numbers consist of the total allowances without the last figure –i.e. if the allowances are £2500, the code number is 250. The code number shows the amount of free pay in Table A.

Payment of Salaries or Wages

From 1 January 1989, workers lost their statutory right to demand payment of wages in cash. The change was made in the 1986 Wages Act, in the hope that it will lead to more people having their wages paid direct into a bank account. Some employees prefer to stick to cash for personal reasons – part-time workers for instance, whose pay is so low it does not justify a bank account, and there are still 5 million workers with bank accounts who prefer to receive their wages in cash. The alternatives are cheque, credit transfer or direct debit (through a current account) or by Girobank. The obvious advantages to employers are increased security and saving of time and money.

TABLE A—FREE PAY

Code	Total free pay to date (£)	Code	Total free pay to date (£)	Code	Total free pay to date (£)	Code	Total free pay to date (£)	Code	Total free pay to date (£)	Code	Total free pay to date (£)	Code	Total free pay to date (£)	Code	Total free pay to date (£)
0	NIL	61	11·91	121	23·45	181	34·99	241	46·52	301	58·06	361	69·60	421	81·14
1	0·37	62	12·10	122	23·64	182	35·18	242	46·72	302	58·25	362	69·79	422	81·33
2	0·56	63	12·29	123	23·83	183	35·37	243	46·91	303	58·45	363	69·99	423	81·52
3	0·75	64	12·49	124	24·02	184	35·56	244	47·10	304	58·64	364	70·18	424	81·72
4	0·95	65	12·68	125	24·22	185	35·75	245	47·29	305	58·83	365	70·37	425	81·91
5	1·14	66	12·87	126	24·41	186	35·95	246	47·49	306	59·02	366	70·56	426	82·10
6	1·33	67	13·06	127	24·60	187	36·14	247	47·68	307	59·22	367	70·75	427	82·29
7	1·52	68	13·25	128	24·79	188	36·33	248	47·87	308	59·41	368	70·95	428	82·49
8	1·72	69	13·45	129	24·99	189	36·52	249	48·06	309	59·60	369	71·14	429	82·68
9	1·91	70	13·64	130	25·18	190	36·72	250	48·25	310	59·79	370	71·33	430	82·87
10	2·10														
11	2·29	71	13·83	131	25·37	191	36·91	251	48·45	311	59·99	371	71·52	431	83·06
12	2·49	72	14·02	132	25·56	192	37·10	252	48·64	312	60·18	372	71·72	432	83·25
13	2·68	73	14·22	133	25·75	193	37·29	253	48·83	313	60·37	373	71·91	433	83·45
14	2·87	74	14·41	134	25·95	194	37·49	254	49·02	314	60·56	374	72·10	434	83·64
15	3·06	75	14·60	135	26·14	195	37·68	255	49·22	315	60·75	375	72·29	435	83·83
16	3·25	76	14·79	136	26·33	196	37·87	256	49·41	316	60·95	376	72·49	436	84·02
17	3·45	77	14·99	137	26·52	197	38·06	257	49·60	317	61·14	377	72·68	437	84·22
18	3·64	78	15·18	138	26·72	198	38·25	258	49·79	318	61·33	378	72·87	438	84·41
19	3·83	79	15·37	139	26·91	199	38·45	259	49·99	319	61·52	379	73·06	439	84·60
20	4·02	80	15·56	140	27·10	200	38·64	260	50·18	320	61·72	380	73·25	440	84·79
21	4·22	81	15·75	141	27·29	201	38·83	261	50·37	321	61·91	381	73·45	441	84·99
22	4·41	82	15·95	142	27·49	202	39·02	262	50·56	322	62·10	382	73·64	442	85·18
23	4·60	83	16·14	143	27·68	203	39·22	263	50·75	323	62·29	383	73·83	443	85·37
24	4·79	84	16·33	144	27·87	204	39·41	264	50·95	324	62·49	384	74·02	444	85·56
25	4·99	85	16·52	145	28·06	205	39·60	265	51·14	325	62·68	385	74·22	445	85·75
26	5·18	86	16·72	146	28·25	206	39·79	266	51·33	326	62·87	386	74·41	446	85·95
27	5·37	87	16·91	147	28·45	207	39·99	267	51·52	327	63·06	387	74·60	447	86·14
28	5·56	88	17·10	148	28·64	208	40·18	268	51·72	328	63·25	388	74·79	448	86·33
29	5·75	89	17·29	149	28·83	209	40·37	269	51·91	329	63·45	389	74·99	449	86·52
30	5·95	90	17·49	150	29·02	210	40·56	270	52·10	330	63·64	390	75·18	450	86·72
31	6·14	91	17·68	151	29·22	211	40·75	271	52·29	331	63·83	391	75·37	451	86·91
32	6·33	92	17·87	152	29·41	212	40·95	272	52·49	332	64·02	392	75·56	452	87·10
33	6·52	93	18·06	153	29·60	213	41·14	273	52·68	333	64·22	393	75·75	453	87·29
34	6·72	94	18·25	154	29·79	214	41·33	274	52·87	334	64·41	394	75·95	454	87·49
35	6·91	95	18·45	155	29·99	215	41·52	275	53·06	335	64·60	395	76·14	455	87·68
36	7·10	96	18·64	156	30·18	216	41·72	276	53·25	336	64·79	396	76·33	456	87·87
37	7·29	97	18·83	157	30·37	217	41·91	277	53·45	337	64·99	397	76·52	457	88·06
38	7·49	98	19·02	158	30·56	218	42·10	278	53·64	338	65·18	398	76·72	458	88·25
39	7·68	99	19·22	159	30·75	219	42·29	279	53·83	339	65·37	399	76·91	459	88·45
40	7·87	100	19·41	160	30·95	220	42·49	280	54·02	340	65·56	400	77·10	460	88·64
41	8·06	101	19·60	161	31·14	221	42·68	281	54·22	341	65·75	401	77·29	461	88·83
42	8·25	102	19·79	162	31·33	222	42·87	282	54·41	342	65·95	402	77·49	462	89·02
43	8·45	103	19·99	163	31·52	223	43·06	283	54·60	343	66·14	403	77·68	463	89·22
44	8·64	104	20·18	164	31·72	224	43·25	284	54·79	344	66·33	404	77·87	464	89·41
45	8·83	105	20·37	165	31·91	225	43·45	285	54·99	345	66·52	405	78·06	465	89·60
46	9·02	106	20·56	166	32·10	226	43·64	286	55·18	346	66·72	406	78·25	466	89·79
47	9·22	107	20·75	167	32·29	227	43·83	287	55·37	347	66·91	407	78·45	467	89·99
48	9·41	108	20·95	168	32·49	228	44·02	288	55·56	348	67·10	408	78·64	468	90·18
49	9·60	109	21·14	169	32·68	229	44·22	289	55·75	349	67·29	409	78·83	469	90·37
50	9·79	110	21·33	170	32·87	230	44·41	290	55·95	350	67·49	410	79·02	470	90·56
51	9·99	111	21·52	171	33·06	231	44·60	291	56·14	351	67·68	411	79·22	471	90·75
52	10·18	112	21·72	172	33·25	232	44·79	292	56·33	352	67·87	412	79·41	472	90·95
53	10·37	113	21·91	173	33·45	233	44·99	293	56·52	353	68·06	413	79·60	473	91·14
54	10·56	114	22·10	174	33·64	234	45·18	294	56·72	354	68·25	414	79·79	474	91·33
55	10·75	115	22·29	175	33·83	235	45·37	295	56·91	355	68·45	415	79·99	475	91·52
56	10·95	116	22·49	176	34·02	236	45·56	296	57·10	356	68·64	416	80·18	476	91·72
57	11·14	117	22·68	177	34·22	237	45·75	297	57·29	357	68·83	417	80·37	477	91·91
58	11·33	118	22·87	178	34·41	238	45·95	298	57·49	358	69·02	418	80·56	478	92·10
59	11·52	119	23·06	179	34·60	239	46·14	299	57·68	359	69·22	419	80·75	479	92·29
60	11·72	120	23·25	180	34·79	240	46·33	300	57·87	360	69·41	420	80·95	480	92·49

see page 2

TABLE B

TAX DUE ON TAXABLE PAY FROM £1 TO £360

Total TAXABLE PAY to date	Total TAX DUE to date	Total TAXABLE PAY to date	Total TAX DUE to date	Total TAXABLE PAY to date	Total TAX DUE to date	Total TAXABLE PAY to date	Total TAX DUE to date	Total TAXABLE PAY to date	Total TAX DUE to date	Total TAXABLE PAY to date	Total TAX DUE to date
£	£	£	£	£	£	£	£	£	£	£	£
1	0.25	61	15.25	121	30.25	181	45.25	241	60.25	301	75.25
2	0.50	62	15.50	122	30.50	182	45.50	242	60.50	302	75.50
3	0.75	63	15.75	123	30.75	183	45.75	243	60.75	303	75.75
4	1.00	64	16.00	124	31.00	184	46.00	244	61.00	304	76.00
5	1.25	65	16.25	125	31.25	185	46.25	245	61.25	305	76.25
6	1.50	66	16.50	126	31.50	186	46.50	246	61.50	306	76.50
7	1.75	67	16.75	127	31.75	187	46.75	247	61.75	307	76.75
8	2.00	68	17.00	128	32.00	188	47.00	248	62.00	308	77.00
9	2.25	69	17.25	129	32.25	189	47.25	249	62.25	309	77.25
10	2.50	70	17.50	130	32.50	190	47.50	250	62.50	310	77.50
11	2.75	71	17.75	131	32.75	191	47.75	251	62.75	311	77.75
12	3.00	72	18.00	132	33.00	192	48.00	252	63.00	312	78.00
13	3.25	73	18.25	133	33.25	193	48.25	253	63.25	313	78.25
14	3.50	74	18.50	134	33.50	194	48.50	254	63.50	314	78.50
15	3.75	75	18.75	135	33.75	195	48.75	255	63.75	315	78.75
16	4.00	76	19.00	136	34.00	196	49.00	256	64.00	316	79.00
17	4.25	77	19.25	137	34.25	197	49.25	257	64.25	317	79.25
18	4.50	78	19.50	138	34.50	198	49.50	258	64.50	318	79.50
19	4.75	79	19.75	139	34.75	199	49.75	259	64.75	319	79.75
20	5.00	80	20.00	140	35.00	200	50.00	260	65.00	320	80.00
21	5.25	81	20.25	141	35.25	201	50.25	261	65.25	321	80.25
22	5.50	82	20.50	142	35.50	202	50.50	262	65.50	322	80.50
23	5.75	83	20.75	143	35.75	203	50.75	263	65.75	323	80.75
24	6.00	84	21.00	144	36.00	204	51.00	264	66.00	324	81.00
25	6.25	85	21.25	145	36.25	205	51.25	265	66.25	325	81.25
26	6.50	86	21.50	146	36.50	206	51.50	266	66.50	326	81.50
27	6.75	87	21.75	147	36.75	207	51.75	267	66.75	327	81.75
28	7.00	88	22.00	148	37.00	208	52.00	268	67.00	328	82.00
29	7.25	89	22.25	149	37.25	209	52.25	269	67.25	329	82.25
30	7.50	90	22.50	150	37.50	210	52.50	270	67.50	330	82.50
31	7.75	91	22.75	151	37.75	211	52.75	271	67.75	331	82.75
32	8.00	92	23.00	152	38.00	212	53.00	272	68.00	332	83.00
33	8.25	93	23.25	153	38.25	213	53.25	273	68.25	333	83.25
34	8.50	94	23.50	154	38.50	214	53.50	274	68.50	334	83.50
35	8.75	95	23.75	155	38.75	215	53.75	275	68.75	335	83.75
36	9.00	96	24.00	156	39.00	216	54.00	276	69.00	336	84.00
37	9.25	97	24.25	157	39.25	217	54.25	277	69.25	337	84.25
38	9.50	98	24.50	158	39.50	218	54.50	278	69.50	338	84.50
39	9.75	99	24.75	159	39.75	219	54.75	279	69.75	339	84.75
40	10.00	100	25.00	160	40.00	220	55.00	280	70.00	340	85.00
41	10.25	101	25.25	161	40.25	221	55.25	281	70.25	341	85.25
42	10.50	102	25.50	162	40.50	222	55.50	282	70.50	342	85.50
43	10.75	103	25.75	163	40.75	223	55.75	283	70.75	343	85.75
44	11.00	104	26.00	164	41.00	224	56.00	284	71.00	344	86.00
45	11.25	105	26.25	165	41.25	225	56.25	285	71.25	345	86.25
46	11.50	106	26.50	166	41.50	226	56.50	286	71.50	346	86.50
47	11.75	107	26.75	167	41.75	227	56.75	287	71.75	347	86.75
48	12.00	108	27.00	168	42.00	228	57.00	288	72.00	348	87.00
49	12.25	109	27.25	169	42.25	229	57.25	289	72.25	349	87.25
50	12.50	110	27.50	170	42.50	230	57.50	290	72.50	350	87.50
51	12.75	111	27.75	171	42.75	231	57.75	291	72.75	351	87.75
52	13.00	112	28.00	172	43.00	232	58.00	292	73.00	352	88.00
53	13.25	113	28.25	173	43.25	233	58.25	293	73.25	353	88.25
54	13.50	114	28.50	174	43.50	234	58.50	294	73.50	354	88.50
55	13.75	115	28.75	175	43.75	235	58.75	295	73.75	355	88.75
56	14.00	116	29.00	176	44.00	236	59.00	296	74.00	356	89.00
57	14.25	117	29.25	177	44.25	237	59.25	297	74.25	357	89.25
58	14.50	118	29.50	178	44.50	238	59.50	298	74.50	358	89.50
59	14.75	119	29.75	179	44.75	239	59.75	299	74.75	359	89.75
60	15.00	120	30.00	180	45.00	240	60.00	300	75.00	360	90.00

Deductions Working Sheet P11   Year to 5 April 19 _____

Employer's name

Tax District and reference

Complete only for occupational pension schemes newly contracted-out since 1 January 1986.
Scheme contracted-out number

| S | 4 | | | | | | |

National Insurance Contributions *

Earnings on which employee's contributions payable 1a	Total of employee's and employer's contributions payable 1b	Employee's contributions payable 1c	Earnings on which employee's contributions at contracted-out rate payable included in column 1a 1d	Employee's contributions at contracted-out rate included in column 1c 1e	Statutory Sick Pay in the week or month included in column 2 1f	Statutory Maternity Pay in the week or month included in column 2 1g	Month no
£	£	£	£	£	£	£	6 April to 5 May **1**
							6 May to 5 June **2**
							6 June to 5 July **3**
							6 July to 5 Aug **4**
							6 Aug to 5 Sept **5**
							6 Sept to 5 Oct **6**
							6 Oct to 5 Nov **7**
Total c/forward	Total c/forward	Total c/forward	Total c/forward	Total c/forward	Total c/forward	Total c/forward	

P11

276

Employee's surname *in CAPITALS*		First two forenames	

National Insurance no.	Date of birth *in figures* Day Month Year	Works no. etc	Date of leaving *in figures* Day · Month Year

Tax code †	Amended code †				
	Wk/Mth in which applied				

PAYE Income Tax

Week no	Pay in the week or month including Statutory Sick Pay/ Statutory Maternity Pay 2	Total pay to date 3	Total free pay to date as shown by Table A 4	Total taxable pay to date Ø 5	Total tax due to date as shown by Taxable Pay Tables 6	Tax deducted or refunded in the week or month *Mark refunds 'R'* 7	For employer's use
1	£	£	£	£	£	£	
2							
3							
4							
5							
6							
7							
8							
9							
10							
11							
12							
13							
14							
15							
16							
17							
18							
19							
20							
21							
22							
23							
24							
25							
26							
27							
28							
29							
30							

* You must enter the NI contribution table letter overleaf beside the NI totals box - *see the note shown there.*

† If amended cross out previous code.

Ø If in any week/month the amount in column 4 is more than the amount in column 3, leave column 5 blank.

277

FRINGE BENEFITS

Fringe benefits (also known as 'perks', short for 'perquisites') are offered by many firms to their employees in addition to salaries or wages, and in some cases make a job more attractive than the money earned.

Fringe benefits are taxable and are offered only on a limited basis per year. If they are in the form of goods manufactured by the firm, they are not for resale to other people outside the family of the employee.

Other Types of Fringe Benefits

- luncheon vouchers,
- travel,
- car or car allowance towards use of own car,
- private health insurance,
- private education,
- housing,
- low-interest loans.
- flexible working hours

Flexible Working Hours

This is a system whereby office workers can vary their starting and finishing times to suit their own convenience, so long as they work an agreed minimum number of hours per week. They may prefer to start early (0800 hours) and finish early (1600) to fit in with family commitments (children at school, for example) or start later (1000) and finish later (1800) to avoid rush-hour traffic.

There are usually periods when all workers have to be in the office. One is in the morning (perhaps 1000–1200) and the other in the afternoon (perhaps 1400–1600). These periods are known as 'core time'. The lunch hour may be taken at any time between the two core periods. Different workers may choose different lunch hours so that, for instance, the reception desk always has someone in attendance.

Time may be 'banked' by working overtime – hours in addition to the agreed minimum, and half-days taken by arrangement with the firm. Banked time is generally limited to a certain number of hours per week.

Clocking in and out is an essential part of flexible working hours in order to keep an accurate record of time actually spent in the office.

Flexible working hours have proved to be popular with office workers, especially women, who are able to fit in working time with looking after school-age children and shopping. They are also popular with office workers who travel long distances as they can fit in travelling time with less busy periods on rail or road.

SICKNESS BENEFIT

In June 1982, notes from doctors for illnesses lasting less than a week were abolished. A scheme was introduced whereby employees should complete a form to declare themselves ill and unfit for work. They do not require their employer's signature on this form and are on their honour to tell the truth about their illness.

Forms are available from: the Department of Social Security (DSS), doctor's receptionists and hospitals. They have to be returned to a Social Security office to entitle the holder to sick pay. In addition, companies may ask their staff to complete a form such as the one shown overleaf.

To get sick pay, an employee has to be ill for four consecutive days. For illnesses lasting more than a week, a doctor's sick note is still required. A doctor will still sign a sick note for fewer than four days, but will charge £1.40.

Since April 1983, employees have been required by law to provide sick pay from the fourth day of an illness. Payments for the first three days of an illness by an employer are voluntary. Many firms pay an employee while he is ill and deduct any sick pay he receives in addition on his return.

Anyone injured at work because of an accident gets sick pay under this scheme – not industrial injury benefit, as hitherto.

EMPLOYMENT LEGISLATION

The Redundancy Payments Act, 1965 is consolidated under the Employment Protection (Consolidation) Act, 1978, which covers the following:

- contracts of employment,
- protection against unfair dismissal,
- rights to maternity pay and reinstatement after pregnancy,
- sick pay.

It also lays down regulations preventing victimisation for union activities.

Other employment legislation is the:

- *Equal Pay Act, 1970* which did not come into effect until the end of 1975. It applies to all kinds of work (not just office work) and is intended to

SELF-CERTIFICATION of SICKNESS

Employer:

PLEASE READ THESE NOTES CAREFULLY. IF THERE IS ANYTHING YOU DO NOT UNDERSTAND, ASK YOUR SUPERVISOR.

As soon as you return to work after a sickness absence of 7 days or less, you must complete this Self-Certification form
Any entitlement to Statutory Sick Pay (SSP) will depend on the evidence of sickness you provide below

a) Complete this form in your supervisor's presence, using BLOCK CAPITALS
b) The 'Period of Sickness' dates must be the first and last days of your ACTUAL SICKNESS, even if these occurred on
   rest days, Public Holidays, or other days you would not normally work
c) Certify your reason for absence, then sign and date the form; your supervisor will then countersign it as a witness to
   your signature

Note: If your sickness exceeds 7 calendar days, ask your Doctor for a Medical Certificate as evidence that you were unfit for work

Job Title/Department/Section	Number	Date of Birth			Forename(s)	Surname	
		Day	Month	Year		Mr. Mrs. Ms. Miss	

I CERTIFY THAT I WAS UNFIT FOR WORK BECAUSE OF	ILLNESS	Put X in correct box
	EMPLOYMENT ACCIDENT	
	OTHER ACCIDENT	

PERIOD OF SICKNESS
Enter first and last dates of sickness, even if not normal working days

From _____ am/pm _____ / /19 To _____ am/pm _____ / /19

Did you become sick whilst at work? YES/NO   If YES did you do any work that day? YES/NO

PERIOD OF ABSENCE
Enter dates absent from work

From _____ am/pm _____ / /19 To _____ am/pm _____ / /19

Give SYMPTOMS of illness, or describe accident and cause

TREATMENT Did you see a Doctor or visit a Hospital?   YES/NO

If YES give name and address of Doctor or Hospital and state treatment	If NO describe any treatment or medicine you took to help your recovery

SSP/STATE BENEFITS | Has the DSS given you an explanatory letter headed Statutory Sick Pay? i.e. Form ref. BF218, BF219, BF220, BM7 or BM8 | YES/NO | If YES, please hand the letter to your supervisor

I certify that the above is a true and correct record of my sickness and absence and understand that further enquiries may be made at the discretion of management   Date   /   /19

The above details were completed and signed in my presence   Date   /   /19

If an Employment Accident has been certified above, check the Notification of Accidents and Dangerous Occurrence Regulations

NOTES   Office use only

SSP DETAILS	Nat. Ins. Number						Is evidence of incapacity acceptable?	YES
No. of days Sickness	Date Notified		/	/				NO
No. of days Qualifying	How Notified						If NO, give reasons	
SSP/State Benefit Linking	Attach DSS form BF218, BF219, BF220, BM7 or BM8 if provided by employee			DSS form ref.				
				Last date of SSP Exclusion				

280

eliminate discrimination with regard to pay and conditions of employment between men and women.

- *Employment and Training Act, 1973,* which established the Manpower Services Commission (MSC), now the Training Agency running training services for the general public.

Redundancy Payments

To qualify for redundancy payment, an employee must have worked full-time for the employer for a continuous period of two years (five if the employee worked part-time for a minimum of eight hours per week). The statutory minimum payment is calculated by age and years of service as follows:

- For each year of service while aged 18–21, ½ week's pay.
- For each year of service while aged 22–40, 1 week's pay.
- For each year of service while aged 41–64 (men) or 59 (women), 1½ week's pay.

CONTRACT OF EMPLOYMENT

The law does not insist that a Contract of Employment should be in writing, but it encourages employers to set out a summary of the main terms in writing, and these must be set out within 13 weeks of the employee starting work. In the event of a dispute between employee and employer, an Industrial Tribunal may regard an employer who has not put the terms of an employment contract in writing with disfavour – the benefit of the doubt may well be given to the employee.

A Contract of Employment is important because it is the peg from which all employees' rights hang, and it is far better from both the employer's and the employee's point of view if it is in writing. Both of them then know where they stand and there can be no dispute over terms and conditions.

Under Section 1 of the Employment Protection (Consolidation) Act, 1978, the following *must* appear on a Contract of Employment, when there is one:

Job title
Wages or salary
Hours of work
Holidays and holiday pay
Sickness or injury pay

Pension and pension schemes
Notice to terminate employment on either side.

Other points which *may* be included are:

Date of commencement of employment
The person to whom a grievance can be made
The right to belong to a trade union of choice
The right *not* to belong to a trade union.

Other points may be included – much depends upon the size and type of the organisation, and agreements with the relevant trade union.

The minimum periods of notice which must be given to employees are based on length of service: after four weeks' service – one week's notice *and then* one week's notice for each completed year of service up to a maximum of 12 weeks' notice.

SECRETARIAL TIPS

1 If the firm's name is to remain anonymous when advertising for a new member of staff, instead of a box number, give the telephone number and a name to ask for when ringing.

2 Send an applicant a small map of the area around the firm with the letter calling her for interview.

3 Telephone the person whose name has been given as a reference – quite often opinions are given verbally which would not be written down.

4 Arrange a telephone test by asking the applicant to answer any calls in your absence from the interview room. Tell her what to say, and get another member of staff to ring the number with a message to pass on to you (make allowances for nervousness).

5 Reimburse travelling expenses at the end of the interview – possibly out of petty cash (see Chapter 11).

6 In a small firm, make sure that you or someone else meets a new employee and shows her where: to hang her coat; the cloakroom is; her desk is; the stationery supplies are.

7 In a large firm, the receptionist must be informed of the name of the new employee and time of arrival.

QUICK REVISION

1 Several ways of advertising a job vacancy are internally, applying to Jobcentres or employment agencies, Prestel, and ....

2 A letter calling an applicant for interview should set out date, time, address and ....

3 A list of applicants with times of appointments will be needed by the ....

4 A job description is compiled by the present holder of the job, and by the ....

5 The interviewer should have in front of her the job description, CV, job specification, completed application form and ....

6 In addition, prepare ....

7 Allocate a reasonable amount of time for each applicant and allow ....

8 If travelling expenses are involved, reimburse applicants ....

9 A letter of appointment should include title of post, date of commencement, salary, holiday entitlement, and ....

10 A Contract of Employment may be in the form of a letter of appointment, or a notice on the wall of the office or it may be ....

11 An induction course is planned to ....

12 A new employee should bring ....

ASSIGNMENTS

1 You work as a personal assistant in a small firm which is beginning to expand. You have a junior typist working with you, but need more help with routine correspondence which would be dictated by you. You have been authorised to advertise.

(a) Draft a job description.

(b) Draft an advertisement, including brief details and what you would regard as a suitable annual salary.

(c) Draft a letter asking suitable applicants to call, leaving blanks for names, addresses, times and dates to be inserted later.

(d) Make a list of questions to ask at the interview.

(e) Draft a message to be telephoned through to each applicant as a test of telephone ability.

(f) A shorthand-typing test will be essential as part of this interview – what would be fair to the applicant and give a clear idea of her proficiency?

2 (a) Write a letter of application for the above position.

(b) Take it in turns to interview applicants.

(c) Draft a suitable letter informing applicants who are unsuccessful.

CHAPTER 16

Meetings

TYPES OF MEETINGS

Meetings absorb employees' time which would normally be spent on their own duties. Therefore the date, time and place of a meeting should be announced as far in advance as possible. A programme of what will be discussed at a meeting (the agenda) is often combined with the notice (see p. 288).

Meetings may be *formal,* such as a board meeting attended by the chairman and directors of a company or a shareholders' meeting at which the chairman of the company is in charge, or *informal,* attended by a few managers and their assistants.

In addition, all clubs and societies have a committee which meets regularly to arrange functions for the members. This committee is elected by members of the society at the annual general meeting (AGM), as also are the committee officers, chairman, treasurer, and secretary.

Informal meetings in firms, which are the ones most frequently held, do not appoint a treasurer (no funds are involved as in societies or clubs) but all have a chairman and a secretary, whose roles are very important in the conduct of all meetings.

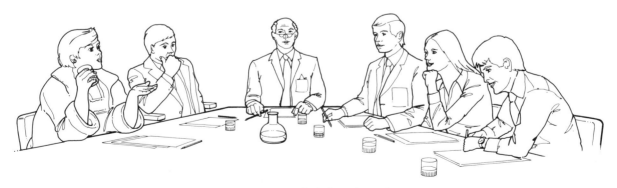

An informal meeting

Below is an example of a combined agenda and notice of meeting for a youth club.

COMMITTEE MEETING OF THE MIDCHESTER MANUFACTURING COMPANY YOUTH CLUB

to be held in the Committee Room of the Midchester Works Canteen at 2000 on Thursday, 20 November 199-

AGENDA

1 Apologies for absence

2 Minutes of last meeting

3 Matters arising out of the Minutes

4 Correspondence

5 Treasurer's Report

6 Secretary's Report

7 To discuss sports programme for summer 199-

8 To discuss raising of subscriptions

9 To discuss Christmas pantomine

10 Any other business

11 Date and time of next meeting

Jane Marsh
Secretary

THE SECRETARY'S RESPONSIBILITIES

Well before a meeting:
- circulate the notice of meeting and agenda,
- circulate copies of the minutes of the previous meeting,
- book room in which meetings will be held,
- arrange for refreshments (if needed),
- prepare cards with names of committee members (if appropriate),
- type out chairman's agenda (see p. 290),
- prepare attendance register (see p. 291).

Immediately before a meeting:
- ensure that telephone calls are re-routed and that personal callers are seen by someone else,

- check that room booked for meeting is free and place notice on door 'MEETING – please do not disturb',
- collect files, papers, etc., which will be needed during the meeting,
- place supplies of plain paper and pencils round the table for committee members to take notes,
- arrange for water, glasses and ashtrays to be available.

During the meeting:
- have notebook and spare pencils or pens at hand,
- have a table to write on if possible,
- make sure you can hear all that is said,
- circulate the attendance register and make sure everyone signs it,
- note apologies for absence (if any),
- make notes of the *decisions* which are arrived at and names of people taking part in them. There is no need to take down all that is said during discussions. When an opportunity arises, read through what you have written and write names or technical words clearly in longhand in the margin of your notebook.

After the meeting:
- gather up files, documents, minute book, attendance register and name cards,
- consign any rough notes left to the wastepaper bin (some may be confidential so tear them all up into small pieces),
- remove notice from outside the door,
- leave room tidy, gathering up used glasses, cups onto a tray, type minutes (see p. 290) as soon as possible. Let chairman have a rough draft in double or treble line spacing and checked with the agenda to ensure that nothing has been left out.
- give final copy of minutes to chairman for his approval,
- circulate copies of minutes when approved (if this is normal practice),
- file copy of minutes in minutes book and cross-reference the topics covered (see p. 291).
- enter date and time of next meeting in your's and your employer's diary and book room (if date fixed).

THE CHAIRMAN'S ROLE

Some women object to being called a 'chairman' and prefer 'chairwoman' – it is a question of personal preference. The word 'chairman' will be used throughout this chapter to avoid confusion. The chairman's role is vitally important at a meeting, because he is there not only to prevent time-wasting arguments, and irrelevant discussions, but to ensure that the items on the agenda are taken in their proper order. He may take part in discussions, but has to stay strictly impartial, although he has a casting vote if he wishes to use it. The chairman's ruling must be taken as final in all matters of order and precedence. He or she may be challenged, but this must be by at least four members. The chairman must not allow discussion unless there is a 'motion' (see p. 293) before him. Speakers are obliged to address the chair, and if the chairman intervenes, the speaker must at once stop speaking.

Voting can be done in three ways: by voice (if it is obvious that the voting is unanimous), by show of hands; by ballot if secret voting is required.

A shareholders' meeting

AGENDA AND NOTICE OF MEETING

The secretary and the chairman draw up an agenda together. It must be sent out well before the date of the meeting, so that members have time to plan ahead.

An agenda is in the following order:
1. Minutes of the last meeting.
2. Matters arising from the minutes.
3. Apologies for absence.
4. Correspondence (if this applies).
5. Other matters to be discussed.
6. *Any other business.
7. Date, time and place of next meeting.

*This allows any matters *not* on the agenda to be raised, but they should be only of minor importance.

```
VINER'S WINE MERCHANTS LTD
Commercial Road
PORT TALBOT
West Glamorgan
SA13 5GL


A meeting of the directors of the above company will be held on
Tuesday 16 November 199- at 1430 in the board room.

AGENDA


1    Minutes of the last meeting
2    Matters arising:
     (a) Falling sales in Midlands
     (b) Australian wine imports
3    Apologies for absence
4    Opening of new branch in Kent
5    Any other business
6    Date and time of next meeting
```

Notice of Meeting

A notice of meeting may take the form of a memo for an informal meeting to be held in a firm. Below is an example of a notice in this form.

```
MEMORANDUM

From  Sales Director              Ref AB/CD

To    Area Sales Managers         Date 20 May 199-


MONTHLY SALES MEETING

The above will be held on 15 June 199- in the Board Room at 1000

AGENDA
1    Sales figures for April/May 199-
2    Sales Conference scheduled for August 199-
3    Opening of new branches in Newcastle, Cardiff and Bristol
4    Any other business
```

Chairman's Agenda

This is similar to the normal agenda, but the layout allows him space to write notes at the side of items under discussion (see p. 290) and may also include additional information so that he can take part in discussions without having to refer to files.

VINER'S WINE MERCHANTS LTD
Commercial Road
PORT TALBOT
West Glamorgan
SA13 5GL

A meeting of the directors of the above company will be held on Tuesday 16 November 199- at 1430 in the board room.

AGENDA		NOTES	
1	Ask Mr S Smithson, Company Secretary to read the minutes	1.	
2.	Matters arising. It is expected that questions may be asked about:	2.	
	(a) Falling sales in midlands	(a)	
	(b) Australian wine imports	(b)	
3.	Ask Mr Smithson to read apologies	3.	
4.	Opening of new branch in Kent	4.	
	(a) Suitable premises have been located in Tonbridge Wells	(a)	(details attached)
	(b) Alternative situation is in	(b)	(details attached)
5.	Any other business	5.	
6.	Chairman to declare meeting closed	6.	

MINUTES

Minutes are a record of the proceedings of a meeting, and are required by law for a limited company (see p. 3). Their purpose is to provide an accurate and concise record of the business transacted at a meeting.

The agreement of the committee is signified when the chairman has asked if all present agree that the minutes are correct. If there is no dissentient voice, his signature is proof that they are and he is said to have 'confirmed' or 'approved' the minutes as a true and accurate record.

Information in minutes is always recorded in the third person and past tense (see p. 292). The details will usually follow the agenda (see p. 288) and include:

- name of group, type of meeting and day, date, time and place,
- name of chairman (or whoever is presiding as chairman),
- name of secretary,
- names of committee (listed alphabetically),
- names of any others in attendance who may have been invited to give advice,
- minutes of last meeting (read by secretary, or, to save time, circulated beforehand with the agenda),
- matters arising,
- apologies for absence,
- business to be discussed in order listed on agenda,
- any other business (i.e. not on agenda),
- date, time and place of next meeting (unless it is a formal AGM, when obviously it is not possible to settle it beforehand).

At the foot of the minutes is a space for the chairman's signature, with his name typed below it, followed by 'Chairman'. The date is written at the time of signing.

Minutes of formal meetings are numbered consecutively for a series of meetings, and quite often the method used is the number of the minute followed by the year, e.g. the first item for January 1990 would be 1/90 and the last item in 1990 might be 150/90, depending upon the number of items minuted. Topics are often cross-referenced at the back of the minute book, with the subject headings listed alphabetically. The minute book is confidential and should be locked away when not in use.

The secretary should record each motion and resolution passed, together with the names of the proposers and seconders. If he thinks it important, the chairman may, at his discretion, ask for a particular point to be 'minuted'. Some discussions are very lengthy and it is not necessary to record all that is said.

TERMS USED IN CONNECTION WITH MEETINGS

There are a great many of these, and most secretarial handbooks (e.g. Chambers *Office Oracle*) list them in full. Below is a selection of those most commonly used:

Ad hoc committee	A special purpose committee.
adjournment	Postponement of completion of business, or meeting.

MINUTES OF MEETING

A meeting of the directors of Viner's Wine Merchants was held on Tuesday 16 November 199- at 1430 in the board room.

PRESENT

Mr David Lloyd (Chairman)   Mr Peter Richards
Mr Paul Anchor   Mr S. Smithson
Ms Marion Davis   Mrs L. Mason (Secretary)
Mr Arthur Jones

The minutes of the last meeting, held on 18 October 199- were read, approved and signed by the Chairman.

MATTERS ARISING

1. Falling sales in Midlands. It was pointed out by Mr Richards that two retail outlets had been closed and that until alternatives had been found, sales would continue to be affected. RESOLVED: That the Midlands Area Manager should be instructed to expedite negotiating two replacement retail outlets.
2. Australian wine imports. Mr Paul Archer reported in detail on sales of Australian wine, which are increasing steadily in all areas. RESOLVED: That imports be increased by 10% for the current year, with a review in 199-

APOLOGIES FOR ABSENCE

An apology was received from Miss Elizabeth Knight, who is ill.

OPENING OF NEW BRANCH IN KENT

Mr Jones reported on the premises in Tonbridge Wells and Southborough, pointing out that the situation of the latter was more favourable and rates and rent lower than in Tonbridge Wells. RESOLVED: to open a new branch in Kent in Southborough in August 199- and to finalise negotiations regarding premises as soon as possible. Other details to be discussed at December's meeting.

ANY OTHER BUSINESS

Mr Smithson raised the question of the regular wine tasting events, to which customers are invited, and pointed out that it is debatable whether the policy of making no charge was now justified by the ensuing sales. RESOLVED: to provide a buffet supper with the various wines for sampling, and make a charge of £5, starting with the wine tastings planned for 199-.

DATE OF NEXT MEETING

It was decided to hold the next meeting of the directors on 14 December 199- at 14.30

Chairman .... Date ....

292

amendment	An alteration to a motion.
ballot	A secret vote.
co-option	An invitation to someone to serve on a committee because of specialist knowledge.
ex officio	'By virtue of office' – an ex officio member is entitled to sit on a committee because of another position he or she holds.
hon sec	Honorary secretary – an unpaid secretary.
joint committee	Co-ordination of two or more committees.
lie on the table	A motion that a particular matter should 'lie on the table' means that it is discussed and finalised at a later date.
motion	A proposal put forward at a meeting. The mover of the motion is called the proposer and the supporter is called the seconder.
nem. con.	Means 'no one dissenting', i.e. no votes are cast against a motion although some members may have abstained from voting.
proxy	Someone may be appointed to vote on behalf of absent member, subject to approval.
quorum	The minimum number of members who must be present at a meeting to make it valid, as laid down in the regulations of the organisation.
rider	An addition to a resolution after it has been passed. It adds to, not alters the sense of, a resolution.
teller	Person who counts votes at a meeting.

SECRETARIAL TIPS

1 At a formal meeting, it is usual for the secretary to sit on the right-hand side of the Chairman.

2 Make sure that spare plain paper is available (A5 size will be adequate) to use in case a ballot is taken.

3 It is helpful to keep a separate shorthand notebook for meetings – dated and ruled after each meeting.

4 Check that any follow-up actions decided upon at the meeting have in fact been taken.

5 A loose-leaf book for minutes, which can easily be extended, is useful.

6 If it is necessary that someone in a meeting *has* to be contacted because of an emergency, a note should be passed to the member concerned, who can slip out quietly without disturbing the others.

QUICK REVISION

1 A secretary's responsibilities start well before a meeting is held and consist of circulating notice of meeting and agenda, circulating copies of minutes of previous meeting, booking room for meeting and ....
....

2 Immediately before a meeting a secretary should make arrangements for telephone calls to be re-routed and personal callers to be seen by someone else, check that room booked for meeting is free, collect files needed during the meeting, and ....
....

3 During the meeting, the secretary should ensure that she can hear clearly, that apologies for absence are noted, ensure that notebook and spare pencils or pens are to hand, and ....

4 After a meeting, the secretary is responsible for gathering up files, documents, minute book attendance register and name cards; removing notice from outside door; typing minutes; gathering up used glasses, and cups; and ....
....

5 The list of items to be discussed at a meeting is ....

6 Minutes are the ....

7 A supply of plain A5 paper may be needed at a meeting for a ....

8 A loose-leaf book is useful for minutes because ....

9 If a member of a meeting has to be contacted in an emergency, the correct procedure is ....

10 Follow-up actions taken at a meeting should be ....

ASSIGNMENT

Draw up the agenda which would have been circulated for the meeting of the Midchester Manufacturing Company Social Club held on Thursday 20 November 199- in the Canteen at 2000. The minutes are below:

```
MINUTES   of the Meeting of the Committee of the Midchester
          Manufacturing Company Social Club held on Thursday 20
          November 199- in the Canteen at 2000.

Present:   J Allan (Chairman)
           P Carter
           H Jones
           L Williams (Treasurer)
           G Ziebarts (Secretary)
```

1.	APOLOGIES	There were no apologies for absence.
2.	MINUTES	The Minutes of the meeting held on Thursday 23 October 199- were approved and signed by the Chairman.
3.	MATTERS ARISING	There were none.
4.	CORRESPONDENCE	The Secretary read a letter from Mr H Moore who has left the firm and regrets that he has to resign from the Committee. It was agreed that a letter should be sent to Mr Moore to thank him for all his help with the work of the Committee.
5.	TREASURER'S REPORT	This had been circulated and was accepted.
6.	SECRETARY's REPORT	This had been circulated and was accepted.
7	SPORTS PROGRAMME	A sub-committee was formed who agreed to deal with the preliminary arrangements for this. The sub-committee to consist of P. Carter, H. Jones and L. Williams.
8.	RAISING OF SUBSCRIPTIONS	It was agreed to defer discussion of this until the Annual General Meeting in February 199-.
9.	CHRISTMAS PANTOMIME	As last year's Christmas pantomime had not been successful financially and in fact had made a loss, it was agreed not to go ahead with the one for 199-.
10.	ANY OTHER BUSINESS	Concern was expressed by several members about the fall in membership of the Social Club and it was agreed to advertise in the Works Magazine as soon as possible to try and interest new employees in the Club.
11.	DATE AND TIME OF NEXT MEETING	This was fixed for Thursday 18 December at 2000 in the Works Canteen.

Signed . . . . Chairman

Date . . . .

CHAPTER 17

Planning Ahead

DIARIES

One of the most important duties of a competent secretary (many experienced secretaries have said *the* most important) is looking after the diaries in an office. Diaries give the day's programme at a glance, and this is a vital part of their use. In addition, they enable a secretary to space out her employer's engagements, and to allocate adequate time between callers, visits, meetings, lunch engagements and dinner engagements, to ensure that he or she has time to deal with correspondence and, above all, to carry out the work for which they are trained. A busy executive is not helped if there are no spare moments free during a working day because of an over-zealous or inexperienced secretary arranging a too-tight daily schedule.

Space should always be allowed after meetings and discussions which may run over their allotted time. If appointments have to be cancelled, because of illness or other emergencies, an apology should be telephoned as soon as possible, and a new appointment made.

The Three Diaries

Two large diaries are essential – one on the desk of the executive, for his use, and one for his secretary's use, on her desk, by the telephone. Both diaries must contain the same entries, so a frequent check during the day by the secretary is an important part of looking after diaries, when any engagements made by her boss must be transferred to her own diary, or, when she has made engagements for him, these must also be entered in *his* diary. This is relatively easy to do during even the busiest day once it has been incorporated into routine, and is so important that it must be given priority.

What is much more difficult but equally important is the transfer of any appointments which may have been made over lunch or dinner, and jotted down in a pocket diary – (the *third* diary) by an executive. Tact and diplomacy are called for on the part of the secretary. A regular, brief enquiry about the pocket diary, timed perhaps at the end of the morning's dictation (the right

time is crucial!), should be sufficient. If her boss continues to make appointments without revealing them, a firmer comment is called for from his secretary, for this 'third diary' (if not amalgamated into general diary planning), can throw into chaos those carefully organised programmes of meetings, etc. arranged weeks, perhaps months, beforehand. Executives who are unaware of what an experienced secretary's duties may be are the least co-operative about their pocket diary.

Diary Entries

Entries in diaries must be plainly written (or printed, if handwriting is not clear). Appointments made by telephone should be confirmed in writing (the same day if possible), and full details of the visitor or person to be visited entered in the diary – name, initials, title (e.g. Works Manager, Chairman, Mrs, or Miss), name and address of firm or private address, telephone number (with code if outside area), and extension number. Vague notes such as 'Miss Jones 10 am', will not mean very much a week later. A secretary's diary will require additional notes for herself.

Friday 20 March 199___

0930	Mrs Mary Wyman, Office Equipment Ltd, Kingston-upon-Thames (Buyer)
1100	Mr K Knight, Assistant Manager, Lloyd's Bank, High Holborn.
1300	Lunch at the Hilton International, with 3 directors from J Law & Sons, Glasgow.
1430	Meeting with Accountants, Thompson and Gregory, Whitaker Lane, Aldwych.
1630	Mr K Evans, Sales Manager, Everton Engineering Co., Bristol.
1930 for 2000	Dinner at the Plaza Restaurant, Piccadilly Circus, with 2 directors from Rank Xerox, London. Wife to accompany me

Page from an executive's diary

Friday 20 March 199___

0930	Mrs Mary Wyman, Office Equipment Ltd, Henley Road, Kingston upon Thames (Buyer) Tel 245 491 EX 15
1100	Mr K Knight, Assistant Manager, Lloyds Bank PLC, High Holborn, London Tel 665 430 Ex 73
1300	Mr Barber to lunch at the Hilton International with 3 directors from J Law & Sons Ltd, Mackenzie Street, Glasgow Tel 537 888
1430	Mr Barber to attend meeting with his accountants, Thompson & Gregory, Whitaker Lane, Aldwych Tel 987 554
1630	Mr K. Evans, Sales Manager, Everton Engineering Co Ltd, Ship Street, Redlands, Bristol Tel 993 871 Ex 42
1930 for 2000	Dinner at the Plaza Restaurant, Piccadilly Circus with 2 directors from Rank Xerox, Hammersmith, London, Mrs Barber included.

A typical page in a secretary's diary

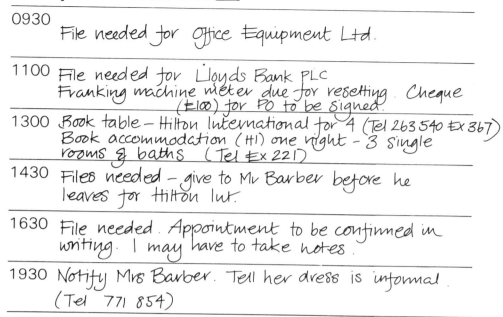

Other personal notes for a secretary might include her own dental appointment, a reminder to return a file borrowed from the Filing Department, or a meeting of the Social Club committee of which she is a member.

The average commercial diary usually gives very little space for essential details. Usually, too, these diaries run from January to December (perhaps providing a few extra weeks before and after the beginning and ending of the year), and it therefore becomes impossible to use the diary to plan very far ahead after the autumn. Five-year diaries are available, but they are equally short of space for details of each engagement. A more efficient arrangement for diaries is for the pages to be duplicated and kept in loose leaf binders – one for the executive and two for the secretary. She can then use one of her pages to duplicate her employer's, and one for her own personal reminders (see illustrations on p. 298 and above). Loose leaf pages have the additional advantages that they can be typed on, when appointments have been finalised, and extra sheets added, when engagements become more frequent than usual, or involve more complex arrangements.

Diary pages (or diaries) should be filed at the end of each year, or when they have ceased to be used. They form an extremely useful record of events with times as well as dates, and in a court case several years ago, a diary was accepted as evidence of an executive's whereabouts on certain days by the presiding judge. Diaries should be kept for a minimum period of at least 5 years, but the decision about disposing of them must be made by the executive.

In a large firm, the receptionist inside the main entrance keeps a diary of all callers expected that day in her appointments book. The information about these appointments is given to the receptionist by the secretaries, ideally the day before, but at the very latest, first thing each morning. A quick check in the diaries on her own desk and that of her employer must be one of the first duties a secretary carries out when she arrives each morning.

OTHER REMINDER SYSTEMS

A helpful and simple reminder system is a list of engagements for the day, week or month, typed in duplicate, with one copy on the executive's desk and one kept by his secretary – both prominently displayed. These must be updated whenever necessary, otherwise they are worse than useless, they are misleading.

Computers can be used as electronic desk diaries. When appointments have been made they can be entered on the computer, seen on the VDU, and printed out when required. A computer can also be programmed to enter appointments arranged at regular times during the year and special events (e.g. birthdays) for each successive year. Also, appointments being entered on a computer at times which should be left free will be rejected automatically (holidays, for instance). The obvious disadvantage to an electronic diary is that it may be too easy for other people to read, so it must be used with discretion in order to preserve confidentiality.

A more direct way of reminding executives, secretaries and other employees who may be involved in important commitments, is by the use of coloured wallcharts. If the chart is large and detailed enough, it can act as an 'at-a-glance' check of appointments for several months ahead. Many charts are metal and the multicoloured stickers are small magnets in different shapes and sizes which can easily be attached and moved around when necessary. Colour coding is useful on a wallchart of this kind – conferences, meetings, exhibitions, business trips and staff holidays can be shown on the chart with a 'legend' at the side explaining which colour (or shape) indicates which kind of event. A visual reminder system of this kind is also useful for the other members of staff, in addition to executives and their secretaries, who may be involved in the organisation of forthcoming events (see Chapter 7 on charts).

A filing memory aid (otherwise called a 'tickler' or 'bring forward' system) could also be used. Twelve suspended pockets in a filing cabinet drawer (or in a concertina file on a desk top – see p. 101) is a helpful reminder system.

The pockets are useful for filing copies of letters and memos, as well as rough drafts and notes referring to events scheduled to take place weeks or months ahead. Each pocket is labelled with the name of the month. Into each pocket are placed details, in date order, of conferences, business trips, meetings, anniversaries, school holidays, visits of VIPs, and social engagements.

A daily check must be made regularly on a follow-up system by the secretary to ensure that anything in that day's folder has been, or is being, dealt with. At the beginning of each day, after the diary check, yesterday's reminders can then be placed at the back of the folder.

BRING FORWARD SHEET   Date for action _____

Subject of reminder   _____

Special notes   _____

_____

_____

_____

Member(s) of staff concerned   _____

_____

_____

ACTION TAKEN   _____

BY   _____

DATE   _____

SECRETARIAL TIPS

1 Write provisional entries in a diary in pencil. If they have to be altered (or cancelled) they are easily erased, avoiding messy alterations.

2 Try not to make appointments during periods normally allocated to routine tasks, such as giving dictation.

3 When appointments are not kept, telephone and try to find out why.

4 Use the calendar for special reminders (such as an important anniversary), by circling round the date with a highlighting pen.

QUICK REVISION

1 The two important uses of diaries are ....

2 Two steps to be taken if an appointment has to be cancelled are ....
....

3 The danger of the 'third diary' is ....

4 The action to be taken the same day as appointments are made by telephone is
....

5 Diary entries should contain full details such as: ....
....

6 In large firms, who else needs information about the day's appointments, besides an executive and his secretary? ....

7 An electronic diary can be used for forward planning but has the disadvantage of
....

8 When a diary is finished with, it should be filed because ....

9 A 'tickler' or 'bring forward' system is a helpful memory aid because it contains pockets in which ....

10 A quick and easy 'special reminder' is by ....

ASSIGNMENTS

1 You are personal assistant to Mr Geoffrey Barber, Managing Director, GPR Developments Ltd, 78 East Square, Chelmsford, Essex CM1 1JN. Tel: (0245) 355211. Sign all the following letters yourself. For the purpose of this assignment, you can assume that these appointments will take place about one month ahead.

   (a) Type a letter confirming arrangements made by telephone for the lunch at the Hilton International, Park Lane, London, with three directors from J. Law & Sons, Glasgow. (Refer to: Secretary's own reminders, p. 299).

   (b) Confirm in writing appointment with accountants, Thompson and Gregory.

   (c) Type a letter to the Plaza Restaurant, Piccadilly Circus, London, confirming arrangements made by telephone for dinner at 1930.

2 You are Mandy Brown. You have been secretary to John Harris, Technical Director of Messrs Bullfrog, Croak & Pond, for six months.
   One morning, the Chairman's secretary rings to ask if Mr Harris can meet the Chairman and an important client within the next two or three days. The 'VIP' is a potential customer with a large order to place and he is looking for technical information before deciding with which of three firms he will place the order. Your firm is one of the three possibilities. Your diary shows your boss is free for lunch tomorrow (in fact, the whole day is free). In your boss's diary is the entry 'Ian', which doesn't mean anything to you.

You confirm with the Chairman's secretary that your boss will be able to meet him and the VIP for lunch tomorrow, and enter this in both your diary and John Harris'.

Your boss does not return to his office all day (this was anticipated) and the following morning, he does not appear (this was not anticipated). At 0957 he calls (from a payphone) to say he is off to see a client in Dundee, and will be away for 3 days. He rings off before you have a chance to tell him about the important lunch with the Chairman.

(a) What has caused the problem?

(b) What immediate action should you take?

(c) Make detailed suggestions to ensure this situation does not arise again.

3 The diary page below is from an executive's own diary. What important details have been omitted from the entries which have been made?

Wednesday 5 September

0900	
1000	J Saunders for interview
1100	Meeting in Executive Suite
1200	
1300	Lunch with Managing Director of Office Equipment Ltd.
1400	
1500	P. Upland calling
1600	
1700	Pick up wife

CHAPTER 18

Travel

In a firm without a Travel Department, a secretary's duties may include the arranging of business journeys for her employer and/or herself. Even in a small firm, the Managing Director or Sales Manager may often frequently travel abroad.

ITINERARIES

Three main decisions have to be made for any journey, whether in the UK to a nearby city, or overseas to several capital cities:

- destination.
- method of travel (air, road, rail or a combination of all three). Travel by sea is used infrequently today, partly because of the time factor, and partly because passenger liners are not available.
- date of departure.

After the above has been definitely decided, a check-list should be typed out in alphabetical order, as follows:

- dates(departure and return),
- destination,
- health documents (e.g. inoculations/vaccinations update),
- hotels,
- insurance,
- itineraries,
- meetings/conferences,
- money,
- passport and visas,
- tickets,
- travel method,

and each item ticked as it is dealt with, so that nothing is forgotten. Then a new folder should be labelled with the name of the executive who is travelling, destination, dates of departure and return. Into this folder can be placed all the documents connected with the business trip.

The itinerary has to be agreed next, in consultation with your executives. It may need redrafting several times, depending upon the length of the trip, transport arrangements and the number of commitments (meetings, for example) abroad.

An itinerary must include:

- Date and time of departure.
- Airport, airline, terminal number and flight number (for air travel).
- Coach and seat number (for rail travel).
- Time of arrival at each stopping place.
- Name of person meeting on arrival (if it applies).
- Names, addresses and telephone numbers of hotels.
- Engagements – names, addresses and telephone numbers of people being visited.
- Date of return.

ITINERARY

Mr E Styles Sales Director - visit to Bristol, Birmingham, Manchester and Glasgow

Monday 20 January - Friday 24 January 199-

Monday 20	Depart LONDON Paddington, Platform 7, Coach D, Seat 11. Dinner in restaurant car.	1845
	Arrive BRISTOL Temple Meads station. Stay over-night at Central Hotel, Lower Castle Street, Tel: (0272) 249218 room booking confirmed by telex 15 January.	2057
Tuesday 21	Appointment with Mr Kenneth O'Brien, Production Manager, The O'Brien Steelworks Ltd, Victor Road, Bedminster, Tel: (0272) 31129.	1030
	Depart BRISTOL Temple Meads, Platform 2, Coach B, Seat 3.	1500
	Arrive BIRMINGHAM New Street Station.	1620
	Appointment with Ms Sally Gray, Office Adminis-trator, The Midland Secretarial Agency, Frederick Road, Edgbaston, Tel: (021) 622 1508.	1700
	Stay overnight at Imperial Hotel, Queensway, Tel: (021) 634 8711.	

Wednesday 22	Depart BIRMINGHAM New Street Station, Platform 1, Coach K, Seat 15. Lunch in restaurant car.	1140
	Arrive MANCHESTER Piccadilly Station. Book into Thistle Hotel, Palatine Road, Northenden, Tel: (061) 225 3765.	1340
	Appointment with Chief Buyer, Mr George Williams, Shaw & Short Ltd, Wholesalers, Whitaker St, Tel: (061) 226 8019.	1500
	Dinner with Mr Williams, Thistle Hotel. Stay overnight at Thistle Hotel.	1930
Thursday 23	Department MANCHESTER Victoria Station, Platform 5, Coach H, Seat 9. Refreshments in buffet car.	0755
	Arrive GLASGOW Central Station. Lunch with Mr Ian M'Bride, Purchasing Officer, Macmillan & Mcmaster Ltd, at the Royal Hotel, Bothwell St, Tel: (041) 226 5566.	1129
	Visit with Mr M'Bride to Macmillan & Mcmaster, Castle Bank St, Tel: (041) 225 5533.	1530
	Depart GLASGOW Central Station, Platform 3, Sleeping Berth, Coach A, Berth 10 - available from 2230 onwards.	2300
Friday 24	Arrive LONDON Euston Station. Sleeping Berth to be vacated by 0800.	0653

It is most important that time is allowed between each engagement for rest, also for correspondence, reports and possibly drafting speeches. Time should always be allowed after long flights for recovery from 'jet lag', which may make travellers irritable, sleepy and hungry at odd times, until their bodies have adjusted to the new time scale.

How to Lessen the Effects of Jet Lag

Before a flight:

- If flying east, go to bed earlier than usual and get up earlier. Eat meals earlier.
- If flying west, go to bed later and get up later than normal. Eat meals later.

(Note that flying directly south does not cause jet lag, but flying south-east or south-west does. Unfortunately, most long journeys involve this.)

During a flight:

● Sleep, if possible. If not, relax. Drink plenty of fruit juice and water and avoid alcohol. Plenty of fruit in place of normal food also helps.

After a flight:

● Try to fit in sleeping and eating with the new time zone, rather than taking naps and snacks at odd times. Exercise within 24 hours of arrival will counteract the effect of jet lag. Arriving on a Saturday ensures a free weekend and gives time for re-adjustment and rest.

Tests have shown that jet lag can cause up to a 10 per cent decrease in mental speed, accuracy and vigilance, so it is important for business people on long business trips to try to offset the worst effects.

Time Zones

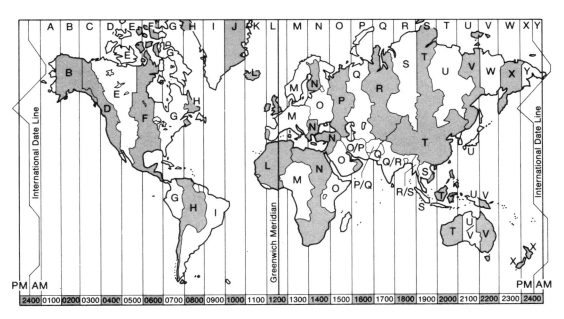

World times at 12 noon GMT

Draft itinerary in hand, travel agents can be contacted to check air and rail travel times. Make sure that times on itinerary are local time (of country of destination), and not Greenwich Mean Time (GMT). Some countries (France, for example), are ahead of the UK in summer because of daylight saving.

Travel by sea is used infrequently these days, because of the time factor. Bear in mind public holidays abroad – more numerous and often quite different from British Bank Holidays. When travel times are agreed, the final travel itinerary can be typed and reservations made for plane or train via a travel agent. Book as far in advance as possible, especially if a journey has to be made during school holidays. Also, try to avoid the crowded London airports (Heathrow and Gatwick) on Sundays, Mondays, Fridays and Saturdays, especially in the summer, particularly between 8 am and noon. If travel at the weekend is unavoidable, Heathrow is better than Gatwick.

DOCUMENTS

Passport

Check that passports do not need renewing. It is usual for business people who travel on their firm's behalf to carry a ten-year passport, although, if one were needed quickly, a one-year passport would be quite adequate for travel in Europe. Ten-year passports can be obtained from passport offices in Belfast, Glasgow, Liverpool, Newport, Peterborough and London. Application forms for new passports can be obtained from most post offices, and local job centres. It is advisable to apply at least a month before a new passport is needed, longer if possible.

Visas

Visas may be needed for some countries and must also be arranged well beforehand. Allow 4–6 weeks for obtaining a visa. The relevant Embassy or Consulate may be written to direct; travel agents are very helpful. A valid passport is essential to obtain a visa. It is also important to check that a businessman will be allowed to enter a country (this does not mean that he is a wanted criminal!). It may be that he is Jewish and certain Arab countries will not permit him to leave the airport. In EEC countries, only British citizens can travel without visas – Commonwealth citizens have to have a visa, e.g. an Australian needs a visa to go to Paris.

HEALTH

Vaccination, immunisation or inoculation are necessary for certain countries outside Europe. The Department of Health will supply leaflet SA 35 giving details of inoculations for travellers abroad. It is possible to obtain last-minute inoculations at a centre in London run by Thomas Cook on any day except Sundays, and certificates are issued at once. Even though there are no definite requirements, if there is any danger of cholera, hepatitus, etc.,

308

injections are strongly advised. Smallpox certificates are no longer required anywhere in the world.

Insurance

Insurance cover is essential against accident, loss, theft, car breakdown and, above all, illness. Many countries have no Health Service similar to the one in the UK, and even a short, simple illness such as a stomach upset can be expensive. The UK has a reciprocal health arrangement with EEC and EFTA countries, under which medical expenses in Europe are reimbursed on returning to the UK, but arrangements about this have to be made beforehand, in this country, from the Department of Health and Social Security. Travel agents will arrange insurance, and there are comprehensive policies available which will cover all of the above risks.

CURRENCY AND TICKETS

Currency

Currency (money) can be in the form of:

- Travellers' cheques.
- Foreign currency (in some countries this is limited, e.g. in December 1987 it was only £14 in Greece!). It should be ordered a few days beforehand.
- Eurocheques.
- Credit cards – American Express, Barclaycard, Access.
- Letter of credit (where a large sum of money has to be transferred to a foreign city).

Travellers' cheques take a few days to organise, so should be arranged well beforehand, bearing in mind that the business person has to go to the bank (or wherever he or she may be obtaining them from) to sign them before they are handed over. This cannot be done by the secretary. A note of the serial numbers of travellers' cheques should be kept separately, in case of a claim due to loss or theft.

Tickets

Collect these in good time (several days before travelling) if possible and check and double-check them. Place tickets in travel folder, with copy of itinerary.

HOTEL BOOKINGS

These should be confirmed by letter when made by telephone. Many hotels can be contacted by telex. Rooms are booked from the day of arrival to the day of departure, and the hotel should be given the following details:

- Time of arrival, especially if late in the evening and food is needed.
- Time of departure.
- Whether transport is required from hotel to airport or station.
- Type of room: with private bath or shower; single or double. Air-conditioning would be particularly important in a hot climate.
- Car parking: if travel is by car, make sure there is car parking available; book a parking space, or a lock-up garage, if necessary.
- Special diets: mention if vegetarian, fat-free, diabetic or any other type of special diet is required.

Place confirmations (copies of letters or telexes) of hotel booking in travel folder. It will be important for the businessman to be able to produce these on arrival at the destination as confirmation of bookings.

Finally...

For a business trip lasting several days, type out daily itineraries on A6 sized cards convenient for slipping into pocket or handbag giving brief details of times of appointments, names of hotels and flight or train departure times, with address and telephone number of each local embassy or consulate (if abroad, and most particularly in Third World countries).

```
ITINERARY

Ms Diana Devinson's schedule for Thursday 4 April 199-

0830   depart Paddington Station, London
1117   arrive Hereford
1215   Lunch at Queen's Hotel, Hereford
1430   Tour round Haldane's Hosiery Works
1600   Tea at Haldane's Hosiery Works
1715   depart Hereford Station
2003   arrive Paddington Station
```

Make out a *folder* for each city or country (for a long trip). Place *documents in order* of requirement. Type *baggage labels* – stick-on and tie-on – and a supply for *inside* each piece of luggage, in case the outside ones are lost. *Place labels in envelopes* clearly marked with description of contents. Type a *list of car hire firms* in each city together with name and telephone number of a travel agent.

Place in a separate wallet documents needed en route:

- tickets,
- passport,
- health documents,
- travellers' cheques,
- foreign currency.

A mini first-aid kit is a boon on long journeys, containing:

- aspirin or paracetamol,
- plasters,
- bandages,
- cotton wool,
- throat pastilles,
- antiseptic ointment,
- scissors,
- tweezers,
- safety pins,
- stomach pills,
- indigestion tablets,
- travel sickness tablets (if appropriate),
- insect repellant,
- anti-malaria tablets (if appropriate),
- water sterilisation tablets (if appropriate).

RAIL AND ROAD TRAVEL

Travelling by Rail

Travelling by train is preferred for long journeys in the UK by many business people, as it enables them to work free from the pressures of driving; sleeping berths are available on many trains to large cities.

When arranging a journey by rail:

- Book a seat, checking whether first or second class is required, and whether smoker or non-smoker.
- For a long journey, check restaurant facilities and book a sleeping berth for an overnight journey.

- Make sure that there is only one railway station in the city where your boss will get off the train. Some cities have more than one (London is an example) and your boss will not be pleased if the car sent to meet him or her has arrived at the wrong station!

Road Travel

Inland

If your employer is driving all the way to his destination, it is useful to have a route worked out with the mileage. The AA or RAC will supply routes, if requested, for members, or their handbooks can be used. On a long road journey, an overnight hotel may be necessary. In addition to an overnight stop, a suitable place for lunch, tea or coffee should be indicated.

Overseas

- Green insurance card is required for international driving abroad; UK insurance is only valid in the UK. In some countries an international driving licence is also required. A GB plate should be displayed (there is an on-the-spot fine for not complying in Italy and Switzerland).
- Check current driving regulations in force with regard to seat belts, advance warning triangles, shading of headlights and speed limits. Shading of headlights is compulsory in France.
- Check headlamps and foglamps for driving on the right-hand side of the road.
- Take up-to-date road maps and an A–Z of any large cities to be visited.
- Take first-aid kit (obligatory in Austria and West Germany).
- Car spares such as plug, points, fan belt, etc. can be useful in an emergency in an isolated area.
- A driving licence translation is required in Italy, which can be obtained from the AA, RAC, Italian Embassy or State Tourist Office in Italy.

TRAVELLING WITH YOUR EXECUTIVE

If you go with your executive, your role will be to take over some of the burden of the detail of the trip, so allowing him or her to concentrate on the important work which is the object of the journey. It is not an easy assignment and will be helped if you have a knowledge of the language of the country to be visited. It is important to organise your wardrobe so that you have the right clothes for hot climates and for social occasions, as you may be expected to accompany your executive. Most of your time, however, will be taken up by dealing with correspondence, attending meetings with your executive, taking the minutes, and writing reports.

312

In Your Executive's Absence

Answer any letters which you can. Pass on technical letters to the executive's assistant (or deputy), or write and explain that the executive is away and will deal with the matter on his or her return (give date of return). Visitors and telephone callers should be referred to someone who can attend to their requirements, if you are unable to do this yourself. Committees should be informed in advance of your executive's absence. You may be able to attend meetings in his or her place – offer to do so if you think it is feasible.

Any emergencies which arise while the executive is away must be dealt with tact and common sense. Refrain from contacting them (perhaps at great expense) if it can possibly be avoided. Unless it is an emergency which necessitates the executive returning at once, it will only add to an executive's worries while away to be burdened with office problems.

Making Use of Any Spare Time

Time at your disposal while your executive is away can be put to good use as below:

- Making 'dead' files or re-organising filing system.
- Updating the 'follow-up' system.
- Having your typewriter serviced/arranging to see a more up-to-date one.
- Going to any convenient exhibition of office equipment and collecting an up-to-date supply of leaflets and prices.
- Visiting your local library to see if there are any reference books which would help you with your job.
- Re-doing your index of frequently used telephone numbers.

TRAVEL REFERENCE BOOKS

ABC Guide to International Travel	Published 4 times a year, gives all information necessary for travellers by air – inoculations, vaccinations, visas, currency.
ABC Railway Guide *ABC World Airways Guide*	Give detailed information about trains and flights and are issued every month.
AA Large Atlas	Gives information about climate, products, population, terrain, principal cities.
Large scale road maps of the area to be visited	Must be as up-to-date as possible.
Guide books of the area to be visited	Must be as up-to-date as possible.

AA or RAC Handbooks	(Free for members only) contain useful maps, information about hotels, ferries, distances between cities and population, in the British Isles.
Bus and Train Timetables	Must be up-to-date.
A–Z Maps of Cities	Contain detailed street maps.
Hints to Businessmen	This is free and produced by the Department of Trade and Industry. It contains information on embassies and consulates, visas, and advice on the customs of various countries.
Statesman's Yearbook	Contains current information on countries of the world and international organisations. Published yearly.
Good Food Guide	Is published annually, and covers restaurants and hotels in the UK.

Also useful for travel information is Prestel (see p. 53) and Ceefax (see p. 54).

SECRETARIAL TIPS

1 Some firms have an account with a travel agent, who will carry out much of the work of making travel arrangements. If your job involves making frequent travel arrangements, and your firm does not have an account, suggest it to your employer.

2 Place tickets for air or rail travel in large, clearly labelled envelopes so that they do not get mislaid or slide into an inaccessible corner.

3 Remind boss about any inoculations 6–8 weeks before departure, if possible.

4 Remind boss to confirm next onward flight on arrival at each destination (even though booked in UK) *before* leaving airport, and to do this at each successive departure point.

5 Make a note of mileage at the start of a car journey for subsequent travel expenses claim.

6 Make a note for future reference when booking a seat on a train, whether a smoker or a non-smoker is required.

7 British Telecom's Weatherline gives information about weather conditions in the British Isles, and a local weather forecast from the Meteorological Office – useful in winter at the start of a long car journey.

8 With an Executive Travelcard, telephone calls can be made from any telephone. The main advantage is that when staying in a hotel, long-distance calls are billed to the card holder. Hotel charges for long-distance calls are notoriously high.

QUICK REVISION

1 The three factors to be considered before making travel arrangements are ....

2 A folder to contain all the documents connected with a journey should be labelled with ....

3 Time should be allowed between engagements on a business trip for ....

4 Travel documents required for overseas business trips are ....

5 Even for short train journeys, there are three points to check: ....

6 Apart from checking the arrival time of a train, what else should be verified? ....

7 What is useful for a journey to be done by car? ....

8 When confirming a hotel in writing, what must be specified? ....

9 Three reference books useful for a business trip abroad by plane are: ....

10 Five different ways of making good use of any spare time while your boss is away are: ....

ASSIGNMENTS

Photocopy the expenses claim form illustrated on p. 316, then complete the assignment.

1 It is realised that a company car would be available in many of the examples below, but for the purpose of this exercise, assume that 'mileage allowance' is paid at the rate per mile indicated. Find the total expenses claimed in each case, and make out a claim for expenses on a copy of the sheet on the next page. Date each one for last week. Sign on behalf of the person concerned.

    (a) J. F. Ellis – Technical Director. Mileage allowance 26p per mile.

Monday:	25 miles. Lunch £11.50. Hotel 2 nights bed and breakfast £80. Dinner £15.
Tuesday:	Lunch for two £36. Travel 170 miles.
Wednesday:	Train fare £52. Lunch for two £32.
Friday:	Travel 80 Miles. Lunch £8.

ASTON MACHINE TOOLS LIMITED

CLAIM FOR EXPENSES

Name ....   Position held ....

Expenses for week ending ....   Car mileage rate ....

199-	Details	Amount	Daily totals
Monday			
Tuesday			
Wednesday			
Thursday			
Friday			

Analysis of expenses:

Travel _____   WEEKLY TOTAL _____

Telephone _____

Meals and hotels _____

TOTAL _____

Signature ....   Date ....

(b) Mr D. S. Wright – Executive Export Promoter.

Monday: Car hire 3 days at £11 per day plus 9p per mile (total 3 days' mileage – 320 miles). (Note: car hired because abroad – air fare already paid by company, hence not on claims for expenses.) Lunch with clients (2 days) £57 total. Dinner 3 evenings with clients £166 total. Car parking fees £11. Telephone £33.

(c) Mr R. U. Reddy – Sales Representative. Mileage allowance 18p per mile.

Monday: Travel 87 miles. Lunch £6.
Tuesday: Travel 40 miles. Lunch (with client) £18 total.
Wednesday: Travel 130 miles. Lunch £5.40. Dinner £12. Bed and breakfast one night £22.
Thursday: Travel 150 miles. Lunch £6.50.

(d) Mr R. J. Cooper – Export Director

Monday: Taxi from Helsinki airport to Hotel Maarski 40 finmarks @ 7.2 finmarks to the £1. Dinner with clients in Helsinki £150.
Tuesday: Car hire £16 per day (3 days) plus 13p per mile. Dinner with clients £39. Telephone £18.75.
Thursday: Lunch with clients £96. Return car to garage. Total mileage 230 miles. Taxi to airport £4.50. Hotel bill £232. Taxi from airport to home £15.

(e) Mr A. Taylor – Sales Representative. Mileage allowance 20p per mile.

Monday: Travel 230 miles. Lunch with clients £19.
Tuesday: Travel 50 miles.
Wednesday: Telephone £2.48. Travel 32 miles.
Thursday: Train fare £21. Lunch with client £18.70. Taxi fare £3.20.
Friday: Telex £9. Travel 150 miles. Lunch with client £15.

2 Your employer is planning a business trip to the Middle East, visiting Oman, Saudi Arabia and the Yemen Arab Republic, in January. He wants to know:

- For which of the countries a visa will be required.
- London addresses of consulates.
- Languages spoken.
- Currencies.
- Max/min temperatures.
- IDD Code.
- Local time compared with GMT.
- Public holidays in January.
- Vaccinations recommended.
- Any special health risks.
- Regulations regarding alcohol.
- Regulations regarding smoking.
- Business/social hints.

All the information you need is in the extracts from the *ABC International Guide* on pp. 318–25.

OMAN

Local Time: GMT +4
Capital: Muscat
Area Of The World: Middle East
Language: Arabic and English
Electricity: 220/240V AC 50 Hz
Int. Direct Dialling Code: 968
Driving Licence: National (valid for 7 days, for longer periods a local licence must be obtained from Police on presentation of National or International licence).
BBC World Service:

	KHz		
Morning	12095	11955	9410
Daytime	17885	15420	9535
Evening	12095	9410	1413

Currency Rial (OMR 1.00 = 1000 Baizas)
Notes: OMR 1, 5, 10, 20, 50; Baiza: 100, 200.
Coins: Baiza: 5, 10, 25, 50, 100, 200, 500.

Business Hours
Banking: 0800-1200 Sat-Wed; 0800-1130 Thur.
Office: 0730-1400 Sat-Wed; 0800-1300 Thur.
Shops: 0800-1300 & 1600-2000; Souks (markets) 0800-1100 & 1600-1900 (official rest day Friday).

Passport/Visa

Prohibited Entry and Transit: The Government of Oman refuses admission and transit to (a) Holders of Israeli passports and holders of passports containing visa for Israel, valid or expired or entry and departure stamps. (b) Passengers in possession of any data indicating that they have been in Israel or are in communication with Israel.

Passports: Required by all and endorsed 'Oman, Sultanate of Oman' or 'all countries'. Endorsement showing Muscat or Muscat and Oman are not acceptable. Passports must correspond and be exactly as shown on the N.O.C. (No Objection Certificate). If N.O.C. is based on an old passport and the passenger is travelling on a new passport, the old passport should be attached to the new passport when entering Sultanate of Oman. Entry overland requires the express permission of the Government of the Sultanate of Oman. Passengers who arrive with different passport or no spare pages are subject to deportation.

Visas: Required by all except: Omani and GCC Nationals born in their respective countries. Visas are not required by businessmen, doctors, engineers, lawyers and their immediate families (wife and children provided they travel together), who are originally nationals of the G.C.C. (Gulf Cooperation Council) countries, provided their passport indicates their status in the profession column. No visas are issued for touristic purposes. The Oman Immigration Authorities have advised carriers that they will be fined OMR 1000 for every passenger arriving without a visa or who does not have a No Objection Certificate. Such passengers will be refused admission. Carriers will not confirm bookings for any passenger without evidence of these documents. Visas are issued by representative of Oman but only on submission of N.O.C.

Transit: Exempt from visa requirements are passengers who continue their journey to a third country, provided the transit time is a minimum of 2 hours and a maximum of 12 hours. Tickets with reserved seats and other documents for their onward journey must be held and their passport will be retained during the transit period. They are not allowed to leave the airport.

Business Visa: If the visit is sponsored, application should be made to sponsor for No Objection Certificate giving details of passport, date and place of birth, private and company address, occupation, approx. date of visit and date of last visit. The sponsor should send the NOC to the visitor, who should present it to the embassy for a single entry visa stamp. If the visit is unsponsored application should be made at an early date to the General Manager, Oman Chamber of Commerce and Industry, P.O. Box 4400, Ruwi-Muscat Hx 389 MB a/b AL & HORFA. Holders of visit visas are not permitted to enter with a work visa before completion of one year from the last visit. Work visa is for two years and before completion of the same, entry is prohibited for those who hold another work visa under new sponsorship. The visa and NOC only valid for entry to Oman by air/sea. For entry through borders (by road) a Road Permit is required in addition to visa/NOC. A Business/Visit Visa can be extended up to a maximum of 90 days only. For stay exceeding 90 days a fine of OMR 10 per day is imposed and prosecution is liable.

Note: No person is permitted to enter Oman overland without written permission of the Immigration Department. Permission to travel to Salalah by Gulf Air must be sought first in writing from the Office of the Governor. Non-compliance with visa regulations will result in heavy fines.

Customs
Currency
Import & Export: No restrictions.
Import Allowances: (a) A reasonable quantity of tobacco products. (b) 8 oz. perfume.
Prohibited: Alcoholic beverages (one bottle alcoholic beverage can be imported provided passenger is non-Omani and non-Muslim), firearms (unless with prior permission). Obscene literature.
Only one piece of hand baggage is permitted.

Air Travel
International Airport: Muscat (Seeb) 25mls/40kms. Taxi.
Airport Tax: Depart International OMR 3.00. Exempt: Diplomats and passengers transiting within 24 hours.

Climate:
Muscat	Jan	Feb	Mar	Apr	May	Jun	Jul	Aug	Sep	Oct	Nov	Dec
Temp °C Max	25	25	28	32	37	38	36	33	34	34	30	20
Min	19	19	22	26	30	31	31	29	28	27	23	20
Humidity % am	72	73	71	64	58	72	77	82	75	69	69	70
pm	71	73	70	68	60	72	77	80	77	74	72	71
Rainfall (mm)	28	18	10	10	0	3	0	0	0	3	10	18

Health
Vaccination Certificates Required: Yellow Fever if arriving within 6 days of leaving or transiting infected areas.
Immunisation Recommended: Cholera, Malaria, Typhoid, Polio.
Health Risks: Risk of Malaria all the year below 1000 metres including urban areas.
Precautions To Be Taken: Boil or sterilize drinking water and milk. All food should be well cooked. Avoid bathing in fresh water.

Public Holidays
1990: Apr 26-28* Eid-Al-Fitr; Jul 2-4* Eid-Al-Adha.
*Dates are dependent on a lunar calendar and may differ by 1 or 2 days from dates given.

Business And Social Hints
There is a formality about the conduct of business and men must wear suits and ties for meetings and functions. Appointments should be made well in advance and adhered to. It is considered impolite to be late. There is frequently an exchange of visiting cards by those attending meetings. The Omanis are happy when visitors can speak some Arabic but English is widely used in business. At other times both men and women should dress circumspectly as in any Muslim country. Smoking is permitted in Oman but there are many buildings where it is restricted. It is advisable to look for signs to this effect. Alcoholic drink is usually obtainable in good hotels and restaurants, elsewhere it is banned by law. Gratuities of not less than 10% are customary for porters, cab-drivers and restaurant staff.

SAUDI ARABIA

Local Time: GMT +3
Capital: Riyadh
Area Of The World: Middle East
Language: Arabic (all correspondence with Government Departments must be in this language), English
Electricity: 125/215V AC 50/60 Hz
Int. Direct Dialling Code: 966
Driving Licence: International or National (valid for 3 months). Women are not permitted to drive.

BBC World Service:

	KHz		
Morning	12095	11955	9410
Daytime	17885	15420	9535
Evening	12095	9410	1413

Currency Saudi Riyal (SAR 1.00 = 20 Qursh = 100 Hallalah)
Notes: SAR: 1, 5, 10, 50, 100, 500.
Coins: Qursh 1, 2; Hallalah: 1, 5, 10, 25, 50.

Business Hours
Banking: 0830-1200 & 1700-1900 Sat-Wed; 0830-1200 Thur.
Office & Shops: 0900-1300 & 1630-2000 Sat-Thur. (Ramadan 2000-0100)
Government Offices: 0730-1430 Sat-Wed.1900.

Passport/Visa

Prohibited Entry and Transit: The Saudi Arabian authorities refuse admission and transit to (a) Holders of Israeli passports. (b) Holders of passports valid for Israel and containing a visa (either valid or expired) or any indication that the passenger has been in Israel. (c) Jewish passengers. (d) Holders of passports of North Yemen who are no originally citizen of North Yemen unless holding valid visa. (e) Those arriving in apparent intoxicated state, the delivering carrier will be held responsible and their regular operation to Saudi Arabia might be jeopardized due to violation of the Islamic laws. (f) Those who do not comply with the Saudi Arabian requirements regarding general appearance and behaviour.

Note: If a pilgrim arrives without the required health documents the pilgrim will either be quarantined or be vacinnated at the airport. Neither the pilgrim not the carrier will be charged for quarantine fee. Pilgrims must enter Saudi Arabia via Jeddah or Medina only. This regulation is applicable both outside and during the pilgrim season.

Passports: Required by all except: Moslem pilgrims holding pilgrim passes (all pilgrims must be in possession of tickets with confirmed reservation for the onward or return journey). Holders of Laissez-Passer issued by U.N. and holders of Seaman Book (travelling on duty). Passports must be valid for at least 6 months beyond estimated stay in Saudi Arabia.

Visas: Required by all except: Nationals of Saudi Arabia, Bahrain, Kuwait, Qatar, Oman or United Arab Emirates. Holders of re-entry permits and 'Landing Permits' issued by Saudi Arabian Ministry of Foreign Affairs.

Additional information: No foreign passenger who is working as a domestic servant in Saudi Arabia should be transported to Saudi Arabia unless he holds a valid Non-Refundable Return Ticket. Wives and housemaids must be met at the airport by husbands or sponsor and hold confirmed onward reservations to their final destinations. All women proceeding to Saudi Arabia for working purposes must have return tickets except those who are working with Saudi Government. Agencies.

Transit: Passengers will not be allowed to leave the transit lounge at international airports unless holding an Entry Visa as well as a Transit Visa. Visa not required by: (a) Passengers proceeding to a third country and having a confirmed ticket to a third country. They should leave by the same or next connecting flight (max. connecting time for Dhahran, Jeddah and Riyadh 12 hours) and are not allowed to leave the transit lounge at the airport. One landing only permitted in Saudi Arabia, except holders of diplomatic passport with valid transit visa from Saudi Consulate. To avoid discomfort overnight e.g. in the case of a missed connection it is advisable to hold a transit visa for Saudi Arabia. There are very limited catering facilities at Dhahran, Jeddah and Riyadh transit lounges. (b) Merchant seamen holding a valid passport or Seaman's Book travelling on duty and arriving in Saudi Arabia by ship and proceeding by first connecting aircraft, complete procedure to be arranged by shipping agent concerned in Saudi Arabia. Or by aircraft and proceeding to join their ship in a Saudi port provided: (1) their ship is already in port or will arrive within 24 hours after the arrival of the seaman involved and the passenger is met by the shipping agent. (2) The station manager of the arriving airline in Saudi Arabia is informed prior to arrival of name of passenger, shipping company and name and address of agent, flight number and date of arrival - if passenger arrives on Thur or Fri emphasize this, thus enabling the station manager of the delivering airline to take necessary measures on the preceding working days. A copy of the telegram/telex must be attached to the passenger ticket. Also applicable to the wife of the captain, even if not holding seaman book or visa in passport provided escorted by husband and holding legal documents proving marital status.

Transit passengers hosted by airlines to hotels: Passengers who proceed to the Kingdom and have transit visa valid for three days from the Saudi Arabian Consulate and the transporting carrier would like to host them in a hotel, the immigration has no objection if the transporting carrier holds the responsibility of their stay until they travel on the first connecting flight. Not applicable to nationals of: Albania, Bulgaria, China People's Rep., Cuba, Czechoslovakia, German Democratic Rep., Hungary, Korea Dem. People's Rep., Mongolian People's Rep, Poland, Romania, USSR, Viet Nam Socialist Rep. and Yugoslavia.

Exit Permits: These are required for nationals and alien residents of Saudi Arabia except for members of the US armed forces who are already registered in Saudi Arabia. One passport photo is required and issue is by the Chief of Police about three days after application.

Customs
Currency
Import & Export: Israeli currency prohibited.

Import Allowances: (a) 600 cigarettes or 100 cigars or 500 gr. tobacco. (b) A reasonable amount of perfume. The importation of the following food stuffs are permitted: fruits, nuts, sweets, honey and other easily accessible food in easy-to-open cans.

Prohibited: Alcoholic beverages (also applies to transit passengers, pig meat and by-products, contraceptives, firearms or other lethal weapons, cultured or natural pearls, drugs of a narcotic nature and diet pills except medicines for personal use and provided holding prescription, horses (unless special permission granted), all types of live birds (except certain rare species e.g. Habari bird).

Air Travel
International Airports: Dhahran 5mls/8kms. Taxi. Jeddah (King Abdul Aziz Int.) 11mls/18kms. Bus, taxi. Riyadh (King Kahled Int.) 22mls/35kms. Bus, taxi.

Airport Tax: not applicable.

Climate:

Riyadh	Jan	Feb	Mar	Apr	May	Jun	Jul	Aug	Sep	Oct	Nov	Dec
Temp °C Max	21	23	28	32	38	42	42	42	39	34	29	21
Min	8	9	13	18	22	25	26	24	22	16	13	9
Humidity % am	70	63	65	64	51	47	33	35	42	47	60	75
pm	44	36	36	34	31	30	19	19	24	25	33	52
Rainfall (mm)	3	20	23	25	10	0	0	0	0	0	0	0

Health
Vaccination Certificates Required: Yellow Fever if arriving within 6 days of leaving or transiting countries any part of which is an infected area and all passengers arriving from Angola, Bolivia, Brazil, Chad, Colombia, Gambia, Ghana, Kenya, Malaysia, Nigeria, Peru, Somalia, Sudan, Zaire and Zambia. Cerebro-Spinal Meningitis (CSM) by pilgrims and other passengers arriving from infected areas.

Quarantine: Persons without a valid **Yellow Fever** certificate – if required – will be vaccinated upon arrival and are subject to quarantine. A **Cholera** vaccinaiton is imposed during Hajj.

Immunisation Recommended: Cholera, Malaria, Typhoid, Polio.

Health Risks: Risk of Malaria throughout the year in provinces other than the Eastern, Northern and Central Provinces, the high altitude areas of Asir Province, and the ruban areas of Western Province (Jeddah, Mecca, Medina, Taif).

Precautions To Be Taken: Boil or sterilize drinking water and milk. All food should be well cooked. Avoid bathing in fresh water.

Public Holidays
1990: Apr 26-28* Eid Al-Fitr; Jul 2-4* Eid Al-Hajt; Sep 23 National Day.
*Dates are dependent on a lunar calendar and may differ by 1 or 2 days from the date given.

Business and Social Hints
Business is conducted in a serious and formal manner and an appointment must always be made in good time. Smart suits and ties are expected for meetings and functions. Punctuality is advisable. The exchange of visiting cards frequently takes place by all concerned. Dress should be circumspect for both men and women at all times. Smoking is quite usual but there are restrictions in some buildings. Alcoholic drink is strictly forbidden by law throughout the country. Gratuities of not less than 10% are usual for cab drivers, porters and restaurant staff.

YEMEN ARAB REPUBLIC

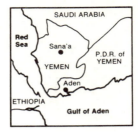

Local Time: GMT +3
Capital: Sana'a
Area Of The World: Middle East
Language: Arabic, some English
Electricity: 125/215V AC 50/60 Hz
Int. Direct Dialling Code: 967
Driving Licence: International.
BBC World Service:

	KHz		
Morning	12095	11955	9410
Daytime	17885	15420	9535
Evening	12095	9410	1413

Currency Yemeni Riyal (YER 1.00 = 100 Fils)
Notes: YER: 1, 5, 10, 20, 50, 100.
Coins: Fils: 1, 5, 10, 25, 50.

Business Hours
Banking: 0800-1200 Sat-Wed; 0800-1130 Thur.
Offices: 0800-1230 & 1600-1900 Mon-Wed; 0800-1100 Thur.
Shops: 0800-1300 & 1600-2100 Sun-Thur.

Passport/Visa
Prohibited Entry and Transit: The Government Authorities of the Yemen Arab Republic refuse entry and transit facilties to (a) Holders of Israeli and South African passports. (b) Holders of passports containing visas, valid or expired, for Israel or South Africa or any indication e.g. entry or exit stamps tha the holder has visited these countries.
Passports: Required by all except holders of (a) Laissez-Passer (travelling on duty) issued by United Nations. (b) Seaman's Books (travelling on duty) issued by any country except Israel or South Africa.
Visas: Required by all except: Nationals of Yemen Arab Rep., Yemen People's Dem. Rep., Algeria, Bahrain, Egypt, Iraq, Jordan, Kuwait, Oman, Qatar, Saudi Arabia, Syria, UNited Arab Emirates and ACC countries holding return or onward tickets and suffient funds for their stay to a minimum of US$500 and holders of re-entry permits.
Issue: By representatives of Yemen Arab Rep. in Algeria (Algiers), China People's Rep. (Beijing), Czechoslovakia (Prague), Djibouti (Djibouti), Egypt (Cairo), Ethiopia (Addis Ababa), German Democratic Rep. (Berlin), Germany Federal Rep. (Bonn), India (New Delhi), Iraq (Baghdad), Italy (Rome), Japan (Tokyo), Jordan (Amman), Kuwait (Kuwait), Lebanon (Beiruit), Libya (Tripoli), Morocco (Rabat), Netherlands (The Hague), Pakistan (Islamabad), Qatar (Doha), Saudi Arabia (Jeddah, Riyadh), Somalia (Mogadishu), Sudan (Khartoum), Switzerland (Geneva), Syria (Damascus), Tunisia (Tunis), UAE (Abu Dhabi), United Kingdom (London) and USA (New York & Washington).
Transit Visa: Not required by those continuing their journey to a third country by the same aircraft and not leaving the airport.
Re-entry Permit: Required by all alien residents and holders of a visa wishing to return. To be obtained from the Immigration Dept. before departure.
Exit Permit: Required by all passengers staying longer than 1 month days. To be obtained from the Immigration Department in town, free of charge.

Customs
Currency
Import: Local currency prohibited. However nationals of Y.A.R. may import up to a max. of YER 2000. Foreign currency in excess of USD 2000 must be declared on arrival.
Export: Foreign – no restriction, but amounts in excess of USD 2000 only if declared on arrival.
Import Allowances: (a) 200 cigarettes or 50 cigars of ½lb tobacco. (b) 2 pints alcoholic beverage (aliens only). (c) 1 pint perfume or toilet water.

Air Travel
International Airports: Sana'a 8mls/13kms. Bus, taxi. Taiz (Al-Janad) 2.5mls/4kms. Bus, taxi. Hodeidah 4.5mls/7kms. Bus, taxi.
Airport Tax: Not Applicable.

Climate:

Kamaran Is.	Jan	Feb	Mar	Apr	May	Jun	Jul	Aug	Sep	Oct	Nov	Dec
Temp °C Max	28	28	30	32	35	36	37	36	36	34	31	28
Min	23	23	25	26	28	29	29	29	29	28	26	24
Humidity % am	79	77	76	74	70	66	64	67	71	68	74	77
pm	70	65	65	60	56	55	52	55	58	57	63	68
Rainfall (mm)	5	5	3	3	3	0	13	18	3	3	10	24

Health

Vaccination Certificates Required: Cholera if arriving within 5 days from or via infected areas. **Yellow Fever** if arriving within 6 days from or via infected areas or all African countries except Algeria, Egypt, Libya, Morocco and Tunisia. Immunisation Recommended: Cholera, Malaria, Typhoid, Polio.
Health Risks: Risk of Malaria Sep-Feb throughout the country excluding Hajja and Sada provinces. Rabies.
Precautions To Be Taken: Boil or sterilize drinking water and milk. All food should be well cooked. Avoid bathing in fresh water.

Public Holidays

1990: Apr 26-28* Ei-Al-Fitr: May 1 Labour Day; Jul 2-4 Eid-Al-Adha; Sep 26 National Day; Oct 1* Prophets Birthday.
*Dates are dependent on a lunar calendar and may differ by 1 or 2 days from date given.

Business And Social Hints

There is some formality about the way in which business is conducted. It is necessary to arrange an appointment in good time and having done so, to be punctual. Men should wear smart suits and ties for meetings and other functions. An exchange of visiting cards by those present is customary. On other occasions, westerners should dress in conservative fashion. Smoking is quite acceptable but there are considerable restrictions on the sale of alcoholic drink, this is limited to the visitor's hotel room, as it is prohibited by law to Y.A.R. citizens. Gratuities of not less than 10% are usual for cab drivers, porters and restaurant staff.

London Addresses of Consulates & Overseas Representatives

JORDAN: 6 Upper Philimore Gardens, W8 7HB. Tel: 937 3685/7. Hours: 1000-1400.
KENYA; Kenya House, 24/25 New Bond Street, W1. Tel. 636 2371/5.
  Hours: 0930-1200, 1400-1530.
KOREA REPUBLIC: 4 Palace Gate, W8 5NF. Tel. 581 3330. Hours: 1000-1200, 1400-1600.
KUWAIT: 46 Queen's Gate, SW7. Tel. 589 4533. Hours: 0930-1600.
LAO PEOPLE'S DEM. REP.: see separate list at end.
LEBANON: 15 Palace Gardens Mews, W8 4QQ. Tel. 727 6696. Hours: 0930-1230.
LESOTHO: 10 Collingwood Road, SW5 0NR. Tel. 373 8581. Hours: 0900-1300, 1400-1600.
LIBERIA: 2 Pembridge Place, W2 4XB. Tel. 221 1036.
LIECHTENSTEIN: see Switzerland.
LUXEMBOURG: 27 Wilton Crescent, SW1X 5SD. Tel. 235 6961. Hours: 1000-1200 (Visas). 1000-1230, 1430-1630 (General Enquiries).
MACAU: Suite 01-01, 22 Devonshire Street, W1N 1RL. Tel: 224 3390. Tlx. 28955 MEDINT G. Fax. 01 224 0601. Hours: 0930-1700.
MADAGASCAR DEM. REP.: 16 Lanark Mansions, Pennard Road, W12 8DT. Tel: 746 0133. Fax: 01-746 0134. Hours: 0900-1300.
MALAWI: 33 Grosvenor Street, W1X 0DE. Tel: 491 4172/7. Tlx: 263308 KWACHA G. Hours: 0930-1700.
MALAYSIA: 45/46 Belgrave Square, SW1X 8QT. Tel: 235 8033. Hours: 0900-1300, 1400-1700. Passports: 0945-1245.
MALI: see separate list at end.
MALTA: Malta National Tourist Office, Suite 207, College House, Wright's Lane, W8 5SH. Tel: 938 1140. Tlx: 266083. Hours: 0900-1730. High Commission Tel: 938 1712.
MAURITANIA ISLAMIC REP.: see separate list at end.

MAURITIUS: 32/33 Elvaston Place, SW7 5NW. Tel: 581 0294.
Hours: 0930-1300, 1400-1700. Tourist Info: 49 Conduit Street, W1. Tel: 437 7508/9.
MEXICO: 8 Halkin Street, SW1X 7DW. Tel: 235 6393. Hours: 0930-1300, 1500-1600.
MONACO: 4 Audley Square, W1Y 5DR. Tel: 629 0734. Hours: 1000-1330, 1430-1730.
MONGOLIA: 7 Kensington Court, W8 5DL. Tel: 937 0150. Hours: 1030-1230, 1430-1630
(closed Wed).
MOROCCO: 97-99 Praed Street, W2. Tel: 724 0719.
MOZAMBIQUE: 159 New Bond Street, W1. Tel: 493 0694. Hours: 0900-1300.
MYANMAR: 19A Charles Street, W1X 8ER. Tel: 499 8841. Hours: 1000-1300.
NEPAL: 12A Kensington Palace Gardens, W8 4QU. Tel: 229 6231, 229 1954. Hours: 1000-
1200.
NETHERLANDS: 38 Hyde Park Gate, SW7 5DP. Tel: 584 5040. Hours: 1000-1330
(Consular Section).
NEW ZEALAND: New Zealand House, Haymarket, SW1 4TQ. Tel: 930 8422. Tlx: 24368. Hours:
0930-1600.
NICARAGUA: 8 Gloucester Road, SW7 4PP. Tel: 584 4365. Consulate Tel: 584 3231.
Hours: 0930-1330.
NIGER: see separate list at end.
NIGERIA: 56-57 Fleet Street, EC4Y 1BT. Tel: 353 3776. Hours: 0930-1300 (Visa Section).
NORWAY: 25 Belgrave Square, SW1X 8QD. Tel: 235 7151. Hours: 0900 1230, 1330-1500.
Visa Section: 1000-1230.
OMAN: 44a/44b Montpelier Square, SW7 1JJ. Tel: 584 6782. Hours: 0900-1300.
PAKISTAN: 35 Lowndes Square, SW1X 9JN. Tel: 235 2044. Hours: 1000-1300.
PANAMA: 24 Tudor Street, EC4Y 0AY. Tel: 353 4792/3. Tlx: 8812982 PANCON G.
Hours: 0930-1700.
PAPUA NEW GUINEA: 14 Waterloo Place, SW1Y 4AR. Tel: 930 0922/6. Tlx: 25827 KUNDU.
Fax: 01 930 0828. Hours: Visas 0900-1300.
PARAGUAY: Braemar Lodge, Cornwall Gardens, SW7 4AQ. Tel: 937 6629. Hours: 1000-1500.
PERU: 52 Sloane Street, SW1X 9SP. Tel: 235 6867. Hours: 1000-1300.
PHILIPPINES: 9a Palace Green, W8 4QE. Tel: 937 3646. Hours: 0900-1300.
POLAND: Visa Section, 19 Weymouth Street, W1. Tel: 580 0476. Hours: 1000-1400
(closed Wed).
PORTUGAL: 3rd Floor, Silver City House, 62 Brompton Road, SW3 1BJ. Tel: 581 8722/4.
Hours: 0900-1330.
QATAR: 115 Queen's Gate, SW7 5LP. Tel: 581 8611. Hours: 0930-1600.
ROMANIA: 4 Palace Green, W8 4QD. Tel: 937 9667. Hours: 1000-1200.
RWANDA: see separate list at end.
SAO TOME & PRINCIPE: 42 North Audley Street, W1A 4PY. Tel: 499 1995. Tlx: 262513.
Hours: 0900-1200.
SAUDI ARABIA: 30 Belgrave Square, SW1X 8QB. Tel: 235 0303, 235 0831.
Hours: 0900-1230.
SENEGAL: 11 Philimore Gardens, W8 7QG. Tel: 937 0925/6, 937 3139. Hours: Visa Section:
0930-1330. Collection: 1600-1630.
SEYCHELLES: High Commission/Tourist Office, 111 Baker Street, 2nd floor, Eros House, W1M
1FE. Tel: High Commission: 224 1660. Tourist Office: 224 1670. Hours: 0900-1230, 1330-
1700 (Tourist Office only).
SIERRA LEONE: 33 Portland Place, W1N 3AG. Tel: 636 6483. Hours: 0930-1200, 1400-1700.
SINGAPORE: 5 Chesham Street, SW1X 8ND. Tel: 235 9067/9. Hours: 1000-1230, 1400-
1600.
SOMALIA DEM. REP.: 60 Portland Place, W1N 3DG. Tel: 580 7148/9. Hours: 0930-1630.
SOUTH AFRICA REP.: South Africa House, Trafalgar Square, WC2N 5DP. Tel: 839 2211.
Hours: 1000-1200, 1400-1600.
SPAIN: 20 Draycott Place, SW3 2RZ. Tel: 581 5921/3. Hours; 0930-1200.
SRI LANKA: 13 Hyde Park Gardens, W2 2LU. Tel: 262 1841. Tlx: 25844. Hours: 0930-1300.
SUDAN REP.: 3 Cleveland Row, St James, SW1A 1DD. Tel: 839 8080. Hours: 0900-1500.
Visas: 0930-1200.
SWAZILAND: 58 Pont Street, SW1X 0AE. Tel: 581 4976/8.
Hours: Mon-Thu 0900-1630 (1600 Fri).
SWEDEN: 11 Montagu Place, W1H 2AL. Tel: 724 2101. Hours: 0900-1230, 1400-1600.
SWITZERLAND: 16/18 Montagu Place, W1H 2BQ. Tel: 723 0701. Hours: 0930-1230.
SYRIA ARAB REP.: 8 Belgrave Square, SW1X 8PH. Tel: 245 9012. Hours: 1000-1100.
TAIWAN, REP. OF CHINA: Free Chinese Centre, 4th Floor, Dorland House, 14-16 Regent
Street, SW1Y 4PH. Tel: 930 5767. Tlx: 24324 FCCLDN G. Hours: 1000-1300.

TANZANIA: Visa Section, 43 Hertford Street, W1Y 7TF. Tel: 499 8951. Tlx: 262504.
  Hours: 1000-1230.
THAILAND: 29-30 Queen's Gate, SW7 5JB. Tel: 589 0173. Visa Section: 589 2857 2944.
  Hours: 0930-1230, 1400-1600.
TOGO: 30 Sloane Street, London SW1. Tel: 235 0147/9. Hours: 0900-1300, 1330-1630.
TONGA: 12th Floor, New Zealand House, Haymarket, SW1Y 4TE. Tel: 839 3287.
  Hours: 0900-1200, 1300-1700.
TRINIDAD & TOBAGO: 42 Belgrave Square, SW1X 8NT. Tel: 245 9351. Hours: 0930-1730.
TUNISIA: 29 Prince's Gate, SW7 1QG. Tel: 584 8117. Hours: 0930-1300.
TURKEY: Rutland Lodge, Rutland Gardens, SW7 1BW. Tel: 589 0360. Hours: 0930-1200.
TURKS & CAICOS ISLANDS: Represented by The West India Committee, 48 Albemarle
  Street, W1X 4AR. Tel: 629 6355.
UGANDA: Uganda House, 58-59 Trafalgar Square, WC2N 5DX. Tel: 839 5783/9.
  Hours: 0930-1730. Visas: 0930-1300.
UNITED ARAB EMIRATES: 48 Prince's Gate, SW7 2QA. Tel: 589 3434. Hours: 0930 1430.
U.S.A.: Visa Unit, 5 Upper Grosvenor Street, W1A 2JB. Tel: 499 3443. Visa Enquiries: 499 7010.
U.S.S.R.: 5 Kensington Palace Gardens, W8 4QS. Tel: 229 3215/6.
  Hours: 1000-1230 (not Wed).
UPPER VOLTA: see Burkina Faso.
URUGUAY: 48 Lennox Gardens, SW1X 0DL. Tel: 589 8835. Hours: 0900-1600.
VENEZUELA: 56 Grafton Way, W1P 5LB. Tel: 387 6727. Hours: 0930-1500.
VIET NAM SOCIALIST REP.: 12-14 Victoria Road, W8 5RD. Tel: 937 1912.
  Hours: 0900-1230, 1400-1700.
YEMEN ARAB REP.: 41 South Street, W1Y 5PD. Tel: 629 9905/8. Hours: 0930-1500.
YEMEN PEOPLE'S DEM. REP.: 57 Cromwell Road, SW7 2ED. Tel. 584 6607/8.
  Hours: 0900-1530. Visa Section: 0900-1300.
YUGOSLAVIA: 7 Lexham Gardens, W8 5 JU. Tel: 370 6105. Hours: 1000-1300.
ZAIRE: 26 Chesham Place, SW1X 8HG. Tel: 235 6137. Hours: 0900-1200.
ZAMBIA: Zambia National Tourist Office, 2 Palace Gate, W8 5NG. Tel: 589 6343/4.
  Tlx: 28956. Hours: 0930-1300, 1400-1700. Visas: 0930-1300.
ZIMBABWE: 429 The Strand, WC2. Tel: 836 7755. Tlx: 262115. Prestel: 344191.
  Hours: 0900-1700. High Commission. Tel: 836 7755.

Reproduced from the *ABC Guide to International Travel*, Church St, Dunstable, Beds LU5 4HB, UK.

3 Mr P. Hunt, Production Manager, is to be away on a business trip from Monday, 1
   March to Saturday 20 March 199-. Type out his itinerary from the following
   information which is somewhat out of order!
   Mr Hunt will travel back from New Zealand by Qantas, arriving at Heathrow at 2200.
   He will depart from Heathrow at 0730 and fly first to Helsinki by British Airways. He will
   stay at the Hotel Polar Espoo in Helsinki. His plane is scheduled to arrive at Helsinki at
   1030.
   From Helsinki he flies to Geneva by Finnair on Thursday, 4 March, leaving Geneva on
   Wednesday 10 March at 1345 for Tel Aviv. His flight number from Helsinki is 034. This
   arrives in Geneva at 1640, having left Helsinki at 1400. His hotel in Geneva is the
   'Splendide'.
   His hotel in Tel Aviv is the Ramada. He flies Swissair from Geneva and arrives at Tel
   Aviv at 1750. His flight number is 4817. At 0700 he flies from Tel Aviv on Monday 15
   March on flight number 55001 and arrives in Wellington, New Zealand at 2300, by
   Ben Gurion Airways. He leaves Wellington on Friday, 19 March at 1545. His hotel in
   Wellington is the Central. His flight number is 2855. His flight number from Heathrow
   on Monday 1 March was 913.
   Hotel telephone numbers: Splendide: 310 247
                               Polar Espoo: 523 533
                               Central: 613 492
                               Ramada: 422 111

CHAPTER 19

Business Entertaining

Business entertaining may consist merely of providing a cup of tea or coffee for a visitor to a firm, or it may be a large lunch party.

The secretary's role could be to assist generally, or to act as hostess. In any case, all arrangements must be completed before the function starts, whether the secretary attends it or not. Specialist outside caterers or the firm's executive canteen will take over the actual organisation of a function.

FORMAL AND INFORMAL

The simplest type of informal entertaining is tea or coffee served in the office, and it is important to use good china, on a tray with a clean traycloth, stands for teapot and hot water jug, and to provide saccharine for those who are weight-conscious. Biscuits should be on a separate plate for guests to help themselves. When serving coffee, ask guests if they would prefer black coffee, or coffee with milk (there is no such thing as 'white coffee'), and provide brown sugar, which many people prefer. If you are asked to serve, give visitors their tea or coffee first, and then, after serving the staff from your own office, leave, unless you are required to take notes.

A 'working lunch' is another type of informal business entertaining, where a light snack such as sandwiches, with soup, are provided, as well as tea, coffee, soft drinks and jugs of water. A large firm will have its own catering section who will provide these, when asked; if not, outside organisations can be found in Yellow Pages, but try to use one which has had a personal recommendation. Working lunches are often provided for meetings likely to go on all day (see p. 286).

For a more formal type of business entertaining such as a lunch or dinner, the firm's dining room would be used (or executive suite, if there is one). If the firm's own catering staff is to provide the meal, they must be given as much notice as possible, and told the type of meal required – hot, or cold, and the number of people expected. Wines will have to be chosen. If an outside restaurant is to be used, the manager must be given the same information as early as possible.

All arrangements for visitors will have to be made within an agreed 'budget' and most firms have a certain amount of money set aside for business entertaining with very clear limits as to what can be spent and how. If funds are running low (towards the end of the financial year, for example) money must be allocated to the best advantage.

GENERAL ARRANGEMENTS

As soon as the date, time and type of business entertaining have been decided upon, the following must be done:

- Inform firm's receptionist of date and time of arrival of visitor(s).
- Decide on venue – inside firm or outside. If outside facilities are necessary, obtain several estimates, and go to see the accommodation to check on what is offered in each case, making notes. The lowest price is not always the best value. Make sure you have the name, telephone and extension numbers of the person who will be the one with whom to liaise after making a final decision.
- If visit involves a tour of the factory, inform secretaries of any departmental heads who may be involved, and send them copies of itineraries.
- Ensure that responsibility for coffee, lunch, or tea is clear, so that it does not get overlooked!
- If an overnight stay is involved, accommodation and transport to a hotel has to be booked and possibly a dinner arranged, followed by some suitable form of entertainment.
- Make sure that visitors have time to themselves during their stay, if it lasts more than a few hours.
- Interpreters may be necessary for foreign visitors.

Arrangements for an Informal Lunch or Dinner for a Few People

- List guests.
- Send invitations – usually by post.
- Reserve table for provisional number of guests (confirm later).
- Arrange menu and wines (do not forget to ask for non-alcoholic drinks to be available).
- Type (or have printed) place cards if number of guests is more than 4.
- Confirm number of guests to restaurant.

Arrangements for Formal Lunch, Dinner or Dinner-dance

- Make list of guests with the names of their firms and business and any other titles.
- Reserve rooms provisionally, giving approximate number of guests.
- If any speakers, check availability.
- Confirm that guest of honour (if relevant) is available on the proposed date.
- Alter date of room reservation if this is necessary, after contacting guest and speaker.
- Draft invitation and have cards printed.
- Despatch invitations.
- Finalise menu, wines, cigarettes and cigars.
- Order floral decoration (hotel may include this in their charges).
- Table layout. The principal guest is seated on the chairman's right hand.
- Place cards.
- Background music (if any) and programme of speeches for printing.
- Entertainment (if any).
- Notify press (see pp. 340–3 for press release). Invitations to editors and/or reporters.
- If dinner dance, arrange for Master of Ceremonies.
- If any VIPs are arriving by train or plane, arrange for them to be met, and for return transport.

Arranging a Drinks Party

- Order drinks – spirits, wines, non-alcoholic drinks and ice.
- Order food (canapés, and other small 'nibbles').
- Hire glasses and trays, if necessary.
- Book people to serve drinks and food if party is not to be held at an hotel.
- Order cigarettes and cigars.
- Order floral decoration (if any).

INVITATIONS

There are two types of invitation: formal and informal. A formal invitation is shown at the top of p. 329.

Note that the name of the person invited is written by hand; the rest of a

```
Mrs Joanne Ashe requests the pleasure of the company of

. . . . . . . . . . . . . . . . . . . . . . . . . . . . . . . . . . . . . . . . . . . . . . . .
to a buffet lunch on Sunday, 15 December 199-
at 12 to 12.30pm.


The Beeches                                    23 November 199-
Hinton
EVESHAM                                                 RSVP
Worcestershire
B67 3BT
```

formal invitation is typed (or printed), often on a card. 'RSVP' is an abbreviation for 'Répondez s'il vous plaît' (French for 'Please reply').

The reply accepting the invitation is typed without signature or other handwritten addition.

```
Mrs T. J. Foster accepts with pleasure Mrs Joanne Ashe's
kind invitation to a buffet lunch on Sunday, 15 December
199- at 12 to 12.30pm.


2 Downesland Road
Dunsley
REDDITCH
Warwickshire
B83 8RB                                        26 November 199-
```

When refusing an invitation, it is polite to give a reason:

```
Mrs T. J. Foster regrets that she is unable to accept the
kind invitation of Mrs Joanne Ashe to a buffet on Sunday,
15 December 199- as she will be away on holiday at that
time.


2 Downesland Road
Dunsley
REDDITCH
Warwickshire
B83 8RB                                        26 November 199-
```

The reply to an informal invitation takes the form of an ordinary personal letter, whether it is an acceptance or a refusal.

---

2 Downesland Road
Dunsley
Redditch
Warwickshire   B83 8RB

Tel: Dunsley 7130

3 December 199-

Dear Margaret and Richard

I would be so pleased if you could come to a small buffet supper I am giving as a housewarming party on Friday, 19 December, at 7.30pm.

I look forward very much to seeing you both then.

With kind regards

Yours sincerely

Thelma J Foster (Mrs)

A formal business invitation might look like this:

The Directors of Viner's Wine Merchants Ltd
request the pleasure of the company of

. . . .

at a Winter Supper
at the Grand Hotel, Port Talbot
on Friday 5 December 199- at 8pm

Viner's Wine Merchants Ltd   12 November 199-
Commercial Road
Port Talbot
West Glamorgan
SA13 5LG   RSVP

SEATING PLANS

Seating is planned in advance, and details are sent out with the dinner arrangements. A typical seating plan is shown here. Note that the names end in the same place in the first and third columns and start in the same place in the second and fourth columns.

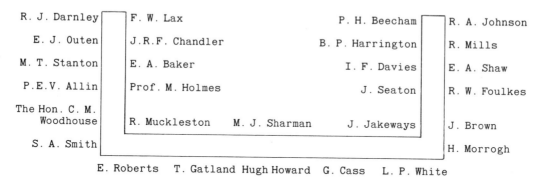

A seating plan

THE SECRETARY'S ROLE

If she acts as hostess, she must be there to greet guests as they arrive and see them as they leave. During the function, she must make sure they are being looked after. If necessary, she helps them to find their right tables. People standing alone should be introduced to each other. At no time during a function should a secretary talk about her own job or her employer's part in the firm. Great tact has to be exercised as well as charm.

After every function the secretary should:

- Collect and return any borrowed equipment - chairs, glasses, trays.
- Settle accounts for orchestra, flowers, hire of glasses, restaurant.
- Send letters of thanks to guest speaker and any organisations which have helped.
- Keep a file for future reference of copies of letters.

SECRETARIAL TIPS

1 Remember some overseas visitors will have restrictions on food for religious or other reasons. The relevant embassies will be helpful about this and any other important customs which should be taken into consideration.

2 Keep a card index with visitors' leisure interests, and any special dietary requirements.

3 In addition to a file for copies of letters in connection with a function, keep notes for

yourself, for future reference, with reminders of things which were overlooked, or could have been done better, or which had gone wrong.

4 A hand-out explaining something about the firm, its history, products and activities will be appreciated, especially by overseas visitors.

5 Not all invitations will be accepted – first bookings *must* be provisional. Some people do not bother to reply!

QUICK REVISION

1 The first step to be taken after the date, time and type of business entertaining have been decided upon is   ....

2 When a hotel booking is involved, what else may have to be arranged?   ....

3 When foreign visitors are expected, special dietary requirements may be necessary and also an   ....

4 The date of a dinner with a guest speaker has often to be arranged around the availability of him/her and also of the   ....

5 What must be done after a function?   ....
        ....

6 What is useful for future reference after a function has taken place?   ....

7 The secretary's role if she acts as hostess at a function is to   ....
        ....

8 People standing alone should be   ....

9 A secretary should also help people by   ....

10 Information about a firm is appreciated by visitors, especially overseas visitors and can be given by means of a   ....

ASSIGNMENT

You are employed by GPR Developments Ltd, 78 East Square, Chelmsford, Essex CM1 1JN (Tel. 0245 355211) as secretary to the Managing Director, Geoffrey Barber. He has asked you to start making arrangements for an informal lunch to be given in 6 weeks' time (use an appropriate date in any correspondence) for 8 people.
The venue will be the Golden Fleece Hotel, Park Way, Chelmsford.

(a) Draft an invitation in the form of a letter, with blanks for names and addresses to be inserted later.

(b) Write to the manager of the Golden Fleece Hotel, reserving a table for 9 (this will obviously include your boss) for the appropriate date and time. The number of guests is provisional, and will be confirmed later.

One of the party is an Israeli and does not eat pork. Ask for sample menus to be sent to you. Another guest does not drink alcohol.

(c) Type a guest list – invent suitable names, including two women, using details of function as main heading and date and time as sub-heading.

(d) Type place cards (you will not be attending the lunch).

(e) Dating letter for 10 days after first one to the Golden Fleece, write again, confirming that the number of guests will be 8 (the Israeli cannot come). Your firm has an account with the hotel and the lunch will go on the account. Remind the manager of the Golden Fleece that a signature only will be required when the account is presented.

CHAPTER 20

Conferences

The main reason for conferences is to exchange ideas and information, but they can also be arranged to:

- exhibit and demonstrate products,
- provide information on any new company developments,
- reward employees for their performance,
- introduce new personnel, planning and policies, solve problems
- provide publicity,
- promote goodwill among employees.

However, over and above all these are the opportunities conferences give to make personal and business contacts, and these justify the time and money which has to be expended. Budgeting is essential, and a close check must be kept on costs to make sure that the budget is not exceeded. Costs have a nasty habit of going up, especially as conferences are usually planned a long time ahead, so a 'contingency' fund is essential to cater for this.

ARRANGEMENTS

A conference may last a week, a weekend or a single day. Avoid bank holidays and if overseas visitors are to be invited, consider their bank holidays also (Chambers *Office Oracle* lists these). The date and the venue have to be decided upon first, and the accommodation booked provisionally. Planning for a conference usually starts months or even over a year ahead, as there is more likelihood of getting exactly what is required in the way of accommodation and facilities when ample notice can be given.

VENUES

Many large hotels offer rooms with everything necessary for conferences and this will be a great help, as much of the organisation can be left to them. It is important to go and see the facilities offered, check hotel bedrooms (if

A conference hall

required) and obtain estimates. It may be less expensive to take over the whole of a small hotel for the period of the conference, but it is essential that the hall to be used for the lectures, demonstrations, etc., is large enough for delegates' comfort.

The location should be convenient for rail and road transport. Car parking is a vital consideration – check that the hotel car parking will be adequate or that an arrangement can be made with the nearest National Car Park.

There are also professional conference organisers, who will attend to everything, but they will be very expensive.

The following will have to be carried out after the date and venue have been decided. Organising a conference is a job for more than one person and as much help as possible should be enlisted:

- Chairperson to be contacted, with a full briefing.
- Accommodation to be booked (provisionally).
- Programme to be drafted.

- Programme to be printed.
- Speakers to be contacted; after receipt of acceptances, a conference 'profile' to be drafted with a brief description of each speaker.
- Invitations to be sent including: a map of the area; a reservation form with tear-off reply slip; programme for each day with speakers; places of entertainment; address and telephone number for enquiries; a leaflet giving general information – (banks, places of worship, post offices, hairdressers, etc., places of interest, telephone numbers of railway stations, airport, coach station, also emergency numbers of nearest doctors, dentist, opticians and hospital).
- List of acceptances/refusals.
- Conference folders, which will include handouts and a list of delegates, together with name badges.
- Receipts to be printed (these are sometimes asked for by delegates whose fees are refunded by their firm).
- List of delegates, when final numbers are known.
- Confirmation of accommodation needed.

A reception desk at the entrance to the conference hall is necessary, where delegates check in, receive their folders (and receipts if required, together with certificates of attendance) and pin-on name badges with name of firm or organisation represented, under delegate's name. A different colour for the name badges of the staff assists delegates in locating them if they need help.

The folder should contain a plan of the venue and conference rooms (if more than one), a few sheets of paper for notes, perhaps a ball-point pen and a clear plan of where various events will take place and at what time. A spreadsheet on a computer is useful to set this out.

A separate area with a supply of leaflets about the firm, additional programmes and timetables is useful, with a member of staff in charge who can answer general enquiries.

Posters, etc., about the conference should be on display stands in or near the reception area.

Where the presence of the press is required (this does not always apply) the local and/or national press representatives should be sent a copy of the programme together with a press release (see p. 340–3).

A hotel specialising in conferences will supply all equipment needed in the form of visual aids, but this availability should be checked beforehand. Some may have to be hired.

Delegates may need some secretarial help, if the conference is to last several days and a room with a typewriter, typist, telephone and a fax machine would be invaluable. An interpreter service for foreign delegates may be required.

SAFETY AND SECURITY

Fire risks are heightened by people smoking and extra electrical equipment with temporary fittings. Fire exits should be marked clearly. Fire doors should always be left open while people are on the premises. Fire extinguishers must be prominently positioned. Extra insurance may be necessary – this should be checked with the hotel management and your firm's accountant.

AFTER THE CONFERENCE

- Letters of thanks to all who have helped are always appreciated and should be sent as soon as possible.
- Certain members of the hotel staff should be tipped – they will probably have worked especially hard and their efforts will have helped to make the conference a success.
- Any hired equipment should be returned at once, after checking that it is still in good working order.

Keep a conference file with copies of letters, lists, profiles, details of hotel or other facilities used and recommendations (or not). If press attended, keep copies of press cuttings and photographs. Include notes for your own use for future conferences, mentioning especially things which went wrong, were overlooked, or could have been improved upon.

SECRETARIAL TIPS

1 When deciding upon an outside venue for a conference, ask the hotel manager for a 'conference package' – this may work out cheaper than normal rates.

2 Many universities offer facilities for conferences during the long summer vacations – food may not be of such high quality as in hotels but costs will be lower.

3 Some holiday camps can be booked when they are closed during out-of-holiday seasons.

4 When choosing a venue, check that noise from adjacent buildings will not annoy speakers, especially during the summer, when double-glazed windows have to be opened. Air conditioned rooms are obviously ideal.

5 Suggest to delegates that they tip guest room maids or housemen themselves. Place tips from your firm in envelopes and hand them personally to other hotel staff.

6 As delegates leave, hand out questionnaires asking for comments on programme and meeting facilities.

QUICK REVISION

1 Conferences are expensive and time-consuming to arrange, but they are justified by
....

2 First decisions to be made when organising a conference are   ....
....

3 The first officer to be appointed is the   ....

4 A conference 'profile' contains   ....

5 Conference folders contain   ....

6 The reception desk at the entrance to the conference hall is necessary because this is where delegates   ....

7 Apart   from   hotels,   other   conference   venues   could   be   ....
....

8 Useful feedback from delegates as they leave can be obtained   ....

9 Two   British   Telecom   services   which   may   be   used   instead   of   conferences   are
....

10 After the conference, send letters of thanks to all helpers, tip hotel staff, return hired equipment and   ....

ASSIGNMENTS

1 You are employed by Shaw & Short Ltd, Whitaker Street, Manchester, M96 8TB, as secretary to the Area Sales Manager. A conference is to be held at the Fox Hotel, Glebelands Road, Sale, to launch a new product. The conference will last for three days. Below is a partially completed draft of the tickets which will be sent to each delegate. Add details which you think will be essential:

SHAW & SHORT LTD
MANCHESTER M96 8TB
Tel: 061 432888 Telex: 990111 Fax: 061 345612

CONFERENCE

. . . .

is a member of this Conference with the official conference

number . . . .

Please have this ticket available for inspection if required
at Conference sessions, functions and meals, etc.

---

2 Draft a questionnaire suitable to be handed out to the delegates as they leave. The delegates come from overseas as well as from many firms in the UK. Invent any other necessary details.

3 Below is a draft of the letter which will be sent to all delegates:

Dear Conference Delegate,

On behalf of Steven Mostyn, Sales Manager, may I welcome you to Sale and to this special Conference. I should like to extend a warm welcome to those of you who have travelled from abroad to be with us, or who are attending one of our Conferences for the first time.

After registering for the Conference, please go to hotel reception, where you will be issued with your room number and key.

Breakfast each day will be served in the hotel restaurant.

Tea and coffee	Royal Suite
Thursday dinner, Friday lunch and Saturday lunch	Royal Suite
The Conference dinner	Grosvenor Suite
The Sales Manager's reception	Royal Suite
All displays and exhibitions	Grosvenor Suite

The hotel staff are anxious to make your stay as comfortable as possible, and will do all they can to assist in any way, but if you have any queries or problems please do not hesitate to ask anyone on the staff of Shaw & Short Ltd for help.

I do hope you enjoy the Conference and that you will find it both worthwhile and stimulating.

Yours sincerely

(a) *When* would this letter be sent?

(b) *What* would be sent with it?

(c) *Who* would sign it (there may be several correct answers to this)?

4 As there will be overseas visitors to this Conference, what other requirement may have to be added to the list of preparations?

CHAPTER 21

Public Relations

PUBLIC RELATIONS OFFICER

It may be part of a secretary's duties to act as Public Relations Officer either for her employer, or for her firm. Public relations means the efforts made by an organisation to create a favourable image, rather than advertising its products or services. Rumours (often unfounded) can spread and become exaggerated unless steps are taken to make sure that the correct information is supplied to the news media (press, television and radio) as quickly as possible. It is also important for a firm to be given favourable publicity (an example might be the sponsorship of an event raising money for charity) and this has maximum impact if the Public Relations Officer briefs the news media – either local or national, depending on the size of the firm and the importance of the event.

PRESS RELEASE

A press release is a way of presenting accurate information to newspapers (local or national) or magazines, on subjects such as:

- Queen's Award for export or technology,
- new products,
- merger with another firm,
- opening of a new branch,
- outstanding achievement by an employee of a firm.

If possible, a press release should be sent on a Monday, when news may be scarce. Copies of a firm's regular newsletter or house journal could be helpful for a local newspaper. The editor can extract and publish interesting news items. Some news is suitable only for local papers, or for trade or technical journals, so it is important to choose suitable media for press releases. An important item may be more suitable for a national newspaper. News agencies which distribute news to radio and television stations, as well as national and provincial newspapers, could be utilised. Accuracy is vitally important, and facts (especially when containing statistics) should be checked thoroughly before the press release is sent.

Specimen Press Release

The PA to the Chairman of the firm of architects, Harley, Knight and Lowndes has been asked to send a Press Release of the 'topping out' ceremony of a new local hypermarket to be held on Friday, 6 November 199-. The Press Release is for a local newspaper:

NEW BLACKPOLE HYPERMARKET

Building of the new hypermarket at Blackpole will be completed on Friday, 6 November, and the occasion will be marked by the usual 'topping out' ceremony on the roof of the hypermarket. The ceremony will be attended by the Mayor of Bestchester, the Managing Director of Greatfare (Mr W. P. Scott) and Mr Richard Lowndes, of Harley, Knight and Lowndes, the firm of architects responsible for the design of the hypermarket.

Edwards & Frame, the local building firm which built the hypermarket, will be represented by a party of workmen and foremen.

The 'topping out' ceremony will take place at 11.30am on 6 November, and will be followed by a lunch for all those present at the Royal Oak, Brackenhill Heath, at 1pm.

This is the first hypermarket of its kind to be built in Bestchester and it will stock not only food and kitchen goods, but furniture, radio and TV equipment, computers, sports goods, clothes and jewellery. Space for parking one thousand cars is planned, together with a restaurant,

```
supervised play area for children and facilities for

leaving babies in prams. There will be ramps and wide

gangways for wheelchairs.


                         – ends –


Mrs T J Foster              From:

                            Harley, Knight and Lowndes

20 October 199-             Architects

                            50/58 Britannia Square

                            Bestchester

                            Telephone 868771 Ext 91
```

Embargo Press Releases

Most press releases are for immediate publication, but occasionally a delay is necessary – when extracts from a speech are included before the day when it is actually delivered. If this is the case, the word 'embargo' myst be typed clearly on the press release, with the date added when it may be published. An 'embargo' press release has two objects – it enables newspaper editors to plan ahead and reserve space to publish information on the most appropriate date, and it can give reporters information about the event so that they know what further information to seek.

Presentation of a Press Release

1 Use good quality paper because attractive presentation is important.
2 Leave plenty of space at the top of the sheet (the editor will choose the headlines; a factual headline may be given, however).
3 Leave wide margins for the sub-editor's use.
4 Type in double line spacing (this makes any alterations easier).
5 Type on one side of the paper only.
6 Paragraphs should be complete on one page and not split over two.
7 If you use more than one sheet of paper, type one of the following at the bottom of each sheet: more follows, mf, more.

8 Finish your article as follows:
   - ends -

9 If a photograph or diagram is to go with the press release, mark the cover PICTURE and write the title of the article on the back of the photograph. Mark also in the article the relevant reference to the picture.

10 Always include the telephone number of someone in the firm who can be contacted by the press for additional information, if required.

11 Ensure that names of people are spelt correctly.

PRESS CONFERENCE

No information should be given to a reporter without authorisation from a responsible executive in a firm. Reporters are very good at asking questions which are designed to extract an unguarded remark. The best reply is 'No comment'. It is a good policy, however, for the Public Relations Officer in a firm to make friends with the press, and when there is information which has sufficient interest for them, to invite them to a press conference.

A press conference should be held in the morning, as early as possible, so that that day's edition of the newspaper can be met.

Reporters and press photographers should be given every assistance when they arrive for a press conference. Some basic written information prepared beforehand for them should be handed to them in a 'press kit'. Photographers will be helped by having someone to set up groups for photographs and giving them names for the captions of their pictures. Reporters should be told where they may have the use of telephones, facsimile machines and teleprinters, preferably near the press conference.

After a prepared statement has been read to the reporters, there should be time for a question and answer session. The secretary should take a verbatim report of this session, so that the accuracy of the facts printed in the newspaper may be checked. Who is asked to a press conference will depend upon the type of publicity coverage required but it could be:

- local newspapers and 'free' newspapers,
- national newspapers,
- trade and technical journals,
- local radio and television networks,
- main news agencies.

Chambers *Office Oracle* gives names, addresses and telephone numbers of news agencies, radio and television stations.

SECRETARIAL TIPS

1 If sending press releases to more than one newspaper, send a slightly different copy to each one. This means that the news item will have more impact than if the same details are repeated exactly.

2 If a press conference is to be a lengthy one, refreshments in some form or another may be needed. It is obvious that these should be of a good quality and employing outside caterers may give a better impression than the firm's own catering staff.

3 Press releases can also be printed in publications abroad. A press release agency will be able to advise about this.

4 Reporters will not be pleased to be invited to your firm unless there is a good 'story', so any invitations should make it clear (without giving too much away) what the press conference is about.

5 No charge is made by newspapers, magazines, etc., for press releases – they are items of news and not advertisements but it is important to choose the newspapers or magazines which have a connection with the piece of news in question.

6 A press conference is the most expensive way to give out information – because of time, facilities and possibly refreshments for the press, so consider a press release first.

QUICK REVISION

1 Public relations means   ....

2 A press release is a way of   ....

3 Four main rules for the layout of a press release are   ....
....

4 What should be added to a press release if a photo is to accompany it?   ....

5 The best day to send a press release is   ....

6 How may a firm's newsletter be useful to the press?   ....

7 An 'embargo' press release has two objects: ....

8 The best time for a press conference is   ....

9 Reporters may need the use of   ....

10 The appropriate time for a question and answer session is   ....

11 During a question and answer session, a secretary should   ....

12 A source of reference for details of news agencies is   ....

ASSIGNMENTS

1 List under the relevant headings, the preparations necessary for a press conference and a general conference arranged for the exchange of ideas.

2 The firm for which you work as a secretary to the Sales Manager has just been informed that it has been given an order worth £2 million for electronic equipment to be supplied to Istanbul, Turkey. The name of the firm is Khan & Sons, and they are carpet manufacturers. Your firm's name is GPR Developments Ltd, 78 East Square, Chelmsford, Essex CM1 1JN, Telephone (0245) 355211, and the Sales Manager is David Ross.

The order is the result of a business trip to Istanbul by Mr Ross.

You accompanied him on this trip, and attended the many and (long) meetings which resulted in the order. You did manage to do some sightseeing, however, and took some photographs both of the city of Istanbul and the factory where the carpets were being made by the traditional methods.

The electronic equipment is going to revolutionise all that.

This large order will mean approximately 50 more job vacancies at the firm in Chelmsford, mainly on the factory floor but also on the office staff.

Type a press release, adding any details which you consider necessary, for the local papers (two free ones, and one weekly).

3 You work as Personal Assistant to the Managing Director (Geoffrey Barber) of GPR Developments Ltd.

Your firm has just been notified that its fourth application for the Queen's Award for Exports achievement has been successful. The number of Queen's Awards for Export or Technology made annually is usually only around 120 and they are very much coveted.

Your firm, currently employing 200 people, manufactures and exports electronic equipment all over the world. It also has a strong home market. It started in 1982 with only 7 employees and now has 200. They are mostly women (176) with 24 men. The firm is situated on the outskirts of Chelmsford and nearly all the employees live locally.

The presentation will be made at the firm's premises by the Lord Lieutenant of the county on behalf of the Queen on a date yet to be fixed.

After the ceremony, your company is allowed to fly the blue and yellow flag and give commemorative gifts to staff. The emblem may be displayed on stationery, products and packaging for the next five years.

Salesmen abroad are allowed to wear the distinctive Queen's Award ties, and have found that they help to open doors.

The feedback from companies about the benefit of winning the Queen's Award states enthusiastically that it brings prestige and increased business.

(a) Prepare a statement based on the above to be handed to reporters at a press conference.

(b) Which newspapers and news agencies would you consider it suitable to invite?

CHAPTER 22

Designing Forms

Forms are necessary when certain information is required in a straight-forward manner. The headings or questions on a form should therefore be clear and unambiguous, so that completing the form is free of uncertainty.

Forms fall into two main categories:

1 Those which require completion by a person outside the firm (e.g. employment application form, questionnaire about firm's products, acknowledgement of order).

2 Forms used internally by employees – petty cash vouchers, telephone message forms, stock requisitions.

When the same details are required on a regular basis, the completion of a form may be the quickest way to obtain them. Callers without appointments can be given a form to complete with the name of their firm, their own name, telephone number, name of firm and name of person whom they wish to see, together with brief details of business to be discussed. This form would complement the callers' register and be helpful to a busy executive.

Designing a Form

1 If your firm already has a number of forms in use, keep to a similar layout and size.

2 Decide on a heading which is self-explanatory and distinctive.

3 Keep side headings and questions easy to understand.

4 Use paper economically – A4 is usual but A5 may be adequate (telephone message form, for example), but make sure there is enough room for all the information asked for.

5 For forms used internally, a lighter weight paper is adequate. Good quality paper must be used for any forms going out of the firm. Light weight paper is necessary for forms which will be interleaved with carbon paper, or which will be NCR (no carbon required) coated for manifold sets (see p. 90).

6 Paper tinted in different colours is useful for identification purposes – a different colour for each copy (if there are several) makes routing to various departments easier to organise.

Computers have made it possible for forms to be printed in offices by means of printers with ink jet printheads, or laser printers, which produce high quality work, incorporating the use of colour, but both printers are expensive. An electronic typewriter or a computer printer with a daisywheel printhead will produce forms suitable for both internal and external use, if well displayed, but no colour can be incorporated.

SECRETARIAL TIPS

1 Allow plenty of space where it is not known how much information may be given (a description for example).

2 It helps both the person completing a form and the user of the information if questions are worded so that the answers may be 'yes' or 'no'.

3 Review forms occasionally; it is often possible the layout could be improved. It does happen, too, that a form is no longer used and should be dispensed with, but keep *one* just in case!

4 Form letters (letters with blanks for details such as name, address and date to be added) are useful for making and confirming appointments as well as similar routine correspondence.

5 Consideration must be given to the design of forms which are to be folded and posted, especially if 'window' envelopes are used.

6 Also, give consideration to the possibility of providing boxes which can be ticked.

QUICK REVISION

1 The heading of a form should be ...., ... and ....

2 Side headings and questions should be ....

3 Paper tinted in different colours is useful for ....

4 Light-weight paper is adequate for forms used internally, and essential for forms which will be ....

5 Forms printed to a high standard incorporating colour can be produced by ....

6 When deciding to dispose of a certain type of form, always ....

7 When forms are to be posted in 'window' envelopes, give consideration to ....

8 Forms are easier and quicker to complete when questions can be answered with either 'yes' or 'no' or ....

9 Allow plenty of space on a form where ....

10 Form letters are ....

ASSIGNMENTS

1 Design a printed postcard to be sent in reply to the invitation below, which enables the guest to indicate date and time when he or she will be attending (or refusing).

The Directors of
Viner's Wine Merchants Ltd
request the pleasure of your company at their

Autumn 199– Wine Tastings
in Their Cellars at Port Talbot

During the week commencing
Monday, 7th November daily until
Saturday, 12th November

Monday to Friday daily, 11.00 a.m. – 7.00 p.m.
Saturday 10.30 a.m. – 1.00 p.m.

Please bring this invitation with you which only admits two, unless prior arrangements have been made.

R.S.V.P.
to Miss Samantha Thompson on enclosed card please

2 Design a questionnaire suitable for sending out to your firm's customers asking for suggestions regarding additions to or improvements in, your firm's products. Your firm is a large one manufacturing ladies' shoes – Fashion Footwear International PLC, Blackhorse Trading Estate, Croydon, CR0 2PR.

3 Design a form applying for membership of a society in the area where you live which meets fortnightly, with speakers on various topics, and whose aim is to raise money for charities of members' choice. Invent the necessary details.

CHAPTER 23

General Assignments

1 You have been employed as a secretary by a small firm for some years, and are thinking of starting up an agency for temporary secretarial and clerical staff. List:
   - the type of equipment you think you would need for yourself and an assistant secretary,
   - stationery,
   - furniture,
   - suppliers in your locality (or nearest suppliers),
   - prices, discounts, delivery dates.

   Draw a map of your area and mark on it likely places which would be suitable for an agency. If your area is unsuitable, draw a map of the nearest one.

   Find out from an estate agent if any offices, or shop premises which could be converted, are for rent and the cost of renting.

2 Your boss has been asked to give a talk to his Rotary Club on his recent visit to the Falkland Islands. He has asked you to let him have details about the following:
   - location,
   - economy,
   - trade with UK,
   - climate and type of terrain,
   - history (including the invasion by Argentina in 1982),
   - total population and ethnic origin,
   - distance from England.

3 Design forms suitable for use by the following:
   (a) Visitors who arrive without appointments.
   (b) Customers who write complaining about the quality of goods supplied to them. Your firm is a large mail order company.
   (c) Students to complete after visiting your firm.

4 Your boss is going to Abu Dhabi and will be staying at the hotel Al Qafa, (Tel: Abu Dhabi 77981).

(a) What will be the correct way to address his mail to Abu Dhabi?

(b) What is the best Post Office service for urgent *valuable* items?

(c) Can he take his favourite brand of whisky with him, or have it sent?

(d) What special instructions are there about parcels to Abu Dhabi?

(e) What number will you dial when you telephone your boss?

(f) If you telephone him at midday, what time will it be in Abu Dhabi?

5 You have just started to work as secretary to Mrs Williams, a self-employed health and safety consultant. Almost immediately, she goes away for a fortnight's holiday sailing around Greek islands, where it will not be easy to get in touch with her quickly. You have, therefore, been left to 'hold the fort'. Your instructions are: to take telephone messages, open and read mail, pay cheques into the bank, and make appointments on suitable days. Her desk diary has been left for you to do this. You have the telephone number of a fellow consultant who has offered to help with any technical details if necessary. He will be available for the first week of your employer's holiday only.

It is impressed upon you that any telephone calls may be from potential clients bringing valuable business and all callers should be treated on this basis.

(a) What will you say when the telephone rings: initially; subsequently?

(b) What will be your order of priority in dealing with the mail?

(c) You receive a telephone call in the first week asking if Mrs Williams is able to give advice about the dust arising when cardboard boxes are flattened. What action do you take? If the telephone call had been made during the second week, what would your reply have been then?

(d) Your employer's home is 70 miles from London. When making appointments, what time would you allocate to (a) London appointments (b) local ones, and why?

CHAPTER 24

Information for Lecturers

TELEPHONE

FREEPOST 800 (BS 3333)
Bristol BS1 6GZ

MAIL HANDLING

All main Post Offices have supplies of up-to-date free leaflets on packing, safeguarding, insuring and sending mail.

BANKING

The Bank Education Service, 10 Lombard Street, London EC3V 98T will arrange (free of charge), for a speaker to come to colleges, with a film, if requested.

SAFETY

ROSPA (The Royal Society for the Prevention of Accidents) publishes a useful booklet (*Care in the Office*) which is inexpensive. Address: Cannon House, The Priory, Queensway, Birmingham B4 6BS.

HEALTH AND SAFETY

Leaflets and posters may be obtained from HMSO bookshops, or: Poster Campaign, PO Box 1144, London SW8 5DS.

NATIONAL EDUCATIONAL RESOURCES INFORMATION SERVICE – (NERIS)

NERIS is a database developed by the Department of Trade and Industry Education Unit. It is stored on a large computer at the Open University, and provides a source of reference for teaching materials for a wide range of subjects, including business studies. Wallcharts, business games, computer software assignments and places to visit are arranged in the form of a bibliographic reference, followed by a review of the material. What is needed to use NERIS, in addition to a microcomputer, is a telephone line, a modem, and a copy of the Marvel II software. Users of Prestel already have access to NERIS.

The database is now also available in the form of a directory.

Further information may be obtained from: NERIS, Maryland College, Woburn, MK17 9JD.

MISCELLANEOUS PUBLICATIONS

A monthly publication which gives up-to-date information about all types of office machinery and furniture is *Office Equipment News* (AGB Publications Ltd) Freepost, *Office Equipment News* Audit House, Field End Road, Eastcote, Ruislip, Middlesex, HA4 9BR. This is issued free to lecturers.

The Inland Revenue office in most larger towns and cities will supply copies of forms on request, for practice purposes.

The AA and RAC may have out-of-date copies of their handbooks which they will pass on to colleges, free of charge.

Local libraries may also be willing to pass on copies of the more expensive out-of-date reference books which are being replaced.

Index

Advertisements for office jobs   32–4
Assignments (general)   349, 350
Audio typing   77–9

Bank accounts   186–7
  bank drafts   207–8
  bank giro credit   201–2
  bill of exchange   208
  cash dispensing machines
    197–8
  cash from branch of another
    bank   208
  cheque cards   197
  cheque crossings   196–7
  cheques – stopping payment
    on   193
  confidentiality   209
  credit cards   198–9
  current account – paying money
    in   200–1
  current account – withdrawals
    from   193–5
  direct debit   199
  electronic funds transfer
    (EFT)   204
  eurocheques   205–6
  foreign currency   206
  insurance – advice on   207
  lending money   209–10
  night safes   206–7
  references from a bank   209
  safe custody of valuables   206
  standing orders   199
  statements of account   203–4
  traveller's cheques   204–5
  wills – acting as executor   207
Business documents   222–8
  credit note   228
  debit note   228
  enquiry   222
  invoice   226–7
  order   225
  price list   224
  quotation   223
  statement   227
Business entertaining   326–33
  drinks party   328

formal and informal
  entertaining   326–7
  invitations   328–30
  seating plans   331
  secretary's role   331
Business organisation
  board of directors   5
  chairman   5
  company secretary   6
  departments within a large
    firm   4–16
  managing director   6
  office services   4, 5
  private limited companies   3
  public limited companies   4
  sole traders   3

Carbon copies   89–90
Conferences   334–9
  arrangements   334–6
  follow-up   337
  reasons for holding   334
  safety and security   337
Curriculum vitae   31

Data Protection Act   88–9
Departments of a company
  accounts department   11–12
  personnel department   6–9
  production department   11
  purchasing department   9–10
  sales department   10–11
  transport department   11
Designing forms   346–9

Employment legislation   279–82
  contract of employment   281–2
  Employment Protection Act,
    1978   281
  Employment and Training Act,
    1973   281
  Equal Pay Act, 1970   281
  redundancy payments   281
  Redundancy Payments Act,
    1965   279

Filing   97–123
  accessories   105–6
  alphabetical   110–12
  aperture cards   116
  bulky items   101
  cabinets   106–7
  card indexes   115–16
  chronological   113
  classification   110–14
  computer disks   116
  computer print-outs   116–17
  cross-referencing   100
  'dead' files   103
  filing clerk   121
  filing supervisor   121
  folders   104–5
  general rules   101–2
  geographical   113
  indexing   114, 116
  in subject order   114
  labelling files   105
  large documents   103–4
  lending of files and papers
    99–100
  microfiche   116
  microfilming   117–21
  miscellaneous file   99
  numerical   112–13
  pending papers   100–101
  photographic material   116
  safety guidelines   108–9
  shredders   103
  terminal digit   114
Flexible working hours   278–9

Girobank   210–12

Information technology   18–19

Location and planning of offices
  cellular offices   21–2
  centralisation   25
  office conditions   20–21
  offices inside a building   20
  open plan offices   21, 23–5
  planning the layout of an
    office   25–6
  siting of firms   20

Mail handling   140–78
  cash on delivery   160
  collators   156
  compensation fee   159
  customs declaration   168–9
  electronic mail   174–5
  folding machines   155
  franking machine   150–3
  incoming mail   141–5
  mail distribution   146–7
  mail room   140, 156
  outgoing mail   147–8
  overseas letters   170
  overseas parcels   168
  parcels   157–9
  parcels delivery by private
    firms   160
  postage book   149
  reference books for the mail
    room   157
  scales   153–4
  secretary's responsibilities
    160–1
  stamp record   150
Meetings   285–95
  agenda and notice of meeting
    288, 289
  chairman's agenda   290
  chairman's role   287, 288
  minutes   290, 291
  secretary's responsibilities
    286, 287
  terms used in connection with
    meetings   291, 293
  types of meetings   285, 286
Money at banks and Post Offices
    186–213

Office automation   18–19
Office furniture   26–8
  work station in an office   28
Office machinery   73–96
  audio-typing equipment   77–8
  calculators   87–8
  computer hardware   84–5
  computer printers   80–1, 86
  computer security   87
  computer software   85
  computer supplies   85–6
  continuous stationery attach-
    ment   90
  disks, care of   86–7
  image scanner   94
  ink duplicators   93
  office copiers   91–2
  offset-litho duplicators   94
  spirit duplicators   93
  typewriters   73–7
  visual display unit (VDU)   79–83
  word processor   79–80
Office services
  audio-typists   14
  copy-typists   14

factory office   13
filing department   12–13
  mail room   12
  office juniors   13
  reception   15
  reprography department   12
  shorthand-typists   14
  telephonists   15
  typing pool   12
  VDU operators   14–15

Personnel department   6–9
  employment application form   7
  staff record sheet   8
Petty cash   214–21
  imprest system   215
  petty cash form   216–18
  petty cash voucher   215
Planning ahead   296–302
  diaries   296–300
  other reminder systems
    300–1
Post Office services
  Accelerated Surface Post   171
  Advice of Delivery   165
  bulk airmail   171
  Business Reply Service   167
  Certificate of Posting   162
  Christmas cards and printed
    matter overseas   170
  Consequential Loss Insurance
    165
  Datapost   172–3
  Freepost   167–8
  Intelpost   175–6
  International Reply Coupon   171
  postal orders   210
  postcode address file   162
  poste restante   166
  Recorded Delivery   163
  redirection of mail   166
  Registered Post   163–4
  Special Delivery   173–4
  Swiftair   170–1
  Trakback   160
Public relations   340–45
  press conference   343
  press release   340–43
  public relations officer   340

Reception   63–72
  dealing with callers   63–5
  reception area   65
  reception in a small firm   69–70
  receptionist's desk   66
  reference books   70
  secretary and reception   68–9
  staf 'In' and 'Out' book   67
  visitors' book   67

Safety and security in the office
    256–61
  reporting accidents   259–60

safety legislation   258
secretary's responsibilities
    256–8
Secretary's role   16–18
  future for secretaries   18
  personal qualities   17
  qualifications   17
Sources of information
  firms and organisations   126
  government statistical service
    127
  libraries   127
  newspaper information bureaux
    126
  people   125
  Prestel and Teletext   127
  reference books – general   124
  useful specialised reference
    books   126
Staff recruitment   262–70
  advertising   262–3
  application for employment
    form   264
  check-list for interviewing   269
  induction courses   268
  interviewing   263–6
  job description and specification
    267–8
  references   263
Stationery supplies   179–85
  envelope sizes   181
  paper sizes   180
  requisition   182
  stock control of stationery   181–2

Telecommunications   37–62
  ADC call   44
  alarm call   43
  answering the telephone   37–9
  audio-conferencing   53
  cheap periods for telephoning   42
  computers and the telephone
    55–6
  Confertel   53
  cordless telephone   49
  Datel   54
  emergency calls   46
  facsimile transmission (Fax)
    54–5
  fixed time call   43–4
  flashing lights   49
  Freefone   45
  information services   45
  intercom   48
  internal telephones   53
  international telephone services
    46–8
  loudspeaking telephone   48
  making telephone calls   40–3
  message call   44
  person-to-person call   43
  Prestel   53–4
  private telephone calls   41

radiopaging   50
radiophone   48-9
sources of reference for tele-
     phoning   42-3
switchboards   51-3
tannoy   49
telephone alphabet   40
telephone answering machines
     50-1
telephone charge card   45
telephone credit card   45
telephone equipment   48-53
telephone messages   38-9
telephone services   43-6
Teletext (Oracle and Ceefax)   54
transferred charge call   44
Telegrams   60
Telejet   60
Telemessages   60-1
Teleprinters and telex
     international telex calls   58
     latest developments   58
     reference books   57
     teleprinter keyboard and dialling
          unit   57
Telex Plus   58
Travel   304-25
     currency and tickets   309

documents   308
health   308-9
hotels   310
in your executive's absence   313
insurance   309
itineraries   304-6
jet lag   306-7
reference books   313-14
road and rail   311-12
travelling with your executive
     312

Value added tax (VAT)   218-19
Visual aids   129-39
     bar charts   134
     flow charts   135-6
     histograms   134
     line charts   133
     line graphs   130-3
     pictograms   137-8
     pie charts   129-30
     wall planners   137

Wages and salaries
     contributions to a pensions
          scheme   270
     deductions   270

fringe benefits   278
income tax   270-7
income tax tables   274-5
sickness benefit   279

Written communications
     audio-typing   249
     blind carbon copies   248
     circular letters   240
     circulation slip or distribution
          slip   245
     compliment slips   243-4
     counties of England and Wales
          236
     county abbreviations   237
     dictating   250-1
     envelope addressing   233-7
     form letters   241-3
     forms of address   238-40
     gauging typing space   251-3
     letter and memorandum com-
          position   246-7
     memoranda   244-5
     postal code areas   234
     regions of Scotland and Ireland
          235
     signing on behalf of the writer
          246